FIFTH EDITION

Counseling Strategies and Interventions

Sherry Cormier

West Virginia University

Harold Hackney

Fairfield University

Allyn and Bacon

Boston ■ London ■ Toronto ■ Sydney ■ Tokyo ■ Singapore

Series Editor: *Ray Short*
Editorial Assistant: *Karin Huang*
Marketing Manager: *Susan E. Ogar*
Editorial-Production Administrator: *Annette Joseph*
Editorial-Production Coordinator: *Susan Freese*
Editorial-Production Service and Electronic Composition: *TKM Productions*
Composition Buyer: *Linda Cox*
Manufacturing Buyer: *Megan Cochran*
Cover Coordinator: *Linda Knowles*

Library of Congress Cataloging-in-Publication Data

Cormier, L. Sherilyn (Louise Sherilyn)
    Counseling strategies and interventions / Sherry Cormier, Harold
Hackney. — 5th ed.
      p. cm.
    Hackney's name appears first on the previous edition.
    Includes bibliographical references and index.
    ISBN 0-205-29347-6 (pbk.)
    1. Counseling.   I. Hackney, Harold.   II. Title.
BF637.C6H25   1999
158'.3—dc21   98-29304
                                       CIP

Printed in the United States of America

10 9 8 7 6 5 4   03 02

*This book is lovingly dedicated
to our children:*

*Christiane and Lisanne
Kristen, Jason, and Curtis*

CONTENTS

EXERCISES

PREFACE

Since the fourth edition of *Counseling Strategies and Interventions,* the counseling profession has continued to expand and evolve. An increasing number of training programs have been recognized by various accrediting bodies. For example, professional counseling programs are now accredited by the Council for Accreditation of Counseling and Related Educational Programs (CACREP); counseling and clinical psychology programs are accredited by the American Psychological Association (APA); marriage and family counseling programs are accredited by the American Association of Marriage and Family Therapists (AAMFT); and social work programs are accredited by the Council on Social Work Education (CSWE). All of these organizations monitor the type, duration, and quality of training that helpers receive throughout their training and educational processes.

In writing this fifth edition, we have kept several well-grounded features from the previous editions. First, we have tried to be comprehensive yet concise. Second, the book has been written with upper-class undergraduates or beginning-level graduate students in mind. Also, we have included a variety of learning exercises to help students apply and review what they have learned.

At the same time, we have made some changes, including deletions and additions. We have eliminated out-of-date material and added content that reflects new sources and new thinking about the field. Many recently published sources are included.

Most importantly, we have expanded the coverage of and the emphasis on diversity and multiculturalism. As Robinson (1997) has so aptly pointed out, the two are not synonymous. *Diversity* describes the experiences of clients who are different across dimensions such as age, gender, race, ethnicity, sexual orientation, economic class, religion, and so on. *Multiculturalism* is "willingly sharing power with those who have less power" and using "unearned privilege to empower others" (p. 6). Robinson has also explained that it is possible to have diversity without a commitment to multiculturalism. When this occurs, differences can pull people apart rather than bring them together. For example, some people may devalue the differences found in others, as well as consciously or unconsciously "pull rank" on the basis of privilege and power. Other people may use their differences in a fashion that resembles what contextual family therapists have called "destructive entitlement"—meaning that those who have been treated unfairly may feel entitled to certain things in return. When these kinds of experiences occur, someone feels scapegoated as a function of age, gender, race, religion, sexual orientation, and so on, and alienation results. Only when *both* diversity and multiculturalism are present and apparent are our differences truly valued and esteemed. In this fifth edition, we have attempted to do just that.

Chapter 1 identifies the context of professional counseling—who the professional counselor is and what kinds of activities he or she enters. This context includes a wide variety of roles and functions. It might even seem to the untrained eye that the differences among helpers are greater than the similarities. We attempt to dispel that impression in Chapter 2, where we discuss the helping relationship. It is this helping relationship that proves to be the unifying force for disparate roles and functions.

Although the helping relationship connotes a sense of shared purpose, there is an added expectation for the counselor—the expectation that he or she be both responsible and responsive in exploring the client's needs and concerns. In Chapters 3 through 10, we identify the skills and interventions expected of a beginning professional counselor. Some of these skills are rudimentary; others are more advanced and require coaching and practice. Chapters 3 and 4 define the counselor's responsibility to be aware of and responsive to the client's communication patterns. Effective attending skills place the counselor in a responsible role in the counseling relationship. This responsibility is examined in Chapter 5, which deals with session management.

Chapters 6 through 8 delineate the basic counseling strategies designed to elicit, support, or direct client change. Whether the focus be the client's thoughts, attitudes, or feelings, or more likely a combination of all three, the counselor has certain tools or skills that facilitate the client's growth. Often, these skills enable the counselor to understand the client's problem or the client's world.

Chapter 9 is a pivotal point in the book. It builds on the fundamentals of the early chapters and is the foundation for the remaining chapters of the book. Although the counselor is instrumental in conceptualizing problems (usually with the assistance of a particular theoretical orientation), the goal-setting process is inherently dependent on *mutual* discussion and agreement between counselor and client. Drawing upon mutually accepted counseling goals, the counselor begins the most crucial portion of the relationship: the focus on overt change. This calls for more than relationship skills and more than active listening. There are many counseling interventions—derived both from theory and practice and supported by research—that are synonymous with effective counseling. In Chapters 9 and 10, we explain and suggest classroom activities that will help the reader understand and begin practicing these interventions.

Finally, Chapter 11 focuses on the process of clinical supervision and how beginning counselors may use it to advance their skills. Counselor educators have long used clinical supervision skills in the training of counselors, but the specificity of those skills and the inclusion of the trainee as a participant in successful clinical supervision has not been dealt with in most professional texts. This chapter was authored by Janine Bernard.

As you begin the process of understanding the role of helper and as you acquire the necessary skills required for effective helping, you will come to realize that the ultimate goal is to develop your abilities to the point that they are a natural extension of your existing interpersonal skills. But this will not be the case in the beginning. The interventions and even the conceptualizations may seem unnatural, inconsistent with your existing behaviors, or inappropriate. As you become more accomplished in the craft of counseling, these counseling skills will begin to feel more comfortable, appropriate, and effective. Ultimately, they will become a natural part of your professional practice.

Acknowledgments

We would like to extend our thanks and appreciation to several people who have helped make this fifth edition possible. We thank our editor at Allyn and Bacon, Ray Short, who is an accomplished and experienced editor as well as a wonderful human being. Thanks also to our editorial assistant at Allyn and Bacon, Karin Huang, whose timely and expert help made our jobs so much easier. We also gratefully acknowledge Janine Bernard for her superb revision of Chapter 11, Victoria Railing for her superior assistance with word processing and manuscript preparation, Cory Clark for his thorough library work on the reference list, and Lisanne Cormier for miscellaneous assistance on the manuscript.

S. C.
H. H.

1 The Helping Profession

The helping profession includes a broadly knit collection of professionals and paraprofessionals, each fitting a particular need or segment of society. Some are directly identified as helping professionals, such as psychiatrists, psychologists, professional counselors, marriage and family therapists, and social workers. Others are professionals from other disciplines who enter the helping network for temporary periods of time. Most notable among these are ministers, physicians, nurses, and teachers. When discussing the helping profession, it is important to keep this fluid interplay between career helpers and peripheral helpers in mind. The bond they share is a desire, a need, or even a mission to be of help. This helping activity has both a subjective and an objective quality and can be studied from both perspectives.

Most counseling textbooks devote at least a portion of one chapter to the subject of helping. You might think that a process so inherent to human nature as this act of extending oneself to another person should be self-evident. And yet, people continue to belabor the subject in ways not unlike the poet who talks about love. In a psychotherapeutic context, the process has carried many labels, among which are *treatment, analysis, facilitation,* and *modification*. In the company of such terms, the label *helping* seems innocently harmless, if not simplistic. In fact, the act of helping proves not to be so simple or clear to the participant or observer. In this chapter, we examine the many facets of the helping profession.

What Is Helping?

The process of helping has several dimensions, each of which contributes to the definition of *helping*. One dimension specifies the conditions under which helping occurs. Another dimension specifies the preconditions that lead one person to seek help and another to provide help. Yet a third dimension relates to the results of the interaction between these two persons.

Helping Conditions

The conditions under which helping occurs are quite complex, but in their simplest terms may be described as involving "(a) someone seeking help, (b) someone willing to give help who is (c) capable of, or trained to help (d) in a setting that permits help to be given and received" (Hackney & Cormier, 1996, p. 2).

The first of these conditions is obvious; one cannot help without the presence of someone seeking help. If I do not want to be helped, nothing you can do will be helpful. If I am not sure I want to be helped, then perhaps you will be helpful, provided you can enjoin me to make a commitment to accept help.

The second condition requires the willingness or intention to be helpful. Here, it would be good to differentiate between the *intention* to be helpful and the *need* to be helpful. Many would-be helpers are driven by the need to be helpful and use the helping relationship for their own needs. This is rarely a conscious act. Neediness has a way of camouflaging itself in more respectable attire. But when the relationship is dictated by the helper's needs, the possibilities for helping are minimal.

It is important to recognize and accept your needs. All people have needs for such things as intimacy, power, esteem, admiration, and so on. It is also important to be certain that you are not dependent on your interactions with clients for fulfilling these needs in a primary way. One of the best ways to ensure that you do not depend on clients inappropriately to meet your needs is to take care of yourself and to live a balanced life in which your needs are met through relationships with a partner, family, friends, or even a support group of other helpers. If you are living your own life in a healthy and balanced way, then your clients will not have to provide you with intimacy, approval, and admiration and will be free to receive from you the kinds of things that *they* need.

The third condition reflects the counselor's skills, either learned or natural. It is not enough to be well intentioned if your awareness and behaviors drive people away. Indeed, the primary purpose of pursuing training in the field of helping is to develop, expand, and refine your therapeutic skills.

The fourth condition, a setting in which help may occur, refers to the physical surroundings in which the helper and client meet. Privacy, comfort, aesthetic character of the room, and timing of the encounter all contribute to the setting in which helping transpires.

All four of these conditions occur within a cultural and environmental context in which individual clients may present with a variety of concerns and individual differences, along such dimensions as race, ethnicity, socioeconomic level, gender, religious and spiritual affiliation, sexual orientation, age, developmental stage of life, and so on. Naturally, such differences affect the help-giving and help-receiving process in a variety of ways. For example, some clients' cultural affiliations have a great impact on even the decision to seek or not seek help from a professional counselor. Instead, they may turn to family or tribal elders, religious and spiritual elders, or close family confidants for guidance. Cultural variables also affect the setting in which help giving occurs. For some clients, the idea of going to see a counselor in a professional office is too foreign to consider it as a viable option. These clients may prefer a setting that is more informal and less structured. Also, even your best intentions to be helpful as a counselor are influenced by your own cultural affiliations and may affect the degree to which some clients perceive you as able and qualified to help. If you do not understand your clients' expressions or subtle nuances of their communication patterns, or their cultural values, or their culturally related views of their problems, your best intentions may not be enough.

Carl Rogers (1957) has discussed the "necessary and sufficient conditions" for helping to occur. His description included conditions similar to those listed above. But he also added some personal qualities of the counselor (accurate empathy, unconditional positive regard) and a communication issue—that the client be able to perceive the counselor's understanding and respect for the client. We discuss these relationship conditions in greater detail in Chapter 2.

Settings in Which Counselors Work

As we mentioned at the beginning of this chapter, there are a variety of trained persons and specializations in the helping professions. The following discussion of representative settings and the services they perform will provide some sense of the helping spectrum.

Counseling in School Settings

School counselors are found in elementary, middle or junior high, as well as high schools. Elementary school counselors do provide some individual counseling with children, but they are more likely to work with the total school environment. Much of the elementary school counselor's focus is on working with the teaching staff to construct a healthy psychological environment in the school for young children. This is accomplished through teacher conferences, classroom presentations, parent conferences, and talking to the children (Baker, 1992).

Middle school and junior high school counselors share this total school perspective but tend to spend more time with students, individually and in groups, and somewhat less time with teachers and parents. This slight shift in focus reflects the developmental changes that occur with preteens, who find themselves involved in self-exploration and identity crises.

Counseling in the high school reflects a noticeable shift to the students as individuals. Career and college planning, interpersonal concerns, family matters, substance use, and personal identity issues tend to dominate the students' awareness, and the counseling process attempts to provide an environment in which these issues may be addressed. The counselor's day is therefore much more task oriented. Some students are referred by teachers, but many are self-referrals. The high school counselor often works with student groups on career and college issues, but individual contact is the main medium for other concerns.

In general, the current force of school counseling is in comprehensive programs that focus on primary prevention and healthy development for all students (Paisley & Borders, 1995). There is also an increasing emphasis on providing multiculturally effective school guidance programs that are inclusive of and relevant to a diverse group of students.

Counseling in College Settings

Although much college counseling occurs in counseling centers or psychological services centers, some counselors in higher education settings also work in offices related to student affairs, such as residence halls, career services, academic advising, and so on. A wide variety of problems are addressed, including career counseling, personal adjustment counseling, crisis counseling, and substance abuse counseling. College counselors also see students with mild to severe pathological problems, ranging from depression to suicide gestures to eating disorders. In addition to individual counseling, much reliance is placed on group counseling and on training paraprofessionals to run crisis telephone services and peer counseling programs.

Historically, college counseling has emphasized a developmental framework resulting in "creative outreach and support work on campuses" (Dean & Meadows, 1995, p. 139). Increasingly, however, college counselors are faced with a rising tide of greater psychopathology among college students, a greater diversity among college students, and an increased need for services stemming from societal issues, such as AIDS, sexual abuse and violence, and dysfunctional family experiences (Dean & Meadows, 1995, p. 141). At the same time that the needs for counseling services are at an all-time high, college counseling faces budget cuts and external pressures for accountability. Increasingly, as a result of the shift in health care to "managed care" or health maintenance organizations (HMOs), some colleges are replacing college counselors with off-campus mental health professionals. Currently, many college counselors are faced with survival!

Counseling in Community Settings

Counselors working in community settings usually are master's degree–level social workers (M.S.W.) or mental health counselors (M.A.). Their places of employment are the most diverse of all counseling settings. Family service agencies, youth service bureaus, satellite mental health centers, YWCA counseling services, and substance abuse centers are examples of community settings. Much of what is done is psychotherapy, whether with individuals, families, or groups. In addition, the community counselor may become involved in community advocacy efforts and direct community intervention. The types of problems seen by community counselors encompass the spectrum of mental health issues. Clients include children, adolescents, adults, couples, families, and the elderly. In other words, community counselors see an enormous variety of clients and problems in a typical month. The work demands are often heavy, with caseloads ranging from 20 to 40 clients per week.

Currently, mental health counselors are concerned with the delivery and implementation of services that are both therapeutical and cost effective and are based on developmental notions as much as remediation (Smith & Robinson, 1995). Couples and family counselors as well as addiction specialists also offer services through a variety of community agencies.

Counseling in Religious Settings

Counseling in religious settings is in many ways similar and in some ways different from that in other counseling settings. The similarities include the range of individual and family problems seen, the types and quality of therapy provided, and the counselors' professional qualifications. The differences reflect the reasons why some religious groups establish their own counseling services. There is at least some acknowledgment of the role of religion or spirituality in the individual's life problems. Many religious counselors believe that human problems must be examined and changes introduced within a context of spiritual and religious beliefs and values. The religious counseling center is undeniably attractive for many clients who, because of their backgrounds, place greater trust in the counselor who works within a religious affiliation.

Counselors in religious settings often are ordained ministers who have obtained postgraduate training in counseling. However, increasing numbers of the laity are also entering religious counseling settings. Their training may be similar to that of the community mental health counselor or the couples and family therapist. Indeed, at a recent Invitational Summit Meeting on Spirituality in Counseling (American Counseling Association, 1995b), a set of spiritual competencies were proposed for all counselors, including the ability to use spiritual, religious, and transpersonal beliefs in the practice of counseling. Also included was the need for counselors to understand other spiritual and religious orientations in addition to their own. Wehrly (1995) noted that "belief systems related to religion and spirituality play vital roles in the lives of many people of color. Western-trained therapists may downplay or ignore the importance of these belief systems because minimal attention is given to the importance of religion or spirituality in most U.S. counselor training programs" (p. 11). All of the world's major religions—Buddhism, Christianity, Confucianism, Hinduism, Islam, Judaism, Shintoism, and Taoism—as well as various tribal beliefs have their own core belief systems and life philosophy (see also Axelson, 1993).

Counseling in Industrial Settings

Many professionals consider the private sector to be the new frontier for counseling services. Counseling services occur primarily in the form of employee assistance programs (EAPs) that are administered either within the plant or through a private contract with a counseling agency. EAPs are occurring with increasing frequency in business, industries, governmental units, hospitals, and schools. Although the primary focus of most EAPs is the treatment of substance abuse problems, some have expanded into other types of personal and family problems.

In addition to employee assistance programs, a new type of counseling service has appeared in industry settings: the outplacement counseling service. *Outplacement* refers to the process of facilitating the transition from employment to unemployment or from employment in one corporation to employment in another. The need for outplacement counseling is increasing as corporations downsize their operations to cut costs or to address new goals and objectives. The client may be a top executive, middle manager, line supervisor, or laborer. Counseling takes the form of career counseling and includes the administration of career and personality inventories. The objectives for management clients are (1) to provide data and counseling that will help executives assess their career options and develop plans for obtaining new positions and (2) to support clients through that transition period. The objectives for plant employees who may be affected by plant closings are (1) to identify career alternatives for the employees and (2) to assist the company in designing retraining programs that will help the unemployed workers obtain new jobs. Much that is done in outplacement counseling is similar to what a career counselor would do. However, the outplacement counselor is usually a person who has worked in an industry setting and understands the characteristics of this clientele from firsthand experience.

Counseling in Health Care Settings

An increasing number of counselors are finding employment in health care settings such as hospitals, departments of behavioral medicine, rehabilitation clinics, and so on. Responsibilities of helpers in these settings include such diverse things as providing counseling to patients and/or patients' families, grief work with the terminally ill, and the implementation of psychological and educational interventions for patients with chronic illnesses, people with physical challenges, and so on. An increasing number of addictions specialists are working in health care settings as well. "Wellness" programs are also increasing in numbers in these settings.

Ingredients of Professional Counseling

We have described six settings in which professional counseling occurs. There are many others, of course, including couples and family therapy, rehabilitation counseling, correctional institution counseling, career and employment counseling, geriatric counseling, and the newly emerging area of sports counseling (Miller & Wooten, 1995). In all of these settings, and with the variety of presenting problems that are seen, there is a common core of counselor characteristics, skills, and abilities. These common ingredients may be categorized as the counselor's personal qualities, and his or her interpersonal skills, discrimination/conceptual skills, intervention skills, and cultural competence skills.

The Counselor's Personal Qualities

What are the raw materials, the predisposing conditions that contribute to the development of a highly skilled counselor? Do all counselor trainees possess these raw materials? Corey, Corey, and Callanan (1998) observed that "a counselor's beliefs, personal attributes, and ways of living inevitably influence the way he or she functions as a professional" (p. 34). They identified 10 personal qualities that are found in effective counselors:

1. Goodwill—a sincere interest in the welfare of others
2. The ability to be present for others; the ability and willingness to be with them in their experiences of joy and pain
3. A recognition and acceptance of one's personal power; being in contact with one's own strength and vitality; without need to diminish others or feel superior to them
4. The knowledge that one has found his or her own counseling style, that style being an expression of one's own personality
5. A willingness to be vulnerable and to take risks
6. Self-respect and self-appreciation; a strong sense of self-worth
7. A willingness to serve as models for their clients
8. A willingness to risk making mistakes and to admit having made them
9. A growth orientation
10. A sense of humor

In addition to these qualities, two others are worth considering. One is the counselor's ability to promote the welfare of the client. Another related and personal quality involves open-mindedness and flexibility—that is, the capacity to hear, believe, and respond in an open and nonjudgmental fashion to clients who may have values, beliefs, and life-styles different from your own. This quality is especially important in being able to work effectively with clients of the opposite gender or of a different ethnic origin and with clients with alternative life-styles, including sexual orientation.

As we discussed earlier in this chapter, part of being an effective counselor involves the awareness of your own needs and the ability to put the well-being of your clients first. Helpers in all fields are guided by codes of ethical behavior (*Ethical Standards,* American Counseling Association, 1995a; *Ethical Principles of Psychologists,* American Psychological Association, 1992; *Code of Ethics,* National Association of Social Workers, 1996; and *Code of Ethical Principles for Marriage and Family Therapists,* American Association for Marriage and Family Therapy, 1991). A major guiding principle of all of these ethical codes is the recognition of the importance of being committed to the client's well-being.

The Counselor's Interpersonal Skills

Although personal qualities are basic ingredients for good counseling, possession of these qualities alone does not ensure success as a counselor. There is a second level of characteristics that determine how a counselor is able to relate to others. Egan (1998, pp. 43–55) described some of these qualities as pragmatism, competence, respect, genuineness, and the promotion of client empowerment and self-responsibility. Other interpersonal skills include the ability to listen and to communicate accurately what one has heard without becoming dominant in the interaction and the ability to communicate competence, trustworthiness, and sensitivity to the other person's situation. This array of characteristics must contribute to a general ability to put clients at ease, to elicit client trust, and to work through difficult moments, tasks, and problems.

The Counselor's Discrimination/Conceptualization Skills

As the counseling relationship evolves, the counselor becomes increasingly involved in the client's personal world. From the client's perspective, the counselor *becomes* part of his or her world. This involvement challenges the counselor to be in the relationship and yet to remain objective. Such a challenge is very difficult because it requires the counselor to exhibit congruence, honesty, and professional responsibility, all at the same time.

The counselor must be able to listen, to comprehend, to relate, to think through, to recognize connections and contradictions, to conceptualize what these might mean within some theoretical framework, to react, to instigate, to support, to challenge, and to empathize—all within the span of a counseling session. And this must all be done as believably as it is felt. Otherwise, the counselor will take on a phony or incongruent persona.

The Counselor's Intervention Skills

Counselors must also be able to implement their conceptualization of what would facilitate a client's growth and success with presenting problems. We believe that "all counselors, regardless of theoretical orientation, have a therapeutic plan that they follow, a plan that is related to the assessment of the presenting problem, to their view of human nature and change processes, and to the resulting goals that have been agreed upon" (Hackney & Cormier, 1996, p. 34). These interventions may address the client's feelings and attitudes, the client's thought processes and assessments of life situations, the client's behaviors or efforts to change, or the client's interpersonal relationships and the effect those relationships have.

Some intervention skills are nothing more than common sense and are as common among friends as they are in counseling. Other interventions are unique to the therapeutic relationship and are formed out of the theoretical conceptualizations of human relationships. As counselors grow in experience and training, their repertoire of intervention skills grows, and their ability to recognize when and how to introduce interventions increases.

The Counselor's Cultural Competence Skills

Counselors are seeing an increasingly diverse group of clients—diversity appearing in such dimensions as race, ethnicity, sexual orientation, socioeconomic level, religion and spiritual affiliation, gender, and age. It is estimated that in the twenty-first century such diversity will only continue to grow. As the dimensions of client diversity expand, the competence of counselors to deal with complex cultural issues must also grow. There are many ideas of what it means to be a culturally competent counselor. Montalvo (as cited in Daw, 1997) stated that cultural competence "is the business of spotting obstacles and facilitators to treatments" within a client's culture (p. 9). He illustrated this definition with the following story of a client who was a Vietnam veteran suffering from posttraumatic stress disorder (PTSD):

> The man was shunned by his family because they saw the spirits of the people he had killed in Vietnam. His therapist did some checking around in the man's ethnic group and discovered that the Navajos had a ritual dance for warriors dealing with the spirits of those they had harmed. Rather than EMDR [eye movement desensitization and reprocessing] or another treatment that had probably already been tried, the therapist connected the veteran to a medicine man. When the man opened up to his culture it was helpful to him and also to his family. The family opened their doors to him again. (p. 9)

The Center for Mental Health Services (as cited in Daw, 1997) described culturally competent service providers as those who "are aware and respectful of the importance of the values, beliefs, traditions, customs, and parenting styles of the people they serve. They are also aware of the impact of their own culture on the therapeutic relationship and take all of these factors into account when planning and delivering services" (p. 9).

How do counselors develop cultural competence? The answers to this question are not always simple ones because, as Sue (1998) notes, there are degrees of cultural competence. However, we can make the following recommendations, as summarized by Daw (1997):

1. Become aware of your own cultural heritage and affiliations and of the impact your own culture has on the counseling relationship. Remember that culture affects you and your clients. Pipher (as cited by Farberman, 1997) observed that it is no longer therapeutically useful to focus just on an individual client or on the client's family of origin without consideration of the client's culture.

2. Become immersed in the cultures of people who differ from yourself. Seek opportunities to interact with people who represent different cultural dimensions and be open to what they have to say.

3. Be realistic and honest about your own range of experiences as well as issues of power, privilege, and poverty. Become aware of the great impact that poverty has on ethnicity. Think about the positions you have or hold that contribute to oppression, power, and privilege. Hardy (as cited in Daw, 1997) observed, "It's easier to talk about one's culture than one's power, one's ethnicity than one's privilege" (p. 9).

4. Consider a referral to another counselor when you are faced with a client that you cannot respond to adequately because of your own limited range of experience and knowledge. Remember, as a counselor, it is incumbent on *you*, not your clients, to educate yourself about various dimensions of culture. For example, if you are uninformed about a sexual orientation different from your own and you ask your client to inform you, this essentially constitutes a role reversal and the client is likely to feel frustrated.

In recent years, all of the major professional organizations for helping professionals have offered descriptions of various multicultural competencies required for helpers. (Table 1.1 provides an example from the American Counseling Association [ACA].) We strongly encourage you to familiarize yourself with these competencies and to work on areas in which you need to develop more awareness and greater proficiency and sensitivity.

Training and Credentialing of Counselors

We have already indicated that professional counselors are trained in graduate programs, usually affiliated with higher education institutions, that lead to a master's degree. Traditionally, these programs have required 33 semester credits, but recently, most of them have been upgraded to require 48 to 60 semester credits. These latter programs usually are designed to meet professional criteria established by the Council for Accreditation of Counseling and Related Educational Programs (CACREP). *Accreditation* refers to the process in which a private associa-

TABLE 1.1   Multicultural Competencies and Standards

Goals	Attitudes and Beliefs	Knowledge	Intervention Strategies
Counselor awareness of own cultural values and beliefs	■ Sensitive to one's own cultural heritage and how this influences thoughts, feelings, and behavior. ■ Recognizes limits of abilities. ■ Comfortable with differences in race, ethnicity, culture, and beliefs.	■ Aware of how background affects the definition of "normality" and the process of counseling. ■ Understands concepts of racism, discrimination, and stereotyping. ■ Understands how one has benefited from above dimensions (for European-Americans). ■ Knows how one's own style may be inappropriate for culturally different clients.	■ Seeks educational/training experiences for continued learning, seeks consultation, and refers when necessary. ■ Seeks to understand oneself as racial/cultural being and actively seeks a nonracist society.

TABLE 1.1 (continued)

Goals	Attitudes and Beliefs	Knowledge	Intervention Strategies
Counselor awareness of client worldview	■ Aware of negative emotional reactions and stereotypes relating to other groups; seeks to move to a nonjudgmental posture.	■ Possesses specific knowledge of worldview, cultural style, and cultural identity levels of clients. ■ Understands how cultural issues relate to personal styles, help-seeking behaviors, and whether or not a particular helping intervention is suitable. ■ Familiar with what social and political influences such as poverty, racism, and powerlessness have on client development and how these influence the counseling process.	■ Skilled in latest research and theoretical findings on groups culturally different from self. ■ Seeks appropriate educational experiences. ■ Actively involved with minority individuals in projects, friendships, social/political functions, and celebrations so that perspective of minority experience is more than an academic or helping exercise.
Culturally appropriate intervention strategies	■ Respects clients' religious/spiritual beliefs and values and understands how these affect expressions of distress. ■ Respects indigenous helping practices and minority communities' natural help-giving networks. ■ Sees bilingualism as an asset rather than a liability.	■ Understands how Euro-centric tradition in counseling and therapy may conflict with cultural values of other traditions. ■ Aware of institutional barriers and bias in assessment instruments and techniques. ■ Aware of the influence of varying family and community structures on the counseling process. ■ Understands issues of racism, oppression, and so on.	■ Sends verbal and nonverbal messages accurately and appropriately. ■ Able to determine if clients' "problems" result from external factors, such as racism and bias in others. ■ Uses institutional interventions on behalf of clients. ■ Works with traditional healers and spiritual leaders as culturally appropriate. ■ Refers to good sources when own linguistic skills are insufficient. ■ Conducts training/educational interventions to combat oppression. ■ Educates clients to their personal and legal rights for effective multicultural intervention.

Source: Adapted from ACA Professional Standards by A. Ivey, M. B. Ivey, & L. Simek-Morgan, *Counseling and Psychotherapy.* Copyright 1997 by Allyn and Bacon. Reprinted from *Journal of Counseling and Development,* 1992, *70,* 484–486. Reprinted by permission of Allyn and Bacon and the American Counseling Association. No further reproduction authorized without written permission of the American Counseling Association.

tion grants public recognition to a program that meets established guidelines, based on evaluative data (Sweeney, 1995).

Most training programs begin with a series of courses that introduce the helping professions, settings, client populations, and professional ethics. Early in most programs, a counseling techniques laboratory or prepracticum introduces students to communication skills and entry-level counseling interventions, and provides opportunities to try out these skills in an observable setting (either through a two-way mirror or a closed-circuit video). Such a course includes content that is presented in this text. Typically, this course is followed by a counseling practicum in which students work with real clients under the supervision of a skilled counselor or therapist. That supervision may include live observation, videotaped review, or audiotaped review. Whatever the medium, sessions are reviewed by the supervisor, and feedback is provided to the trainee to permit assessment and professional growth.

Concurrent with these courses, most students take courses in group counseling (sometimes including a group practicum) psychology, educational and psychological testing, and career counseling and development. Toward the end of the program, most trainees are required to complete a one-year internship in a counseling setting related to their program. This may be in school counseling, agency counseling, college counseling, or another related setting. Programs in rehabilitation counseling, social work, and marriage and family therapy differ in some of the didactic content, but the experiential portions are similar. These programs are also accredited by their respective accrediting organization.

In addition to receiving a degree in counseling or a related field, most counselors and other help-giving professionals also seek a means by which they can become a credentialed counselor following their training and degree. Credentialing has become an important issue in recent years because of health care reforms (i.e., managed care) in which the credentials of the counselor are important for obtaining third-party reimbursement. Sweeney (1995) defined *credentialing* as "a method of identifying individuals by occupational group" (p. 120). It involves either certification and/or licensing. Although certification and licensing are similar processes, they differ in several important ways. *Certification,* unlike licensure, is established through independent, nonlegislative organizations that help to regulate the use of a particular *title*. Counselors can be certified through the National Board of Certified Counselors (NBCC), rehabilitation counselors are certified through the Commission for Rehabilitation Counselor Certification (CRCC), and social workers are certified through the National Association of Social Workers (NASW). *Licensure* is a legislatively established basis of credentialing that is considered even more desirable than certification because it regulates not only the *title* but also the *practice* of the profession. Over 40 states have passed legislation to license professional counselors. Social workers also can obtain social work licenses through state legislation, and some states have passed legislation to license marriage and family therapists. It is important to note that licensing laws, in particular, vary among different states and "only by examining a specific law and the rules by which it is administered can one determine the full implications of the law in a given state" (Sweeney, 1995, p. 121).

Summary

This chapter has examined the meaning of helping in the context of human problems and who the helpers are. Professional helpers are found in many settings and encounter a wide variety of human problems. The effective helper brings to the setting certain personal qualities, without which the client would not likely enter into the alliance in which help occurs. But more than personal qualities are necessary to become a professional helper. A person must possess certain interpersonal skills, conceptual skills, intervention skills, and cultural competence skills to be an effective counselor. While the exact parameters of these skills may be defined by the counselor's theoretical orientation, there is no denying that the effective counselor has them and the ineffective counselor does not.

In the chapters that follow, we shall examine these skills and provide you with exercises and discussion questions to help in your integration of the material. Chapter 2 will look at the helping relationship and conditions that enable it to develop in positive directions to facilitate the client's progress. Chapters 3, 4, and 5 address the interpersonal skills of the counselor in regard to attending to clients, recognizing communication patterns, and managing the counseling session. Chapters 6, 7, and 8 focus on the cognitive and affective messages of clients and ways in which counselors can differentiate between and respond to these two types of messages. Chapters 9 and 10 address the counselor's skills in conceptualizing problems and selecting and implementing strategies and interventions. Finally, Chapter 11 looks at the special issues involved in supervisor-trainee sessions, with the aim of helping the beginning counselor to make full use of the benefits of supervision. It is important to note that all of the skills and processes we describe in the following chapters are affected by both the social milieu and the multicultural context of the counselor and client.

DISCUSSION QUESTIONS

1. In a small group of three to five class members, each of you should identify a preferred setting in which you would choose to be a professional counselor. Discuss among yourselves why you chose the particular setting. Does it have to do with your personal qualities? Your perception of the demands of the setting? Your perception of the rewards of working in that setting?

2. Now choose a second-most-preferred setting (other than your first choice). Continue the discussion as directed in Question 1. How did you find your reactions to be different in this second discussion? What might you learn from these differences? Did you perceive the other group members as having similar or differ-

ent reactions to the second choice? What did you learn about them as a result? Share your reactions candidly.

3. Identify a person you have known who was, in your opinion, an exceptional helper. What qualities did this person possess that contributed to his or her helping nature? How do you think these qualities were acquired? Do you have any of these qualities?

4. In your opinion, what does it mean to help? To give help? To receive help? How are these processes related?

5. What has had an impact on your decision to become a helper? Consider the following sources of influence: your family of origin (the one in which you grew up), life experiences, role models, personal qualities, needs, motivations, and pragmatic concerns.

6. What do you have to offer to people struggling both with life issues and with societal issues? How do your gender, race, and cultural affiliation(s) affect this?

RECOMMENDED READINGS

Capuzzi, D., & Gross P. (1997). *Introduction to the counseling profession* (2nd ed.). Boston: Allyn and Bacon.

Corey, G., Corey, M. S., & Callanan, P. (1998). *Issues and ethics in the helping professions* (5th ed.). Pacific Grove, CA: Brooks/Cole.

Corey, M. S., & Corey, G. (1998). *Becoming a helper* (3rd ed.). Pacific Grove, CA: Brooks/Cole.

Hepworth, D., Rooney, R., & Larsen, J. (1997). *Direct social work practice* (5th ed.). Pacific Grove, CA: Brooks/Cole.

Meyers, J. (1995). Professional counseling: Spotlight on specialties (Special Issue). *Journal of Counseling and Development, 74* (2).

Sue, D. W., Ivey, A. E., & Pedersen, P. (1996). *A theory of multicultural counseling and therapy.* Pacific Grove, CA: Brooks/Cole.

Sue, S. (1998). In search of cultural competence in psychotherapy and counseling. *American Psychologist, 53,* 440–448.

Sweeney, T. J. (1995). Accreditation, credentialing, professionalization: The role of specialties. *Journal of Counseling and Development, 74,* 117–125.

Wehrly, B. (1995). *Pathways to multicultural counseling competence.* Pacific Grove, CA: Brooks/Cole.

Woodside, M., & McClam, T. (1994). *An introduction to human services* (2nd ed.). Pacific Grove, CA: Brooks/Cole.

2 The Helping Relationship

Much of what is accomplished in counseling is dependent on the quality of the relationship between counselor and the client. In all the writing on this subject, none offers more than an approach to helping known as the *person-centered approach*. This approach has been described by Corey (1996):

> The person-centered approach focuses on clients' responsibility and capacity to discover ways to more fully encounter reality. Clients, who know themselves best, are the ones to discover more appropriate behavior for themselves based on a growing self-awareness. The approach emphasizes the phenomenal world of the client. With an attempt to apprehend the client's internal frame of reference, therapists concern themselves mainly with the client's perception of self and of the world. (p. 202)

The person-centered approach derives principally from the work of one individual: Carl Rogers. Rogers emerged on the counseling scene at a time when two psychological approaches, psychoanalysis and behaviorism, were dominant. Through his influence, the profession began to focus on the relationship between therapist and client, as opposed to the existing emphasis on either the client's intrapsychic experience or patterns of behavior. In one of his early writings, Rogers (1957) defined what he believed to be the "necessary and sufficient conditions" for positive personality change to occur. These conditions referred to characteristics inherent in a constructive interpersonal relationship, including accurate empathy, unconditional positive regard, and genuineness. These concepts have evolved over the years, and today they are generally acknowledged by most theoretical approaches as core conditions in the therapeutic process.

Accurate Empathy

There are numerous definitions of *empathy* in the counseling literature. Recently, an entire volume was written just on the concept of empathy (Bohart & Greenberg, 1997a). The one that we like is the following: the ability to (1) understand the client's experience and (2) feel with or emotionally resonate to the client's experience as if it were your own but without losing the "as if" quality (Rogers, 1957; Bozarth, 1997).

Empathic understanding involves two primary steps:

1. "Empathic rapport"; that is, accurately sensing the client's world and being able to see things the way he or she does (Bohart & Greenberg, 1997, p. 13)
2. "Communicative attunement"; that is, verbally sharing your understanding with the client (Bohart & Greenberg, 1997, p. 14)

How do you know when the client feels you have understood? Client responses such as "Yes, that's it" or "That's exactly right" indicate some sort of recognition by the client of the level of your understanding. When your clients say something like that after one of your responses, you are assured that they feel you are following and understanding what is occurring.

Learning to understand is not an easy process. It involves the capacity to switch from your own set of experiences to those of your clients, as seen through their eyes, not yours. It involves sensing the feelings they have, not the feelings you have or might have had in the same or similar circumstances. It involves skillful listening, so that you can hear not only the obvious but also the subtle shadings of which, perhaps, even the client is not yet aware.

Empathy also involves having good internal boundaries for yourself. An internal boundary helps to separate personal thoughts, feelings, and behavior from the thoughts, feelings, and behaviors of others (Mellody, 1989, p. 11). Rogers (1957) asserted that empathy is being sensitive to a client's experiencing a feeling. This is sometimes called *resonant empathy* (Buie, 1981). You can feel with the client yet you do not take on the client's feelings and actually feel them yourself. This is an area that occasionally poses problems, especially for beginning counselors. In your eagerness to be helpful, you may find yourself becoming so involved with the client that you get disconnected from yourself and what you are feeling. Instead, you take on the client's feelings and perhaps even find yourself obsessing about the client long after the session is over. Such *immersion* is not helpful because you lose your capacity to be objective in a subjective way about the client's experience. As a result, you may avoid seeing, hearing, or saying important things in the session. If you feel this is happening to you, you can talk it over with a supervisor. You also can get reconnected to yourself during a session by taking a minute to focus internally and privately on what you are feeling and by taking some deep breaths.

Understanding clients' perspectives alone is not sufficient. You also must express verbally to clients your sense of understanding about them. This kind of communication is, in effect, a kind of mirror—feeding back clients' feelings to them, without agreeing or disagreeing, reassuring or denying. Accurate empathy involves not only mirroring your clients' feelings but also some parts of the immediate process. For example, if clients continually ask many questions, rather than discuss the issues that brought them to counseling, it would be appropriate to reflect on the obvious with statements such as:

"You have a lot of questions to ask right now."
"You seem to be wanting a lot of information about this."

"You are asking a lot of questions. I wonder if you are uncertain about what to expect."

Learning to develop accurate empathy with your client and with other people takes time and practice. You must experience the clients' feeling first, understand it as best you can, then react to it using your own words. Effectively used, empathy helps clients to "symbolize, organize, and make sense" of their experiences (Bohart & Greenberg, 1997, p. 15).

Cultural and Relational Empathy

In addition to understanding the client's verbal message, it is also important to consider the impact of gender and cultural backgrounds. There is increasing evidence that men and women talk in different ways (Tannen, 1990) and that cultural/historical backgrounds affect the meaning the client conveys as well as the meaning the therapist interprets. O'Hara (1997) observed that "there is good evidence that people are not all in the world in the same way and that the way people experience themselves and their phenomenal world has differed historically across time and still differs from context to context" (p. 301).

Cultural empathy includes consideration of context and society in which both the counselor and the client live. When context is ignored and attempts to understand are made solely from an individualistic frame of reference, "blaming the victim" can result (O'Hara, 1997, p. 311). As an example of this, consider the way in which the understanding of unwed teenage pregnancy is often confined to the individual teenage girl who presents with the pregnancy. Absent from this empathic quotient is the understanding of larger system issues about why the girl became pregnant in the first place (O'Hara, 1997). Ignoring social context overlooks the relational world in which clients live—the dyads, families, racial-ethnic groups, social class, occupational groups, and genders to which clients belong. As O'Hara (1997) noted, effective counseling is more than just a venture of two people—it is a "multilevel, relational situation" (p. 311). Stone Center theorists have coined the term *relational empathy* to describe this process (Jordan, 1997). Relational empathy involves empathy for oneself, other people, and the counseling relationship. In empathic interactions with the therapist, the client develops self-empathy as well as an increase in empathic attunement to others. This leads to "enhanced relational capacity and to an increase in self-esteem" (Jordan, 1997, p. 345).

Jenkins (1997) stated that there is a considerable degree of "empathic failure" in therapy with ethnic minority clients and that ethnic minority clients, because of their experience of social exclusion, will test the therapist's empathic capacities early on in the counseling process. A Eurocentric counselor may fail these tests because of more limited ways of "knowing" persons of color.

For therapists to work effectively with clients from cultures different from their own, they must be able to step back from the usual ways of knowing and be open to different ways of seeing things (Jenkins, 1997). To empathize effectively with clients of color, therapists must also be able to discuss openly the "racial implications" of the client's struggles (Jenkins, 1997, p. 334).

In working empathically with all clients, Jordan (1997) believes that working with the disconnections and misunderstandings, referred to as "empathic failures," is very powerful. She notes, "Therapists must be honest regarding their mistakes and misattunements.... Disconnections and failures in mutuality and empathy must be named and understood" (pp. 349–350).

EXERCISE 2.1

Accurate Empathy and Cultural Empathy

A. Hearing and Verbalizing Client Concerns

Using triads with one person as speaker, a second as respondent, and the third as observer, complete the following tasks. Then rotate roles until each person has had an opportunity to react in all three ways.

1. The speaker should begin by sharing a personal concern or issue with the listener.
2. The respondent should
   a. listen to the speaker and account for gender, cultural, and historical factors as well as the verbal message.
   b. verbalize to the speaker what he or she heard.
3. The observer should note the extent to which the others accomplished their tasks and whether any understanding or misunderstanding occurred.

Following a brief (five-minute) interaction, respond verbally to the following questions:

SPEAKER: Do you think the respondent heard what you had to say? Did you think he or she understood you? Did the listener seem to understand your culture? Discuss this with the respondent.

RESPONDENT: Did you let the speaker know you understood or attempted to understand? How did you do this? What blocks within yourself interfered with doing so? Did you struggle with the person's cultural affiliations?

OBSERVER: Discuss what you saw taking place between the speaker and the respondent.

Now reverse roles and complete the same process.

B. *Understanding Client Concerns*
This exercise should be completed with a group of 3 to 10 people sitting in a circle.

1. Each participant is given a piece of paper and a pencil.
2. Each participant should complete, in writing and anonymously, the following sentence: *My primary concern about becoming a counselor is*

_____

_____

_____

3. Papers are folded and placed in the center of the circle.
4. Each participant draws a paper. (If one person receives his or her own, all should draw again.)
5. Each participant reads aloud the concern listed, then talks several minutes about what it would be like to have this concern. Other participants can then add to this.

This process continues until each participant has read and discussed a concern. When discussing the concern, attempt to reflect only your *understanding* of the world of the person with this concern. Do *not* attempt to give a solution or advice.

After the exercise, members should give each other feedback about the level of empathic understanding that was displayed during the discussion. Feedback should be specific so participants can use it for behavior change.

C. *Cultural and Relational Empathy*
Consider your capacity to relate to clients who are both similar to and different from yourself along cultural dimensions. Explore and discuss the following three questions, adapted from Hardy and Laszloffy (1995, p. 234):

1. What are your family's beliefs and feelings about the group(s) that comprise your culture of origin? What parts of the group(s) do they embrace or reject? How has this influenced your feelings about your cultural identity?
2. What aspects of your culture of origin do you have the most comfort "owning"? The most difficulty "owning"?
3. What groups will you have the easiest time understanding and relating to? The most difficult?

Shame and the Empathy Bond

Another factor that is increasingly recognized as having a substantial impact on the helping relationship is shame. Shame is viewed as a central component or main regulator of a person's affective life. Normal shame is about values and limits; it is recognized, spoken about, and acknowledged. The shame that is considered problematic and a primary contributor to aggression, addictions, obsessions, narcissism, and depression is hidden shame—shame that is unacknowledged, repressed, or defended against that seems to result in either an attack on others or an incredible self-loathing (Karen, 1992).

According to Lewis (1971), shame is inescapable in the counselor-client relationship and has major implications for the empathic bonding of the counselor to the client. Karen quoted Lewis as follows: "However good your reasons for going into treatment, so long as you are an adult speaking to another adult to whom you are telling the most intimate things, there is an undercurrent of shame in every session" (1992, p. 50). Lewis (1971) asserted that not only do counselors overlook shame in clients and bypass dealing with it but they inadvertently add to a client's "shame tank" through judgmental interpretations. Value judgments about the client's culture can also contribute to a sense of shame. Lewis stated that when this happens, the client becomes enraged at the counselor but, because he or she cannot accept feeling angry toward someone who is a "helper," it is turned inward and becomes depression and self-denigration. Lewis cautioned counselors to be alert to client states of shame so that they can help clients work through and discharge the feeling. In this way, clients can move ahead. Otherwise, they are likely to continue to move in and out of shame attacks or shame spirals, both within and outside of the counseling sessions.

A major precursor to shame appears to be the lack of parental empathy. According to Miller (1985), a child's sense of self-esteem comes largely from the parents' capacity to tune in empathically with the child, to mirror and reflect the child as she or he develops. As Karen (1992) pointed out, in therapy, "the same phenomenon requires a special sensitivity on the part of the therapist. The patient is hypersensitive about acceptance and abandonment and uncertain of whether he can trust the therapist with his wound—a wound that, he no doubt senses, the therapy session has great potential to exacerbate. The therapist must win over the hiding, shameful side of the personality and gradually help it to heal" (p. 65). The counselor does this by creating an empathic bond with the client—that is, an emotional connection, a genuine feeling for the client. Although empathy can be conveyed by certain techniques (such as the verbal expressions we noted earlier), ultimately there is no substitute for the counselor's ability to genuinely care for and feel with the client. Empathy appears to be the critical variable in the healing of pathological shame (Jordan, 1997).

Shame can also be culture bound. Hardy and Laszloffy (1995) pointed out that every cultural group has pride and shame issues—that is, "aspects of a culture that are sanctioned as distinctively negative or positive" (p. 229). These are important issues to identify about a client's cultural group because they help to define appropriate and inappropriate behavior within a cultural context.

Positive Regard

In his early writings, Carl Rogers (1957) described positive regard as unconditional. That quality has been interpreted by Hansen, Rossberg, and Cramer (1994) as "respect[ing] the client regardless of differences in values, differences in worldview; in short, no condition is set upon the client's behaviors and experiences" (p. 82). Egan (1998) elaborated on the concept of respect, noting that it involves the following behaviors:

> Do no harm.
>
> Become competent and committed.
>
> Make it clear you are "for" the client.
>
> Assume the client's goodwill.
>
> Do not rush to judgment.
>
> Keep the *client's* agenda in focus. (pp. 44–46)

More recent writers have relabeled positive regard as *nonpossessive warmth.*

Positive regard, or nonpossessive warmth, is often misconstrued as agreement or lack of disagreement with the client. Instead, it is an attitude of valuing the client. To show positive regard is to express appreciation of the client as a unique and worthwhile person. It is also to be noncritical, to provide an "overall sense of protection, support, or acceptance, no matter what is divulged" (Karasu, 1992, p. 36). As Karasu noted, unconditional or positive regard specifically means that the client's supposedly bad or unacceptable ideas, wishes, and feelings can be expressed without loss of the counselor's respect and attention. In other words, the client can divulge whatever is needed and still be protected from the counselor's "personal reactions, especially those that reflect rejection or disdain" (p. 37).

EXERCISE **2.2**

Positive Regard

A. *Overcoming Barriers to Positive Regard*

Think of expressing to the client (1) those limitations that may be blocking your sense of liking for the client and (2) those strengths that increase your appreciation for the client. The following steps may assist you in expressing this:

1. Picture the other person in your mind. Begin a dialogue in which you express what it is that is interfering with your sense of positive regard. Now, reverse the roles. Become the other person. What does the person say in response? Then what do you say?

2. Complete this process again. This time, express the strengths you see in the other person—what you appreciate about that person. Again, reverse the roles. Become the other person. What does he or she say in response? Then what do you say?

This exercise can be used with any client toward whom you have difficulty experiencing positive regard.

B. Expressing Positive Regard

Take a few minutes to think of a person with whom you currently have a relationship and for whom you experience positive regard. What kinds of things do you do to express your feelings of positive regard for this person? Jot them down.

_____

_____

_____

There is no set answer to the preceding exercise because each person has a different style of communicating good feelings for another person. The first step, though, is positive regard—to feel comfortable enough to *express* warm feelings to someone else. Being free enough to spontaneously share feelings of regard for another human being is a process that can be learned.

Think again for a moment about several of your existing relationships with a few people close to you—perhaps your spouse, parent, child, neighbor, or friend. Then respond, in writing, to the following questions:

What is your level of expression of positive regard to these people?

How often do you say things like "I like you"; "It's nice to be with you"; "You're good for me"; "I enjoy you"; and so forth?

What is your feeling when you do?

What is the effect on the other person?

If your expression of these kinds of statements is infrequent, what might be holding you back?

Either now or later, seek out someone you like and try to express these kinds of feelings to that person. Then think again about the previous questions. Share your reactions with your partner. In doing this, you will probably note that warmth and positive regard are expressed both nonverbally and verbally. Nonverbally, they are shown by facial expression, smiling, and eye contact. In fact, you might think of your entire nonverbal stance as communicating a degree of enthusiasm for the other person.

In counseling, positive regard is sometimes shown when the physical posture of the counselor mirrors that of the client. Verbally, you express your feelings for another person by statements that reflect a sense of caring and affection, best described, perhaps, by the word *nurturance.* Affectional nurturing statements can have a strong effect on the client and on the relationship. They are most effective when used *selectively* and *sincerely.* You know the feeling you have about someone who is always saying nice things—these statements lose their effect when used constantly. Some examples of affectional nurturing statements are:

> **CLIENT:** "I know I shouldn't do that because at those times I'm selfish, yet it's hard for me to always do everything for her first, but I am selfish and that's an even worse way for me to be."
>
> **COUNSELOR:** "I like you even when you're selfish."
>
> **CLIENT:** (Crying) "I'm sorry I'm crying. They [parents] tell me I am a baby for doing it, but I am so worried, but uh, I'll try not to do it."
>
> **COUNSELOR:** "It's all right for you to cry with me."

Think of some affectional nurturing statements on your own. List them here and discuss them with someone:

_____

_____

_____

_____

_____

Genuineness

The notion that the counselor should project genuineness is also difficult to define. Rogers tended to connect it with *congruence,* a condition reflecting honesty, transparency, and openness to the client. Genuineness implies that therapists are real in their interactions with clients. As Corey (1996) noted, this means counselors are "without a false front, their inner and outer experiences match, and they can openly express feelings and attitudes that are present in the relationship with the client" (p. 205).

Through being genuine and congruent, counselors model for clients not only the experience of being real but also the process of claiming one's truths and speaking about them. When this happens, there is usually more vitality and a greater "connection" in the counseling relationship. As Jordan (1997) noted, "We all know the deadened, bored, or anxious feelings that occur in interactions in which people cannot risk being in their truth.... Inauthenticity takes us out of real mutuality" (p. 350).

The beginning counselor may find this condition easier to apply in theory than in practice. Questions such as What if I really don't like my client? Should I let that be known? Wouldn't it destroy the relationship? inevitably rise when genuineness and congruence are examined. The appropriate answer to these questions may not be entirely satisfying. Genuineness dictates that the counselor be honest, but in helpful, rather than destructive, ways.

Expression of your feelings should not take precedence over understanding the client's feelings. The counseling relationship does not have all the mutuality that is present in many other relationships, such as friend to friend, partner to partner, and so forth. Corey (1996) cautioned that genuineness does not mean, however, that the counselor impulsively shares all thoughts and feelings with clients in a nonselective way. A general rule of thumb is to share your feelings when they are persistent and block your acceptance of the client.

Before you can express your feelings, you must become aware of them. For example, ask yourself what it means to be genuine. Can you tell when you are being yourself or when you are presenting an image that is different from the way you actually feel? In order to communicate genuineness to the client, you must first learn to get in touch with yourself and your own truth—to become aware of who you are as an individual and what kinds of thoughts and feelings you have. This involves learning to discriminate between your various feelings and allowing them to come into your awareness without denial or distortion; it means, for example, that when you are happy, you can acknowledge that you are happy and when you are angry, you can be aware of your anger. It also means that you can speak about these "truths."

EXERCISE 2.3

Dyadic Encounter

To assist you in becoming aware of your own thoughts and feelings, select a partner and spend a few minutes with this dyadic encounter experience (Banikiotes, Kubinski, & Pursell, 1981). It is designed to facilitate getting to know yourself and another person on a fairly close level. All you need to do is respond to the open-ended questions as honestly and directly as possible. Both of you should respond to one question at a time. The discussion statements can be completed at whatever level of self-disclosure you wish.

My name is _____ .
The reason I'm here is _____ .

One of the most important skills in getting to know another person is listening. In order to check on your ability to understand what your partner is communicating, the two of you should go through the following steps one at a time.

Decide which one of you is to speak first in this unit. The first speaker is to complete the following item in two or three sentences:

When I think about the future. I see myself . . .

The second speaker repeats in his or her own words what the first speaker has just said. The first speaker must be satisfied that he or she has been heard accurately.

The second speaker then completes the item in two or three sentences. The first speaker paraphrases what the second speaker just said, to the satisfaction of the second speaker.

Share what you may have learned about yourself as a listener with your partner. To check your listening accuracy, the two of you may find yourselves later saying to each other, "Do you mean that . . . ?" or "You're saying that . . . ."

When I am new in a group, I . . .
When I am feeling anxious in a new situation, I usually . . .
You're saying that . . . (listening check)
Right now, I'm feeling . . .
When I am rejected, I usually . . .
The thing that turns me off the most is . . .
Toward you right now, I feel . . .
When I am alone, I usually . . .
I feel angry about . . .
Do you mean that . . . ? (listening check)
I am rebellious when . . .

Checkup

Have a short discussion about this experience so far. Keep eye contact as much as you can and try to cover the following points:

How well are you listening?
How open and honest have you been?
How eager are you to continue this interchange?
Do you feel that you are getting to know each other?

Then continue with the following:

I love . . .
I feel jealous about . . .
Right now, I'm feeling. . .
I am afraid of . . .
The thing I like best about you is . . .
You are . . .
Right now, I am responding most to . . .

Self-Disclosure

Expression of your thoughts, ideas, and feelings follows after your awareness of them. This process might also be called *self-expression* or *self-disclosure*. Self-expression and disclosure are important ways of letting the client know that you are a person and not just a role; however, self-disclosure should be used appropriately and not indiscriminately in the counseling sessions.

It is important not to interpret self-disclosure to mean that you ought to talk about yourself, since the primary focus of the interview is on the client. Thus, genuineness does not mean that you reveal your own experiences and values. It does mean, however, that occasionally it is appropriate and helpful for you to reveal or disclose a particular feeling you may have about the counseling session or about the client. The clue to appropriateness is often determined by the question: Whose needs am I meeting when I disclose this idea or feeling—the client's or mine? Clearly, the former is the much more appropriate instance of the two. There are several different kinds of self-disclosure. These include:

1. The counselor's own problems
2. Facts about the counselor's role
3. The counselor's reactions to the client (feedback)
4. The counselor's reactions to the counselor-client relationship

Usually, disclosure in the latter two areas is more productive. Many times, counselors are tempted to share their problems and concerns when encountering a client with similar problems. In a few instances, this may be done as a reassurance to clients that their concerns are not catastrophic. But, in most other instances, a role reversal occurs—the counselor is gaining something by this sharing with the client. Some research indicates that the counselor who discloses at a *moderate* level may be perceived by the client more positively than the counselor who discloses at a high or low level (Edwards & Murdock, 1994). Thus, too much or too little self-disclosure may limit the client's confidence in you as an effective helper.

Often, clients may ask questions concerning information about the counselor: Are you married? Why did you become a counselor? Are you in school? These are common types of questions clients ask in seeking facts about the counselor. In this case, it is usually best just to give a direct, brief answer and then return the interview focus to the client. However, if this is a common occurrence with the same client, there are other ways of responding. Continual client questioning of this sort often indicates that the client is anxious and is attempting to get off the "hot seat" by turning the focus onto you. There are better ways to handle this than by spending the interview disclosing facts about yourself! Alternative ways of responding include:

1. Reflect on the client's feelings of anxiety: "You seem anxious about talking about yourself now."

2. Reflect on the process: "You seem to be asking a lot of questions now."
3. Make a statement about what you see happening: "I think you feel as if you're on the 'hot seat' and asking me questions is a good way for you to get off it."

EXERCISE 2.4

Self-Disclosure

Think about yourself in the following instances:

1. You have a client who describes herself as shy and retiring. During the third interview, she says, "I'd like to be like you—you seem so outgoing and comfortable with people. Why don't you just tell me how you got that way?" Do you then consider it appropriate to share some of your experiences with her? Do you think your response to this might vary, depending on the client's cultural affiliations? If so, how?

2. You have had one particular client for about seven individual sessions. After the first session, the client has been at least several minutes late for each session and waits until almost the end of the interview to bring up something important to discuss. You feel that he is infringing on your time. This is preventing you from giving your full attention and understanding to the client. You have acknowledged to yourself that this is bothering you. Is it appropriate to go ahead and express this to him?

Take a few minutes to think about yourself as the counselor in these two examples. Now write in the following space what you would do in each example to communicate *facilitative genuineness:*

_____

_____

_____

_____

There are no right or wrong answers to these two examples; each counseling interaction is somewhat different. Ultimately, you, as the counselor, will have to make a decision like this for yourself in each instance. Based on the preceding written material, perhaps you did indicate that it would be more appropriate to express your irritation (the second example) than to disclose your experiences (the first). In the first instance, rather than sharing facts about yourself, there are more productive ways of helping that client reach her goals. For example, she would be more involved if you suggest role reversal. You become the client; have her be the outgoing and comfortable counselor she sees. In the second instance, the client, by being late, is not fulfilling his share of the responsibility or he is indirectly communicating something about his feelings that needs to be discussed.

Some counselors are able to acknowledge their feelings and determine when these can best be expressed in the interview but are not sure how to express these kinds of thoughts and feelings to the client. Self-disclosure or expressions of genuineness are often characterized by sharing and feedback statements—statements that convey to the client your sense of what is going on and your feelings about it. These kinds of statements are illustrated by the following examples:

> "I am glad you shared that with me."
> "If that happened to me, I think I'd feel pretty angry."
> "I don't feel that we're getting anywhere right now."

Other examples of sharing kinds of responses are:

CLIENT: "It's hard for me to say so but I really do get a lot out of these sessions."

COUNSELOR: "That makes me feel good to hear you say that."
or:
"I'm glad to know you feel that way."

Note that in the counselor's sharing statements, the communication is *direct*—it focuses on the counselor's feelings and on the client. It is a better statement than a generalized comment like "I hope most clients would feel the same way." A sharing and feedback statement should avoid the trap of "counselor language." To begin a sharing and/or feedback statement with "I hear you saying," "It seems that you feel," or "I feel that you feel" gets wordy, repetitive, and even phony. Say *exactly* what you mean.

EXERCISE 2.5

Expressing Counselor Feelings

Sharing and feedback communicate to the client that you have heard or seen something going on and that you have certain thoughts or feelings about it that you want to communicate. Sometimes you will want to say not only what you feel about a specific instance or experience but also how you feel about the client. This will be more effective if your feelings are expressed as immediate ones—that is, expressed in the *present* rather than in the past or future. This is the meaning of keeping the process of relationship in the *here and now,* using what is going on from moment to moment in each session to build the relationship. It is represented by the type of statement that communicates, "Right now, I'm feeling . . ." or "Right now, we are . . ."

To experience this here-and-now kind of communication, try to get in touch with yourself this instant. What are you feeling *this very moment* as you are reading and thinking about this page, this paragraph, this sentence? Write down four or five adjectives that express your present feelings. Tune in to your nonverbal cues as well (body position, rate of breathing, tension spots, etc.).

_____

_____

_____

EXERCISE **2.6**

Using Sharing Statements

With a partner, engage in some sharing-type statements that are direct, specific, and immediate. Can you tune in to your feelings as you engage in this kind of communication? What does it do for you and what effect does it have on the other person? Jot down some of these reactions here. List the sharing statements you have made to your partner.

_____

_____

_____

_____

_____

Sharing statements reflect the expression of the counselor's thoughts and feelings. Feedback statements incorporate a description of *client behavior,* as well. Some examples of counselors' feedback-type statements are "When you are continually late to the sessions (client behavior), I feel it is a loss to both of us" (counselor feeling) or "When you talk about school, your face really lights up" (client behavior) and "It feels good to me to see you so happy about that" (counselor reaction).

You probably are aware that these examples have several characteristics fundamental to effective feedback processes. Such statements express a feeling of acknowledgment and *ownership* by the counselor, as in "When something happens, I feel thus and so" or "When I see you _____ , I think _____ ." They avoid judgment and evaluation. Most of all, they do not accuse or blame, as in the following statement: "You are a real problem to work with because you are always late." In other words, they preserve the dignity and self-respect of the other person involved in the relationship. Furthermore, an effective feedback statement does not contain advice; it is not a "parenting" or scolding statement. It also should concern a behavior or attitude the other person has the capacity to change or modify. It would not be helpful, for instance, to use the following kind of feedback statement: "I just don't like the way you look. Why don't you do something about your complexion?"

Feedback is usually more effective when it is solicited. Thus, feedback statements that relate to clients' goals or to aspects of the counseling relationship may be better received by clients because of their involvement in this. In any case, though, you can determine the effects of your feedback by the clients' reactions. If your clients are defensive, give detailed explanation or justification, or make strong denials, this is a clue that your feedback was not solicited and that perhaps you have touched on an issue too soon. At this point in the relationship, clients need an indication of your support and acceptance.

EXERCISE 2.7

Using Feedback Statements

With a partner, try some feedback-type statements that meet the characteristics described in the preceding section. Be sure your responses include a description of your partner's behavior as well as your reactions to it. For example, you might say something like "I appreciate (your feeling) your taking the time to talk with me (partner's behavior)."

List the feedback statements you make to your partner. What are the effects on you? On the other person? On the relationship?

_____

_____

_____

A Climate of Safety

The primary reason why the conditions of a therapeutic relationship are so important is to help clients feel safe. When clients feel safe, they feel trusting and free to be open and disclosive. As Karasu (1992) observed, "This special permission to experience one's psychic life under the interpersonal sheath of a psychologically safe environment gives psychotherapy its unique quality, allowing the [client] to gradually shed the accumulated layers of defensive armor" (p. 37). When clients do not feel safe, they often feel self-protective, guarded, and subdued. It is the counselor's responsibility to offer the kind of climate in which clients feel the sense of safety they need in order to ask for and accept help. If a client has come from a particular kind of family or relationship in which there was a lot of stress, such as abuse or incest, then the counselor's effort to provide a safe environment will need to be even more intentional and more intensive.

Clients, particularly those who have had their trust broken in the past, will often test the counselor. They will likely not believe that the therapist's initial efforts to be understanding, sincere, accepting, and warm are really true. They may want to find out if they really mean something to the counselor—if they really are valued as the therapist says they are. This reason may account for all kinds of client feelings and behaviors that are projected or reflected in or outside a session, including acting out, calling the counselor on the phone, being late to a session, becoming angry, and so on. It is as if clients long for a warm, caring empathic helper but, due to their history, fear this and in their fear, resist, attack, or retreat (Karasu, 1992, p. 21). Efforts to provide a safe therapeutic environment for clients need to be ongoing and persistent. This is also especially true in working with clients who do not have privileges and power from the mainstream culture and who have a history of discrimination and oppression.

Summary

Although the counseling relationship has some marked differences from other interpersonal relationships, it does serve as a model that the client can use to improve the quality of relationships outside the counseling room. You must assume responsibility at the outset of counseling for those qualities that generate and maintain the relationship process. Later, as the client's comfort and social skills get stronger, the relationship becomes more of a mutually responsible process.

Clearly, the counseling relationship cannot succeed without the presence of accurate empathy or understanding of the client's world. When you assume that you understand, but you do not, you and your client detour from a constructive and helpful course and risk the dangers of false conclusions and failure. In a similar manner, if you do not value your client or if you do not consider the client's problems and concerns to be real, you are denying the most reliable information about your client's perceptions. Lacking this information, you cannot help your client develop in more constructive directions. Finally, and underlying both accurate empathy and positive regard, the degree to which you can be honestly and consistently yourself, knowing yourself, and sharing yourself with your client will establish the ultimate parameters of the helping relationship.

Although the behaviors presented in this chapter can be learned and incorporated into your style and repertoire, there is a dimension yet to be acknowledged. The integral human element of the counseling relationship cannot exist by mechanical manipulation of certain behaviors at given moments. Your relationship with each client contains its own uniqueness and spontaneity that cannot, without the loss of both genuineness and sincerity, be systematically controlled prior to its occurrence. Your spontaneity, however, will increase rather than decrease once you have become comfortable with a variety of counseling techniques. While you are learning counselor responses, this ease may not be quite as apparent because you will need to overlearn them. However, once the responses suggested in this book have become second nature to you, your spontaneity as a counselor will begin to emerge. You will be on your way to becoming the helper you hope to be.

DISCUSSION QUESTIONS

1. How do you approach a new relationship? What conditions do you require to be met before you open yourself to a closer relationship?

2. What were the "unwritten rules" in your family and in your culture about interactions with nonfamily members? How might these rules affect the kind of relationship you are able to offer clients?

3. If you were a client, what conditions would you look for in your counselor?

4. Under what conditions do you feel safe? Open and disclosive? Trusting? Does this vary with persons of different ages, gender, values, and ethnic origins?

RECOMMENDED READINGS

Bohart, A., & Greenberg, L. (Eds.). (1997). *Empathy reconsidered.* Washington, DC: American Psychological Association.

Bozarth, J. (1997). Empathy from the framework of client-centered theory and the Rogerian hypothesis. In A. Bohart & L. Greenberg (Eds.), *Empathy reconsidered* (pp. 81–102). Washington, DC: American Psychological Association.

Brammer, L. M. (1993). *The helping relationship* (5th ed.). Boston: Allyn and Bacon.

Edwards, C., & Murdock, N. (1994). Characteristics of therapist self-disclosure in the counseling process. *Journal of Counseling and Development, 72,* 384–389.

Egan, G. (1998). *The skilled helper* (6th ed.). Pacific Grove, CA: Brooks/Cole.

Jenkins, A. H. (1997). The empathic context in psychotherapy with people of color. In A. Bohart & L. Greenberg (Eds.), *Empathy reconsidered* (pp. 321–342). Washington, DC: American Psychological Association.

Jordan, J. (1997). Relational development through mutual empathy. In A. Bohart & L. Greenberg (Eds.), *Empathy reconsidered* (pp. 343–352). Washington, DC: American Psychological Association.

Kahn, M. (1991). *Between therapist and client: The new relationship.* New York: Freeman.

Karasu, T. B. (1992). *Wisdom in the practice of psychotherapy.* New York: Basic Books.

Karen, R. (1992). Shame. *Atlantic Monthly, 269,* 40–70.

Kelly, E. W., Jr. (1997). Relationship-centered counseling: A humanistic model of integration. *Journal of Counseling and Development, 75,* 337–345.

CHAPTER

3

Attending to Clients

Thus far, we have identified several conditions that affect the development of the counseling relationship. Those conditions—accurate empathy, positive regard, and genuineness or congruence—are called *core conditions* because they are central to the therapeutic process. While these core conditions are necessary, the counselor must also bring other skills and knowledge to the therapeutic process. Certainly the first of these skills is the ability to *listen* actively and attentively to the client. This objective is not so simple as it might appear. It involves more than an attentive ear.

Have you ever talked to someone who was fiddling with a pencil, staring around the room, or seemed otherwise distracted as he or she listened to you? If you have—and who has not?—you will recall how this felt. The listener may have heard all that you said, but you probably interpreted his or her behavior as a lack of interest, concentration, or attention. That seemingly to be the case, you probably found it difficult to continue the conversation. Clients exhibit this same sensitivity to whether the counselor is paying attention to what they say. Nonverbal behavior does influence the verbal message with which it is paired, particularly when inconsistencies exist between verbal and nonverbal messages.

This chapter is concerned with the behaviors that do or do not facilitate communication and the core conditions in counseling. In addition, attending skills used by the counselor to assure the client and to support or reinforce the client are examined. These skills are very important for the client who is feeling vulnerable, uncertain, nonconfident, or nontrusting. As Gazda and colleagues (1995) noted, "When verbal and nonverbal messages are in contradiction, we usually believe the nonverbal message" (p. 87).

One precondition for the existence of these reinforcing or supporting behaviors is an awareness of the client's communication. This awareness must then be communicated through your undistracted attentiveness to the client. Attentiveness is one way of saying, "I am following both your message and your metacommunication; I am experiencing as you are experiencing this moment; I am invested and involved in your story." Studies have indicated that attentiveness is related to other counselor attitudes, most notably empathy and involvement. Counselor interest and commitment are related to clients' and observers' perceptions of the counselor's empathy and positive regard.

Communication of Attentiveness

Attentiveness is communicated primarily through four channels: facial expressions, eye contact, bodily positions and movement, and verbal responses (Cormier & Cormier, 1998). Although attending to clients on the surface appears relatively simple, it is easier said than done. Egan (1998) listed a number of obstacles to the attending process:

1. Being preoccupied
2. Being judgmental
3. Having biases
4. Pigeonholing clients
5. Attending to facts
6. Rehearsing
7. Sympathizing
8. Interrupting

In the following sections of the chapter, we describe nonverbal and verbal ways to increase your attentiveness with clients.

The meanings people attach to different gestures or words have been learned. Some of the meanings are fairly standardized; others have distinct regional or cultural variances. For example, do you prefer to have people look at you when you talk to them? Most Euro-Americans do, but some Native Americans do not, and studies suggest that some inner-city African American youths do not. It is important to remember that some cultural groups have sanctions on direct visual contact during some types of interpersonal interactions. When you are telling someone what you think, what would be your reaction if that person began to frown? If the frown was not consistent with your feelings, you probably would begin to question the inconsistency between your message and the listener's response. If you feel strongly about a topic and the other person does not seem to care about it, are you likely to continue telling the person about your feelings? No, since most of us want to know that our feelings are falling on concerned ears.

For these and many more reasons, your behavior can contribute to your client's feelings of security. This increased sense of security that occurs at the same time clients are talking about themselves can become a self-reinforcing phenomenon. Most of you have probably had the experience of entering a new activity and feeling nervous and unsure of yourselves. But as you stayed with the activity and nothing bad (perhaps even some good things) happened, before long, your self-confidence began to grow. So it is with counseling. As the client begins to experience your acceptance, your understanding, and your commitment, the feelings of vulnerability, uncertainty, caution, or lack of trust begin to dissipate. Is this a predictable reaction? Yes, it is, with the majority of clients who are in search of themselves, a better way to live life, or a better way to relate to others.

Facial Expressions

Knapp and Hall (1992) have observed that the face is the primary means by which people communicate information about their emotional states. Facial expressions convey basic emotions such as anger, disgust, fear, sadness, and happiness. Unlike most other aspects of nonverbal attending behavior, facial expressions do not seem to vary much among cultures. These basic emotions seem to be represented by the same facial expressions across cultures, although individual cultural norms may influence how much and how often such emotions are expressed (Mesquita & Frijda, 1992). For example, anger is often conveyed cross-culturally through the eyes and by changes in the area of the mouth and jaw. However, men and women both within and between the same and different cultures may express anger in different ways and at different times. For example, some persons may reject the idea of releasing anger because they have learned it is "unchristian" or "unladylike" (Kelley, 1979, p. 24).

Your facial expressions communicate messages to the client that are as meaningful as those you receive from the client's facial expressions. A primary, though often not intentional, way that counselors use their facial expressions is to reinforce client behavior. Perhaps it would be more accurate to say that the effect of your facial expressions is to reinforce, either positively or negatively, clients' verbal behavior. It is also important for your facial expressions to reflect those of the client—if the client expresses pleasure, you look happy; if the client conveys sadness, you show concern.

Animation

Animation in facial expression gives clients the feeling that you are alert and responding to ongoing communication. It may be that your facial expressions serve as a mirror for clients' feelings as well as an acceptance of them. Certainly, an absence of facial expressions (a deadpan look) will suggest a lack of interest, awareness, or mental presence to clients. The most noticeable expression is the smile. The appropriate use of smiles can have a powerful effect on clients, particularly when paired with occasional head nods. Continuous smiling, however, becomes a negative stimulus. Frequent frowns can communicate disapproval. Occasional frowns, on the other hand, communicate your failure to follow or understand a particular point and are therefore useful.

EXERCISE 3.1

Facial Expressions

A. Facial Attentiveness
With a partner, designate one of you as the speaker and the other as the listener. While the speaker shares one of his or her concerns, the listener's tasks are:

1. Do not respond with *any* facial expression or animation whatsoever while the speaker is talking; maintain complete facial passivity.
2. After two or three minutes, respond with a facial reaction that is opposite of the feelings and concerns being expressed by the speaker. For example, if the speaker is talking seriously, smile and look happy.
3. After another three minutes or so, respond with facial animation and expression that mirror the kind and intensity of feelings being expressed by the speaker.

Discuss the different results produced by these three approaches. Reverse roles and repeat the exercise. What can you conclude about facial attentiveness as a result of this exercise? What have you learned about yourself and your facial gestures? What do you want to change about your facial gestures and how do you intend to bring this change about? If possible, repeat this activity with a person from a distinctly different culture than your own. Do your conclusions change in any way?

B. Recognizing Facial Cues

Find two people with whom to work. Designate one of you as the speaker for round 1; the second as the listener, and the third as the observer. Roles are rotated for round 2 and round 3. For each round, the listener feeds each of the four incomplete sentences to the speaker. The speaker repeats the sentence and adds the first completion that comes to his or her mind. The observer watches for changes and cues in the speaker's facial expressions as he or she works with all of the incomplete sentences in the round. For this to be most effective, when you are in the role of the speaker, take your time, breathe deeply, and say whatever comes into your mind without thinking about it or censoring it. The observer shares the observations with the speaker after the round is over.

1. Anger
   a. When I get angry . . .
   b. I get angry when . . .
   c. I feel disgusted that . . .
   d. One thing that makes me mad is . . .
2. Sadness
   a. When I get sad . . .
   b. I get sad when . . .
   c. I feel "blue" that . . .
   d. One thing that makes me sad is . . .
3. Fear
   a. When I get afraid . . .
   b. I feel afraid that . . .
   c. I get afraid when . . .
   d. One thing that makes me afraid is . . .

Eye Contact

What is the effect of eye contact? Research into interpersonal interaction indicates that eye contact has more than one effect and that these effects do vary across cultures. It may signal a need for affiliation, involvement, or inclusion; it may reflect the quality of an existing relationship; or it may enhance the communication of a complex message. Eye contact can also produce anxiety in the other person. A gaze lasting longer than about 10 seconds can signal aggressiveness rather than acceptance. An averted gaze may hide shame over expressing something seen as culturally taboo.

In some cultures, client eye contact is appropriate when listening. In other cultures, an individual may look away as a sign of respect or may demonstrate more eye contact when talking and less eye contact while listening. Good eye contact—eye contact that reinforces clients and makes their communication easier—lies somewhere between the fixed gaze and "shifty eyes," or frequent breaks of eye contact. Look at clients when they are talking. Occasionally, permit your eyes to drift to an object away, *but not far away,* from the client. Then return your eyes to the client. Let yourself be natural. Do not be afraid to invite the client into the world of your vision. At the same time, avoid making stereotypical judgments about the client's eye contact or lack thereof. As Cormier and Cormier (1998) noted, "Unfortunately, counselors all too often equate avoidance of eye contact with disrespect, shyness, deception and/or depression, but for some clients of color, less frequent eye contact is typical of their culture and is not a sign of any of the above" (p. 81).

EXERCISE 3.2

Eye Contact

Perhaps you can better grasp the effects of eye contact by participating in the following dyadic exercise. With a partner, determine who will be the talker and who will be the listener. While the talker speaks, the listener should listen but avoid eye contact with the speaker. Then discuss the following questions: What are the effects on the speaker? How well did the speaker feel that he or she was able to communicate? Try the exercise again, but this time maintain eye contact with the speaker as described in the previous section. What effect does this have? Reverse roles and repeat the exercise. Discuss how the effects may vary, depending on the gender and culture of the participants.

Body Positions and Use of Space

Body positions serve important functions in a counseling session. Body positions and movement regulate space or distance between the counselor and a client, greeting of a client, termination of a session, and turn taking (that is, the exchange of speaker and listener roles within a conversation) (Cormier & Cormier, 1998, pp. 82–83). Body movement and comfort with physical space (closeness or distance) vary among cultures and with gender. Generally, among White people in the United States, counselors and clients sit face to face. Even an intervening object such as a desk is often considered a distraction. Yet, as Ivey, Ivey, and Simek-Morgan (1997, p. 59) noted, in some Eskimo and Inuit cultural groups, persons sit side by side when discussing a personal issue. Whites usually prefer several feet of distance between chairs; however, those from contact cultures may be more comfortable with closer distances (Watson, 1970). The effects of space also vary with a client's expression of feelings. A client who has just expressed a lot of anger often requires more personal space than someone who is feeling sad or experiencing a lot of pain. In short, the concept of space has no universals.

Gender also dictates what is considered appropriate space. Some females may be more comfortable with a closer distance to the counselor, especially if the counselor is female. However, many female clients may feel intruded upon if a male counselor positions himself too close for comfort. Clients with a history of severe physical and/or sexual abuse may require greater space, particularly at the beginning stage of counseling. To be respectful of all clients, it is important to allow *them* to choose the appropriate amount of distance from the therapist in the counseling interactions. Sue and Sue (1990) provided some contrasts in the use of space cross-culturally:

> For Latin Americans, Africans, Black Americans, Indonesians, Arabs, South Americans, and French, conversing with a person dictates a much closer stance than normally comfortable for Anglos. A Latin-American client may cause the counselor to back away because of the closeness taken. The client may interpret the counselor's behavior as indicative of aloofness, coldness, or a desire not to communicate. In some cross-cultural encounters, it may even be perceived as a sign of haughtiness and superiority. On the other hand, the counselor may misinterpret the client's behavior as an attempt to become inappropriately intimate, a sign of pushiness or aggressiveness. Both the counselor and the culturally different client may benefit from understanding that their reactions and behaviors are attempts to create the spatial dimension to which they are culturally conditioned. (p. 53)

One important aspect to body communication involves the amount of tension conveyed by the body. Astute counselors will note the degree of tension or relaxation in a client's body. A body that is blocking or holding back a feeling may be tense, with shallow, fast breathing. A relaxed body posture indicates comfort, both with the counseling setting and with the topic being discussed. Selective body tension communicates action. It may reflect a "working" moment for you—

involvement with the client, movement toward a goal, or preparation for something new. Body tension that is continuous will probably communicate discomfort with the client, the topic, or yourself. To be comfortable with yourself, it is important to begin from a base of relaxation. Exercise 3.3 may help you to achieve a desired state of relaxation.

EXERCISE 3.3

Relaxing

A. Muscle Relaxation

While sitting down, raise your hand and arms three to four inches above the armrests of the chair and then let them drop. Feel the tension flow out of your arms. Repeat this and try to increase the relaxation. Let your back and buttocks be in contact with as much of the chair as possible. Feel the chair pressing against your body. Tense the muscles in your legs and then release the tension. Feel the surge of warmth in your muscles as your legs relax. Repeat this tensing and releasing of leg muscles several times, each time achieving a little more relaxation. Now take three or four deep breaths slowly. After each breath, slowly release the air from your lungs. Do you feel more relaxed than when you started?

Do this exercise again, this time without any interruptions between different body exercises. This is a good exercise to do just before seeing a client. It is one of the ways by which you can prepare yourself for the session. As you do the exercise more often, you will find it easier and quicker to achieve a surprisingly comfortable state of relaxation.

B. Massage Relaxation

As you engage in this activity, breathe in and out through your nose in an even, balanced way. Rub the palms of your hands together for several minutes or until they feel very warm. Then lightly rest each hand on your head with your thumbs touching each temple. Place your hands on your forehead and smooth out any tension. Then gently massage this part of your head. Lightly massage over and under your eyes, moving your fingers down your nose as you massage under your eyes. Close your eyes and rest the palms of your hands on your eyes. Massage the area around your mouth and cheekbones. Move over to your jawbones and as you massage them, open your mouth and move your jaws around. Next, take your fingertips and massage all around your ears, allowing sounds around you to soften as you do so. Work your hands around to the back of your neck and massage the tension accumulated in this area. When finished, take your hands and shake the tension out, away from your body. This activity can also be done with a partner.

Visible Behavior

Together, facial expressions, eye contact, and body messages constitute the counselor's visible behavior. The impact of visible behavior on communication is considerable, as the following exercise will prove.

EXERCISE **3.4**

The Impact of Visible Behavior

Egan (1976, p. 101) has described an exercise that illustrates the importance of what you see in another person when you communicate. This exercise will give you an opportunity to measure the effect of your facial and body gestures on the person receiving your message. Select as your partner a person you have been wanting to involve in a conversation. Sit down facing each other. Each of you close your eyes and keep them closed throughout the conversation. Talk to each other for about five minutes. Then open your eyes, complete the conversation, and discuss the differences between visual and nonvisual communication. What compensations did you have to make while talking without sight? How successful do you believe you were in your communication attempts? What, in particular, were you missing in terms of visual feedback from your partner?

Verbal Behavior and Selective Attention

The things you say will have an immediate impact on your clients. Many studies have shown that the counselor's responses can mold and shape the direction of the client's responses. In other words, whatever topic you respond to with a verbal acknowledgment, the client will probably continue to talk about it. Topics that you do not respond to often get cut off or interrupted. This process is called *selective attention.* Ivey, Gluckstern, and Ivey (1993) noted that what the counselor chooses to focus on says more about the counselor than the client. These authors also noted that it is important to notice what topics the counselor selectively attends to so that the clients are not inadvertently or unconsciously steered away from topics they need to discuss just because they are uncomfortable to the counselor. If you become aware of this happening, it is useful to consult your supervisor (see also Chapter 11).

Several points should be considered in terms of your verbal impact. Fit your comments or questions into the context of the topic at hand. Do not interrupt clients or quickly change topics. Stay with the topics that clients introduce and help them develop and pursue them. This implies more than a technique; it is a highly conscious awareness of what is going on between you and your client. It is called *verbal following*. Practice verbal following in the following exercise.

EXERCISE **3.5**
Verbal Following

A. Roleplay of Verbal Following
In the roles of counselor and client, choose a partner and sit in pairs. Concentrate on using the verbal reinforcing behaviors discussed in this chapter. In your responses, react only to what the client has just said; do not add a new idea. Let your thinking be as close as possible to that of the client.

Prevent your facial gestures, body gestures, and verbal responses from distracting the client. After five minutes, stop the exercise and discuss the following with your client: What was your client most aware of in your behavior? How well did your client think you understood his or her communication? What, if any, behavior got in your client's way? Now reverse roles and repeat the exercise. What effect did your own gender and culture have on this activity? What about the client's gender and culture?

B. Verbal Following and Shifts in Focus
Shown here are some client statements followed by counselor responses. Describe each counselor response: Do you feel that it is a response to the client's statement? If not, describe the nature of the inappropriate response, such as *shift of topic, focus on others,* or *focus on past.*

> **CLIENT A:** "I think I just have to go away for a while. The pressure is really building up."
>
> **COUNSELOR:** "What would Bob say to that?"

The counselor did/did not (circle one) respond to the client's statement. If the counselor did not respond to the client's statement, the nature of the inappropriate response was _____ .

> **CLIENT B:** "She doesn't really care anymore, and I've got to learn to accept that."
>
> **COUNSELOR:** "You are fairly sure that she doesn't care."

The counselor did/did not (circle one) respond to the client's statement. If the counselor did not respond to the client's statement, the nature of the inappropriate response was _____ .

CLIENT C: "Grades are the biggest problem I have in school. I can't get poor grades and bring shame to my family."

COUNSELOR: "What did you do last year?"

The counselor did/did not (circle one) respond to the client's statement. If the counselor did not respond to the client's statement, the nature of the inappropriate response was _____ .

CLIENT D: "The job I have isn't fun, but I'm afraid if I quit, I might not get another job."

COUNSELOR: "Jobs are really getting hard to find."

The counselor did/did not (circle one) respond to the client's statement. If the counselor did not respond to the client's statement, the nature of the inappropriate response was _____ .

These exchanges illustrate some of the common pitfalls that await the counselor. In the exchange with client A, the response was probably inappropriate. The counselor seems to have jumped topics by bringing up Bob. In addition, the counselor ignored the client's reference to the pressure and its effect on him. The response given to client B could be quite appropriate, though it is not the only possible appropriate response. The counselor is responding directly to what the client said. The inappropriateness of the response to client C is more obvious. The counselor really did not respond to any of the key ideas in the client's statement. Instead, the counselor decided, for some reason, to collect information about the client. Moreover, the counselor also ignored the social and cultural implications of the client's situation. Finally, the response to client D is also inappropriate. The client is talking about feelings ("isn't fun"; "afraid"). The counselor's response has nothing to do with the client. Instead, the counselor shifted the focus to a social commentary on the current economic scene.

EXERCISE 3.6

Culturally Appropriate Behavior for Counselor Attentiveness

Now that you are aware of behavioral descriptions of inappropriate social behaviors and attending behaviors in the counseling setting, can you deduce some appropriate behaviors? Be specific as to nonverbal components (face, eyes, tone of voice, rate of speech, etc.), body-language components (head, arms, body position, etc.), and verbal components (choice of words, types of responses, etc.). List them on a sheet of paper.

For the second part of this activity, go back over your list you just created. Consider instances where your list of counselor attentiveness behaviors may not be culturally appropriate for some clients. Discuss examples you can think of with a partner or in a small group.

Vocal Characteristics and Minimal Verbal Followers

The use of a well-modulated, calm, but energetic vocal tone and pitch will reassure clients of your own comfort with their problems. The use of intermittent one-word phrases (minimal verbal followers) serves much the same purposes as do head nods and eye contact. These are verbal signs that you are listening and following what the client is saying. The more common minimal verbal stimuli are "mm-hmm," "mmm," "ah," and so forth. There is one hazard that should be mentioned: Overuse of these vocal stimuli can produce a parrotlike effect that has negative results. Later chapters will describe how you can use minimal verbal stimuli and other types of reinforcing behaviors to assist clients in developing their thinking.

Summary

One of the major goals in the counseling setting is to listen attentively and to communicate this attentiveness through the use of eye contact, intermittent head nods, a variety of facial expressions, relaxed posture, modulated voice, minimal verbal followers, and verbal responses that follow the client's topics. As we have seen in this chapter, many of these components of attentiveness vary, depending on the gender and culture of both counselor and client.

DISCUSSION QUESTIONS

1. How much do you rely on reactions (gestures or verbal responses) from the other person when you are trying to communicate an important message?

2. What is your typical response when you feel that you are failing in your attempt to communicate with another person?

3. What goals or objectives have you set for yourself in terms of improving your ability to be a good listener? What do you plan to do to achieve these goals?

4. What are some additional examples for social behaviors that you would find distracting if you were involved in a sensitive discussion of your private life?

5. Recall an incident in which you were sharing a significant moment with another person and that person displayed some distracting behavior. What was the effect

of that person's behavior on you? What did you decide was the reason for that person's behavior?

6. What do you notice about nonverbal behavior among persons from varying cultures?

7. What effect does your own culture have on the way you seem to attend and respond to clients?

RECOMMENDED READINGS

Cormier, L. S., & Cormier, W. H. (1998). *Interviewing strategies for helpers* (4th ed.). Pacific Grove, CA: Brooks/Cole.

Egan, G. (1998). *The skilled helper* (6th ed.). Pacific Grove, CA: Brooks/Cole.

Ivey, A., Gluckstern, N., & Ivey, M. B. (1993). *Basic attending skills.* No. Amherst, MA: Microtraining Associates.

Ivey, A., Ivey, M. B., & Simek-Morgan, L. (1997). *Counseling and psychotherapy: A multicultural perspective* (4th ed.). Boston: Allyn and Bacon.

Johanson, G., & Kurtz, R. (1991). *Grace unfolding: Psychotherapy in the spirit of the Tao-te ching.* New York: Bell Tower, a division of Crown Publishers.

Knapp, M. L., and Hall, J. (1992). *Nonverbal communication in human interaction* (3rd ed.). Orlando: Holt, Rinehart and Winston.

4 Recognizing Communication Patterns

We have shown how verbal and nonverbal behaviors are the means by which core conditions such as empathy and warmth are communicated. The next level in this process involves the communication patterns that emerge as the counselor-client relationship develops. Issues related to the locus of control and responsibility in the session, choice of topics, timing, and other therapeutic logistics are undefined at the outset of counseling. In the first few sessions, these issues are resolved, either openly or tacitly, and become apparent through understanding the communication patterns that evolve.

There are many ways to think about patterning in the counseling process. Some patterning takes the form of ritual, whereas other patterning is responsive. That is to say, some of the behaviors become ritualized as a function of routine; for example, the client always chooses the chair facing the window, or the counselor always begins by asking, "What is on your mind today?" and so forth. Other patterns are negotiations between counselor and client, the intent of which may be to settle such matters as "Are we really going to work today?" or "I want you to take charge because I'm feeling overwhelmed."

Frequent topic shifts made by the client in early sessions of counseling may be an expression of client anxiety and of a need to control something about the process. If the counselor is unaware of these shifts in communication and also of the client's underlying affect, progress may be impeded. However, as you will see later in this chapter, communication styles and patterns are greatly influenced by culture and gender, and particular communication patterns do not always have the same meaning.

Ritualized Patterns of Communication

Ritualized patterns may be either situation specific or idiosyncratic to the individuals involved. We have already mentioned examples of situation-specific patterning with the client who, for example, always chooses a certain chair to sit in. This act of repeated choice may arise out of a very simple condition. It was the chair selected by the client at the initial session, and its continued selection in subsequent sessions offers familiar ground and reflects that the client feels no need to make a different choice. However, if the client arrives for the fifth session and, with no explanation, chooses a different chair, the act of choice may contain unspecified meaning. In other words, through the act of choosing, something is communicated, but what is communicated is unclear until the counselor questions the client.

Ritualized Counselor Patterns

The same situation may apply to the counselor. Most experienced counselors develop a style of interaction with their clients. Although their style takes individuals into account, it is nonetheless patterned and, as such, is a kind of trademark of that counselor's work. For example, a counselor may use the first several minutes of the session as relationship time and may communicate this to clients. A different counselor may view the first few minutes as history-taking time. However, should a client arrive in a distraught state, that pattern may be suspended and therapeutic work may begin immediately.

Ritualized Client Patterns

Clients also become involved in ritualized patterns of communication. Often, these patterns evolve out of assumptions about what the counselor wants or expects from the client. For example, a client may assume that the counselor expects to hear an account of the week's worries. The fact that this happened in the second session led the client to think such an account is expected, and so he or she continues the practice in subsequent sessions. Thus, although the activity may have little to do with the ensuing process, it remains a part of the pattern.

Interactive Communication Patterns

Most patterning, and certainly the most significant patterning that occurs in the counseling session, is interactive in nature. It has been suggested by Hackney and Cormier (1996) that most clients approach counseling with two conflicting motivations: (1) "I know I need help" and (2) "I wish I weren't here." Given this dual set of motivations, the client may be expected to convey conflicting and even contradictory communications at times. Similarly, counselors must resolve the potential conflict that was mentioned in Chapter 2 regarding unconditional positive regard and congruence. We mention these conflicting tendencies because they can confuse the communication process. It is essential that the counselor know his or her inner motivations and conflicts. In addition to these inner motivations, interactive communication patterns are also influenced by culture and gender.

Communication and Culture

Many communication patterns are affected by both cultural heritage and gender. Sue and Sue (1990) have noted that different racial-ethnic groups differ in their communication styles. They further observed that communication styles have a great impact on counseling intentions:

> Whether we interrupt one another continually or proceed smoothly, the topics we prefer to discuss or avoid, the depth of our involvement, the forms of interaction (ritual, repartee, argumentative, persuasive, etc.) and the channel we use to communicate (verbal-nonverbal vs. nonverbal-verbal) are all aspects of communication style. Some refer to it as the "social rhythms" that underlie our speech and actions. Communication styles are strongly correlated with race, culture, and ethnicity. (p. 51)

For example, "in traditional Japanese culture, children have been taught not to speak until addressed. Patterns of communication tend to be vertical, flowing from those of higher prestige and status to those of lower prestige and status. Likewise, there are many cultural groups in which restraint of strong feelings is highly valued. It is equated with wisdom and maturity" (Sue, 1992, p. 12). Sue and Sue (1990) have provided other examples of different communication patterns, such as the following: "Many Black clients may use a communication style that is 'high-keyed, animated, confrontational and interpersonal' whereas for many traditional Asian clients 'more subtle forms of communication' are the rule" (pp. 50–51). Unfortunately, a culturally uninformed counselor may view varying patterns of client communication in pejorative ways. For example, a client practicing restraint may be viewed by a culturally uninformed counselor as being "inarticulate, less intelligent, inhibited, lacking in spontaneity, or repressed" (Sue, 1992). Pedersen and Ivey (1993, p. 14) have identified four possible communication barriers in cross-cultural counseling, including verbal and nonverbal language problems, interference from preconceptions and stereotyping, erroneous evaluation, and stress. They cited six specific ways these communication barriers may present:

1. Assuming similarities instead of differences.
2. Verbal language problems occur when another person uses words you do not understand.
3. Nonverbal language problems occur through intentional or unintentional behavior, which is accurately or inaccurately interpreted by others.
4. Preconceptions and stereotypes can become so influential that you see and hear only what you expect, ignoring the real person in front of you.
5. Evaluation biases result from drawing premature conclusions of value judgments about other persons and/or situations before you have all the facts.
6. Stress barriers arise when you feel danger and try to protect yourself against a real or imagined enemy. Multicultural situations are often ambiguous and result in stress because you are not sure what others expect of you or what you can expect of them. (pp. 14–15)

Generally speaking, clients belonging to different cultural groups will be more receptive to counseling communication patterns that are similar to their own and that are respectful of their values. For example, Native Americans, Asian Americans, African Americans, and Latinos tend to prefer more active and directive communication patterns rather than more passive, nondirective communication (Sue & Sue, 1990, p. 69). Misunderstandings and breakdowns in the communication process in cross-cultural counseling dyads are more likely to occur if counselors assume that certain rules and patterns of speaking "are universal and have the same meaning" (Sue & Sue, 1990, p. 52). Communication patterns are also affected by the gender of counselor and client.

Communication and Gender

Communication patterns are also influenced by gender (Tannen, 1993). Gender has been limited to such communication variables as amount of talk time, swearing, interrupting, and use of qualifying questions (O'Donohue & Crouch, 1996). New research reported in various magazines and newspapers in the last several years has noted differences in brain-wave patterns between the genders, resulting in differences in how women and men think. Gender roles, schemas, and the resulting communication patterns are learned in a social and cultural context and are affected by cultural affiliations.

Tannen has described patterns of communication among women as "rapport talk" and among men as "report talk" (Simpkinson & Simpkinson, 1992). In rapport talk, women talk easily about private, intimate topics and about feelings. They talk to create a connection. In report talk, men discuss facts and figures, and share information. They talk to make a point or establish a position. Women tend to be more nonconfrontational in communication with others. They also are often more comfortable in disclosing concerns and troubles and asking for help. Men are often more reticent to request help and place more emphasis on solutions or "fixing" problems. Female clients may be less likely than their male counterparts to speak up in group counseling because they may be more worried about reactions to their "voice" and because they do not use "talk" to enhance their status (Tannen, 1993).

In a ground-breaking book on the effect of gender in couples therapy, Worden and Worden (1998) noted that the two genders differ on issues of autonomy and connection, and expression of anger and power, resulting in differences in communication in the counseling process. These kinds of learned gender roles and schemas are evident in gay, lesbian, and bisexual men and women, as well, since they are also "not immune from the social-psychological construction of gender" (Worden & Worden, 1998, p. 19). Gender and roles and schemata cannot help but spill over or infiltrate into the counseling process, so that both ritualized and responsive patterns between same-gender and different-gender counselor and client pairs are likely to vary somewhat.

Tannen (1990) has stated that observation of such gender differences in language and style of communication helps both genders to be more accepting and respectful of differences. Since style is a learned and somewhat automatic process, awareness of your own style also may help you develop greater flexibility in responding to clients. As Worden and Worden (1998) noted, it is important "to become aware of the context and power of gender roles to powerfully influence what we hear, what we say, and the purpose of communication" as therapists (p. 40).

Like culture, counselors can also perpetuate stereotypes about gender and gender-based communication. For example, a counselor may readily believe a male client's complaint that his female partner talks too much, yet a review of the evidence has found the opposite—men talk more than women (O'Donohue & Crouch, 1996). Such stereotypes about gender patterns in communication can adversely affect the way the counselor views the client's issues and may lead the counselor to draw erroneous conclusions (O'Donohue & Crouch, 1996).

EXERCISE **4.1**

Communication Patterns

A. Cultural Differences
In a small group, discuss ways in which communication patterns may vary among cultures. Relate your observations to the counseling process.

B. Gender Differences
Observe the way men and women talk, even in ordinary, noncounseling conversations. What similarities and differences do you note? How do you think these similarities and differences will affect the counseling situation?

Silence

For most beginning counselors, silence can be frightening. It seems to bring the total focus of attention on them, revealing their most glaring weaknesses as counselors—at least this is how many beginning counselors describe their experiences with silence. As a result, their tendency is to say something—anything—to prevent silence. Typically, a question is asked. Often, it is a bad question—one that can be answered by a minimal response from the client. The answer to the question is relatively unimportant, since the question was not well thought out by the counselor. The counselor may not even be listening to the answer. Such a state of affairs suggests that it is the counselor's responsibility to keep the client talking, that talking is the only evidence that the client is working, and that silence is probably nontherapeutic or a waste of time. None of these assumptions is valid. As Karasu (1992) has noted, the importance of silence is frequently overlooked, as "therapists tend to underestimate the power of listening and overestimate the power of speaking" (pp. 81–82).

Silence has a similar effect on clients. They also perceive silence as a demanding condition and feel a need to fill the gaps of silence with talking. Because clients react to silence in this way, you can use silence as a counseling technique and as a way of responding to clients. Silence has another meaning that is important to acknowledge. After a period of hard work in the session, or after a moment of significant insight, the client often needs time to absorb the experience, to fit it into his or her existing system. This results in an *integration silence,* one in which the client is experiencing fully the therapeutic moment. You may not encounter this in your first counseling sessions, but you will as you gain experience.

Types of Silence

Silence can be a therapeutic moment as well as a self-conscious moment. But what makes one silence different from another? What are the dimensions of silence in a counseling session? Silence can be categorized broadly as counselor induced or client induced. Counselor-induced silence occurs at a time when the focus of the interview is on the counselor. In other words, if the counselor, rather than the client, is feeling responsible for the moment and responds with silence, that is a counselor-induced silence. Conversely, if the client has been talking, assuming responsibility, and then stops, that is a client-induced silence.

Counselor-Induced Silence

Counselor-induced silence can be examined in two contexts: the counselor's intentions and the consequences of the silence. Counselor intentions can vary widely. The underparticipatory counselor gives very little verbally. It is a style of behavior that may reflect the counselor's interpersonal interactions with people in general. It does not reflect therapeutic intentions. Rather, it may indicate a generalized tendency to hide, to withhold, to protect oneself from other people. It arises out of fear.

A second form of silence is that which occurs unsystematically. It is like being at a loss for words. Its intention is probably to give the counselor time to absorb and comprehend all that is going on at the moment. Again, it is not intended by the counselor to be a therapeutic moment, though the effect is often therapeutic. Many times, a counselor will fail to respond to the moment, for personal reasons, and the effect is to encourage the client to continue more deeply into the topic or the feeling. When this happens, the counselor is more apt to feel lucky rather than competent.

The third form of counselor-induced silence is that which the counselor has deliberately presented. It may be that the counselor has been very active and has decided to reduce that activity, thus transferring more responsibility to the client. Or it may be that the counselor senses a momentum on the client's part that will lead to insight, commitment, or new relevant issues. In this case, the counselor chooses not to respond, in order not to interfere with or impede the client's psychological momentum.

Client-Induced Silence

Client-induced silence also has varied intentions and consequences. As noted with counselor silence, client silence is affected by the issue of responsibility and what to do with it. If the client is feeling irresponsible or underresponsible, the intention behind the silence may be antitherapeutic or antigrowth. For example, suppose Betty has developed a life pattern of avoiding some personal issues. When these issues arise, her natural response is to deny or ignore them by deflecting attention from herself. In the counseling setting, she may be aware that these personal issues are the source of her difficulties. Yet her natural reaction continues to be avoidance, deflection, or resistance. In this example, Betty's silence would reflect an attempt to transfer momentary responsibility over to the counselor and away from herself. If she is successful, the consequence would be yet another time when important issues are avoided and underresponsibility is rewarded.

Another reason clients lapse into silence is to try to catch up on the progress of the moment. Counseling sessions sometimes move very quickly, covering a lot of ground, incorporating and relating many issues to one another. There is a need to stop, catch one's breath, observe the progress, or comprehend the implications. This is a very therapeutic type of silence. It allows clients to fit the new growth or insight that has occurred into their existing system. In effect, the client alters the existing system to include what has just been learned. There are also times when client-induced silence results from a client opening some new door to his or her awareness. For instance, Robert, who, with his wife, Carolyn, had been in counseling for several weeks, lapsed into a silence during a discussion of "families of origin" (a technique used to identify styles, expectations, and rules of interpersonal living). After a silence of a minute or more, he stated to the therapist and his wife, "I've been living with Carolyn for six years and thinking that I was overcoming the life I had with my parents. Now I can see that I have been more a reflection of my parents' home than I realized. I wonder what I really do believe in and want from my own family."

Silence also has different meanings from one culture to another. Sue and Sue (1990) stated that there are "complex rules" regarding the cultural appropriateness of the use of silence:

> U.S. Americans frequently feel uncomfortable with a pause or silent stretch in the conversation, feeling obligated to fill it in with more talk. Silence is not always a sign for you, the listener, to take up the conversation. While it may be viewed negatively by many, other cultures interpret the use of silence differently. The English and Arabs use silence for privacy, while the Russians, French and Spanish read it as agreement among the parties. In Asian culture, silence is traditionally a sign of respect for elders. Furthermore, silence by many Chinese and Japanese is not a floor-yielding signal inviting others to pick up the conversation. Rather, it may indicate a desire to continue speaking after making a particular point. Oftentimes silence is a sign of politeness and respect rather than a lack of desire to continue speaking. (p. 56)

Patterns of silence may also vary with gender. A woman may wait for a pause in the conversation to make a point; a man may interrupt a conversation to offer a fact. When expressing feelings, a woman may do so with great verbal facility; a man may pause frequently or present his feelings more hesitantly (Simpkinson & Simpkinson, 1992, p. 30).

How are you to know what kind of silence is occurring? The intention of a client-induced silence must always be inferred. By watching the client closely and by being sensitive to the themes, issues, and feelings being expressed, you will be gathering clues to what is happening. Is the client relaxed? Are the client's eyes fixed on something without being focused? This may mean the client is thinking about or pondering something or examining a new idea, or ruminating around in his or her mind. Or is the client tense, appearing nervous, looking from one object to another and avoiding eye contact? If so, this may mean that he or she is avoiding some topic or idea. Again, we remind you to be careful about assigning universal meanings to client pauses and silent periods, as these meanings do vary with culture, gender, and individuals.

Therapeutic Silence

Skilled counselors often use silence as their best technique for specific situations. This does not suggest that they are inactive. There is always nonverbal behavior that adds meaning to the silence, thereby communicating a therapeutic message to the client. The messages that the counselor may seek to communicate include "I want us to move a bit more slowly"; "I want you to think more about what you just said"; "I don't accept the message you just presented"; or "I care very much about you and your feelings in this moment." Silence can also be soothing to clients. There are other therapeutic messages that can be communicated through silence, but these tend to be the most common.

Pacing the Interview

Counseling interviews can be compared to a musical score. They have variations in theme, timing, activity, and inactivity. As you acquire self-comfort and skills, you will become aware that the different times in an interview have very different qualities. The counselor is a conductor of sorts for this therapeutic score. There are times when the client is hyperactive, babbling, or overreacting, and the desired objective is to slow down the pace of the session. You can always verbally call attention to the client's activity; oftentimes, silence achieves the same objective. You may not respond with total silence. Occasional verbal responses let the client know that you are still a participant. But you may want to monitor your reactions and not respond to all that stimulates you.

The use of silence to pace the session is especially important in initial interviews when the conditions of trust and safety are being built. Especially in these sessions, it is important to let the client determine the pace. As Hutchins and Cole-Vaught (1997) noted, "The helping interview may be one of the few opportunities clients have to express their thoughts and feelings without being rushed or pressed to perform. This luxury of unhurried time allows more complete expression than is typical in most interactions" (p. 104). In using silence to pace a session, it is important to explain the purpose of silence to clients, especially those in beginning sessions, so that they are not scared away (Sommers-Flanagan & Sommers-Flanagan, 1994, p. 71).

Silent Focusing

One of the ways in which silence is most useful is to focus attention on the moment. It is like stopping to listen to an echo. Throughout the book, we will be suggesting ways in which you can help clients hear themselves. Silence is the first of these ways. Sometimes, clients make totally irrational statements. By not responding to the statement, you allow the clients' messages to remain present, to continue to be heard even by the clients themselves. Other times, clients may make a statement of such relevance that you want to give them time to absorb the impact of that relevance. This would be the case when a client has just acknowledged a significant insight and needs time to fit this insight into an existing system of meanings.

Responding to Defenses

Occasionally, clients come to the interview filled with emotions that belong to other people or situations, yet they spill them out on you or the counseling process. Or you may make a statement to which the client responds defensively. These situations often reflect a lack of client awareness, though they are moments when the potential for awareness is great. The temptation for you may be to give the client insight into the situation. Often, it is more meaningful to allow clients to give themselves that insight. This can be done by using silence as your response.

Silent Caring

Silent caring occurs in those moments when no words are an adequate response to the feelings that are present. It may be a moment of quiet weeping for the client, or it may be a moment of heavy melancholy. Whatever the feeling may be, it is one of those moments when experiencing the feeling fully is more important than making it go away. You can communicate your compassion and involvement very clearly with caring silence.

Guidelines for Using Silence

After all is said and done, there are specific therapeutic guidelines to follow in using silence effectively with clients. Sommers-Flanagan and Sommers-Flanagan (1994) have summarized these:

1. When a role-play client pauses after making a statement or after hearing your paraphrase, let a few seconds pass rather than immediately jumping in with further verbal interaction. Given the opportunity, clients often flow naturally

into very significant material *without* your guidance or urging. Give them a chance to associate to new material.

2. As you're sitting silently and waiting for your client to resume speaking, try to tell yourself that this is the client's time to express herself, not your time to prove you can be useful. If you assume the role of an "expert" interviewer, you will probably feel greater responsibility (i.e., as if you need to say the right thing or ask the right question).

3. Try not to get into a rut regarding your use of silence. When silence comes, sometimes you should wait for the client to speak next and other times you should break the silence yourself.

4. Avoid using silence if you believe your client is confused, experiencing an acute emotional crisis, or psychotic. Excessive silence, and the anxiety it provokes, tends to exacerbate these conditions.

5. If you feel uncomfortable during silent periods, try your best to relax. Use your attending skills to look expectantly toward clients. This will help them understand that it's their turn to talk.

6. If clients appear uncomfortable with silence, you may give them instructions to free associate (i.e., tell them "just say whatever comes to mind"). Or you may want to use an empathic reflection of content or feeling (say something like "it's hard to decide what to say next"). (pp. 71–72)

EXERCISE 4.2

Being Comfortable with Silence

In the United States, some people often have to learn to be silent. Perhaps you find silence to be intense and uncomfortable. If so, this exercise will help you become more comfortable with silence. Team up with two other people. One person will be the talker, you be the listener, and the third person can be the timekeeper. Invite the talker to talk about anything he or she wishes. You will listen and respond. But, before you respond, allow a pause to occur. Begin with 5-second pauses. Gradually increase the duration of pauses until you are allowing 15 seconds to pass before responding. The timekeeper should sit in a position from which he or she can signal the number of seconds to you without distracting the talker. After a 10-minute discussion, rotate roles and repeat the exercise until all three of you have had a turn as listener.

As a variation on this exercise, consider your contacts with people you encounter every day. Become conscious of your interaction patterns. Do you interject your reactions as soon as the other person has completed a communication? Do you interrupt the other person, thus preventing the slightest possibility of a silence? During the next few days, monitor your response behavior. When someone speaks to you, pause and think about the message for a few seconds and then give your response. Record any feedback you receive from your friends or acquaintances regarding your communication behavior.

Summary

The practice of professional counseling involves a compromise between personal authenticity and professional skills. Both authenticity and skills are maintained by patterns of behavior that emerge as the counselor matures and grows in experience. Similarly, clients evolve patterns of behavior that reflect both their personal qualities, their problems, and their culture. We have noted how these patterns affect and are affected by the counselor's interventions.

The beginning counselor's most noticeable patterns are those involving interactive qualities as well as cultural and gender factors. As the counselor's comfort level with the counseling setting improves, these patterns may be examined for their effect on the session. More subtle, and perhaps of greater concern, are the counselor patterns that become ritualized. Ritualized patterns exist for expediency's sake. They are the behavioral shorthand that allows more efficient functioning. The problem is that efficient functioning may not be effective functioning, particularly in the helping relationship. Consequently, it is professionally imperative that counselors examine their patterns of interaction with clients, not just early in their careers but throughout their careers.

DISCUSSION QUESTIONS

1. If you are able to eliminate inappropriate social behavior from your counseling repertoire, what impression do you think this will make on your client?

2. What types of messages can be communicated with a silence? How many of these messages might occur in a counseling session? How can you tell one message from another?

3. What do you think your own tolerance/comfort level is with silence? Are you more comfortable with silence that is initiated by you or the client?

4. Provide examples that illustrate how the meaning and use of silence is affected by culture and gender.

5. Discuss some examples in which you have observed communication patterns being influenced by culture.

6. Describe your reactions to the idea that gender affects communications.

RECOMMENDED READINGS

Hutchins, P., & Cole, C. (1997). *Helping relationships and strategies* (3rd ed.). Pacific Grove, CA: Wadsworth, Brooks/Cole.

Karasu, T. (1992). *Wisdom in the practice of psychotherapy*. New York: Basic Books.

O'Donohue, W., & Crouch, J. (1996). Marital therapy and gender-linked factors in communication. *Journal of Marital and Family Therapy, 22*, 87–101.

Pedersen, P., & Ivey, A. (1993). *Culture-centered counseling and interviewing skills.* Westport, CT: Praeger.

Sommers-Flanagan, J., & Sommers-Flanagan, R. (1994). *Foundations of therapeutic interviewing.* Boston: Allyn and Bacon.

Sue, D. W., & Sue, D. (1990). *Counseling the culturally different.* New York: Wiley.

Tannen, D. (1993). *Gender and conversational interaction.* New York: Oxford University Press.

Worden, M., & Worden, B. (1998). *The gender dance in couples therapy.* Pacific Grove, CA: Brooks/Cole.

5 Managing the Counseling Session

We have discussed the qualities of a therapeutic relationship and how effective counselors attend to and understand the client, but we have not yet discussed the *structure* within which all this occurs. Experienced counselors enter each session with a sense of who they are, what they wish to do and to be in the session, and how they will represent themselves to the client. This is true in the first session as well as in the twentieth session. As we mentioned in the previous chapter, experienced counselors develop a personal style that they carry into the relationship. That style provides the structure for how to begin the process—how to develop it and how to end it.

In this chapter, we will consider some awkward and sensitive times in the counseling relationship that require structure. Many counselors and clients have difficulty with beginnings and endings, whether they be the beginning or ending of a counseling interview or the beginning or ending of a counseling relationship. As you read the chapter, you will find suggestions and thoughts that may help you make smoother transitions into and out of these moments. There are two types of beginnings that will be examined: beginning the first interview you have with a client and beginning subsequent interviews. Similarly, we examine the two types of termination: session termination and relationship termination.

The First Interview

Your first interview with a client will have a special set of dynamics operating. It is the beginning of a potentially significant relationship. As such, there are hopes and expectations, fears and reservations, acute awareness of some conditions and an amazing lack of awareness of other conditions—all of which have a bearing on the session. With so many emotional issues operating, you might be wondering how you can possibly have a successful first interview. Counselors deal with this issue in one of two ways. Some counselors choose to work with the relationship dynamics that are operating. Others choose to make the first session an intake interview and collect needed information about the client. Whichever choice you make, you must still attend to the other issue later. If you focus on interpersonal dynamics in the first session, in the second or third interview you will want to collect information. If you use the first session as an intake session, soon afterward you must begin to acknowledge relationship dynamics.

If you wish to focus on relationship dynamics, then the content of Chapter 2 is particularly relevant. Specifically, you will want to achieve an accurate sense of the client's world and communicate that understanding back to your client. Learning to understand means putting aside your own agenda long enough to allow the client's world to enter your awareness. It means not worrying about yourself (Am I doing the right thing? Am I looking nervous? etc.). Until you have had the experience of several beginning sessions, this will be a difficult task. Of course, you will have an underlying set of objectives in this session:

1. To reduce your client's initial anxieties to a level that permits him or her to begin talking
2. To refrain from excessive talking, since that takes time away from your client
3. To listen carefully to what your client is saying and attempt to reconstruct in your thinking the world that he or she is describing
4. To be aware that your client's choice of topics gives insight into his or her priorities for the moment

Initial Moments

In addition to these objectives, there are some logistics that require your attention. In opening the interview, be on time. This communicates respect. The beginning point can be as simple as a smile from you, along with a simple introduction and a motion to show the client where to sit—for example:

> "Hello, I'm Bill Janutolo. Please have a seat here, or in that chair, if you wish."

After introductions, you might allow for a brief pause. This gives your client a chance to talk if he or she is prepared to begin. Or you might proceed to give the first interview some structure. There are questions that must be resolved. How long will the interview be? (Often, the length of the interview depends on the age of the client.) How do you want your client to address you? What should your client expect the sessions to be like? What are your client's rights? What will be your role? Answers to these and other questions provide the structure for the relationship.

Structuring has been defined as the way the counselor defines the nature, limits, roles, and goals within the counseling relationship (Brammer, Shostrom, & Abrego, 1992). It includes comments about time limits, number of sessions, confidentiality, possibilities and expectations, as well as supervision, observation, and/or tape-recording procedures. Describing the counseling process and providing structure reduces the unknowns and thus reduces the anxiety of clients. It also permits clients the opportunity to check out their expectations. Kottler (1991) summarized the ingredients of effective structuring in initial sessions as follows:

1. Providing a general overview and preview of the counseling process
2. Assessing the client's expectations and promoting positive ones
3. Describing the counselor's expectations
4. Orienting the client to new language and new behaviors
5. Helping the client to increase tolerance for frustration and discomfort
6. Obtaining client commitment (pp. 141–144)

Confidentiality

You will want to emphasize the issue of confidentiality to new clients. Does it mean you will talk to no one? What are the implications if you are being observed by a supervisor or if you are tape-recording the session? Will you keep a written record? If so, what are the client's guarantees that the record will be kept confidential? Some of these may not be relevant issues, in which case it would be better not to introduce them as issues. You can discuss this with a colleague or supervisor to determine which issues are relevant and which are not. Here is how one counselor begins a session with structuring:

> "Juanita, we have about an hour together. I'm not sure what brings you here, but I'm ready to answer any questions you have and also to listen to whatever you tell me. You can talk about whatever you wish—this is your time. And whatever you do talk about is kept confidential between you and me."

Exceptions to Confidentiality

According to ethical guidelines for helping professions, the counselor is generally obligated to treat the client's communication in a confidential manner; that is, the counselor agrees to not share information given by the client with other persons. However, there are several exceptions to this general policy, such as when the client's condition indicates harm to self or others (American Counseling Association, 1995a). Some states also have legal statutes that require helpers to report instances of child abuse or to testify under subpoena. Since these statutes vary from state to state, it is important to know the guidelines for your particular state. The important point is to discuss with clients both the protection and the limits of confidentiality as a part of the structuring process.

Encouraging the Client to Talk

After providing this initial structure, you and your client are ready to begin work. The obvious beginning is to get your client to talk, to indicate his or her reason for entering counseling, and perhaps to indicate in some form what he or she hopes to achieve as a result of counseling (the client's first statement of counseling goals). Your beginning will be an invitation to the client to talk. The nature of this invitation is important. A good invitation is one that encourages but does not specify what the client should talk about. This is called an *unstructured invitation* or an *open-ended lead*.

Unstructured Invitations

The unstructured invitation has two purposes: (1) it gives the client an opportunity to talk and (2) it prevents the counselor from identifying the topic the client should discuss. An unstructured invitation is a statement in which the counselor encourages clients to begin talking about whatever is of concern to them, such as:

"Please feel free to go ahead and begin."
"Where would you like to begin today?"
"You can talk about whatever you would like."
"Perhaps there is something particular you want to discuss."
"What brings you to counseling?"

By contrast, a structured invitation—one that specifies a topic—gives clients little room to reflect on the motives, goals, or needs that brought them to counseling. An example of a less desirable structured invitation to talk might be: "Tell me about what careers you are considering." The client is obviously tied down to a discussion of careers by this invitation, thus delaying or even negating a more relevant issue. (*Note:* If careers are what the client wants to discuss, an unstructured invitation allows this topic to emerge as well as a structured invitation would.)

The following exercise will help you develop the skills involved in initiating the interview.

EXERCISE 5.1

Initiating an Interview

This is a class exercise that requires a videotape system. Have class members select partners. Each pair is to decide who is to be the counselor and who is to be the client. The exercise is to last for five minutes. The counselor is to work toward achieving the following goals:

1. Set the client at ease (body relaxed, voice without tension).
2. Help the client to start talking about anything (use unstructured invitation, silence).
3. Get the client to *identify* a current concern (acknowledge that the client came to counseling for a reason; ask about the reason).

Following each exercise, reverse roles and repeat the procedure. Then, when all pairs have had the opportunity to do the exercise, replay the tape and discuss the encounters, using the following format:

1. Ask the counselor for his or her reaction to the tape.
2. Describe those behaviors that were helpful in the exercise.
3. Identify and describe those elements in which there is need for further growth.

Objectives of the First Interview

If your objective in the first interview is to focus on client feelings or interpersonal dynamics, you will find yourself using responses that elicit feelings, describe relationships, and communicate your understanding. These responses include restatement, reflection of feeling, summarization of feelings, requests for clarification, and acknowledgment of nonverbal behavior. These types of response encourage the client to present and explore thoughts and feelings, and give you an opportunity to understand some of the unique perceptions your clients may have.

On the other hand, you may wish to use the first interview to collect as much information as possible about your client, and not become involved with intrapersonal dynamics. This approach characterizes the intake interview and is based on the rationale that the more you know about the client's world, the better you are able to understand and respond to intrapersonal dynamics, particularly those perceptions that may be slightly distorted. An intake interview is highly structured. There are specific topics you want the client to discuss. The types of response that you will use in this interview tend to be open questions, accents, closed questions, and requests for clarification, although the other mentioned responses may also be used on occasion.

Cultural Variables and the First Interview

Whether you choose to focus primarily on establishing a relationship or on gathering information in an initial counseling session often depends somewhat on your setting as well as the client's cultural affiliation. Some settings specify that the initial session be an intake interview; this initial history-gathering session may even be conducted by an intake worker rather than the counselor assigned to work with the client.

The client's culture also influences your focus in an initial interview. Sue and Sue (1991) stated, "In cross-cultural counseling, the culturally different client is likely to approach the counselor with trepidation" and may not self-disclose "until you, the counselor, self-disclose first" (p. 71). This trepidation may be reinforced with White counselors whose sole focus in the initial session is individualistic rather than contextualistic—that is, viewing the client's problems "as residing within the individual rather than society" (Sue & Sue, 1991, p. 72). Moreover, some research reported by Sue and Sue (1991) has found that many Asian American and African American clients prefer a more structured and logical approach (e.g., an intake information session) to an affective and reflective one. In any initial session, regardless of approach, counselors need to exert caution and move slowly, as asking very personal questions in an initial session may be perceived as lacking in respect just as much as reflecting client feelings (Sue & Sue, 1991). It is important to be flexible enough in your counseling style to adapt your style in an initial session to meet the cultural diversity of your clients.

Counselor Responses That Encourage Client Expression

We have already described the unstructured invitation as a response to encourage the client to begin talking. It remains for us to describe the other responses that can be used in the initial interview, depending on your purpose in that session. These responses are also used in subsequent counseling sessions and will be reintroduced in later chapters that describe specific objectives. We will first consider those responses that are most useful when you focus on feeling and dynamics.

Restatement

Although it is important to maintain a listening role, there are certain kinds of responses that communicate not only that you are listening but also that you are a person with an active role. The *restatement* is one of these responses. It is a verbatim repetition of the main thought or feeling expressed by your client's preceding communication. An example is the following interaction:

> **CLIENT:** "I don't know whether to stay in school or to drop out and get a job. But if I did drop out, I don't know what kind of job I could find."
>
> **COUNSELOR:** "You don't know whether to stay in school or to drop out."

In this example, the client has communicated two thoughts: whether to stay in school and uncertainty about finding a job. When the counselor uses a restatement, it is easy to respond to the last thought emitted by the client, since it is the most immediate communication. However, this is a poor criterion. It is better to pick out the *primary* thought or feeling of the client's communication, regardless of its position in the statement. Just as a caution, it should be noted that the overuse of restatements produces a parrotlike effect in the interview. As a guide, the restatement should be used no more than about once or twice per topic without producing this mimic effect.

Reflection of Feeling

The *reflection of feeling* is a paraphrased response to a feeling communicated by the client, either verbally or nonverbally. The statement accomplishes precisely what its name implies: a mirroring of the feelings or emotion present in the client's message. Chapter 7 explores the different levels that this type of response can reflect. For our purposes in opening an interview, the following examples are sufficient.

Reflection of a Verbally Expressed Feeling

CLIENT: "One of my main problems is that I need to come out of myself. And, uh, when I'm with people, or even when I'm alone, I'm at a loss for words. I have nothing to say, you know?"

COUNSELOR: "So when you are with other people, it must feel like there's nothing inside you to come out and be noticed."

Reflection of a Nonverbally Expressed Feeling

CLIENT: (Sitting in chair in slumped position, eyes downcast, forlorn look on face.)

COUNSELOR: "From the way you look, you must be feeling pretty alone, pretty wiped out right now."

Summarization of Feeling

The *summarization of feeling* is similar to the reflection of feeling, with one exception: The former represents a set of feelings that might have been communicated over a period of minutes in the interview. Again, it is a paraphrase by the counselor that pulls together several feelings, as shown here:

CLIENT: "And that gets very uncomfortable, you know, with people. With a big group, I'm fine, listening . . . or if I have something to say I get it out, usually. Usually, it takes me a very long time, and when I do come out, you see, I consider it's not worth saying, and half the time, I think, I don't come out with it. Um . . . and that gets uncomfortable. And then I get the feeling like when I'm with people that if I can't be rambling off an awful lot of information, you know, then I'm not worth anything, you know? And that kind of thing bothers me."

COUNSELOR: "Let me see if I understand all of that. In large groups, you can feel a little safer sometimes if nobody notices you, but if you have something you want to say, it is so hard finding a way to say it that you finally decide it's probably not worth hearing if it's that hard to say. And that gets you to feeling down on yourself again."

In using both the reflection of feeling and the summarization of feeling, remember an earlier caution about the lack of suitability of these two responses in an initial session for some clients of color who may perceive these very affective-oriented responses as disrespectful.

Requests for Clarification

Sometimes, client responses sound cryptic or confused, and you are left wondering just what the client was trying to say. It can be very important to seek clarification at those moments rather than guess or assume that the communication was unimportant. The *request for clarification* asks the client to rephrase the communication. It can be stated in several ways:

> "Could you try to describe that feeling in another way? I'm not sure I am following what you mean."
>
> "When you say 'fuzzy,' what's that feeling like?"
>
> "I think I got lost in that. Could you go through the sequence of events again for me?"

Acknowledgment of Nonverbal Behavior

Acknowledgment of nonverbal behavior is a response that speaks to an obvious client gesture or posture without interpreting the meaning of the behavior. In this way, this response is different from the reflection of nonverbally expressed feeling. Although it is important that you resist any inclination to interpret the client's behavior verbally, you may speculate or ask for clarification of the nonverbal gesture. If the behavior has meaning, your client can tell you what the meaning is. Examples of acknowledgment of nonverbal behavior include the following:

> "You are holding your body really tight right now."
> "You look quizzical. Do you follow what I am saying?"
> "Your body is looking more relaxed now. Are you feeling more relaxed?"

Counselor Responses That Solicit Information

Since the intake interview is intended primarily to solicit information, the types of responses that characterize it include, but are not restricted to, open-ended questions, accents, closed questions, and requests for clarification.

Open-Ended Questions

Open-ended questions require more than a minimal or one-word response by the client. This type of question is introduced with either *what, where, when,* or *how.* You will find that it is very difficult to ask questions that clearly place the focus on your client. Fairly often, it happens that counselors ask questions that allow the client to respond with either a yes or a no. The result is that the client assumes no responsibility for the content of the interview. The purpose of the open question is to prevent this from happening. The following questions are examples of open-ended questions:

"What are you thinking when you are silent?"
"How do you plan to find employment?"
"When do you feel anxious?"

Accents

Accents are one- or two-word restatements that focus or bring attention to a preceding client response. An accent is said in a tone of voice that suggests that the counselor would like the client to elaborate, as in the following:

CLIENT: "I'd like to have more self-confidence, but then I'd only be fooling myself."

COUNSELOR: "Fooling yourself?"

CLIENT: "After I returned from the meeting. I really felt dragged out."

COUNSELOR: "Dragged out?"

Closed Questions

When your objective is to get the client to talk about anything, closed questions are not good responses. However, when you want the client to give a specific piece of information, a closed question can be the best response available, such as:

"How old were you when your parents died?"
"How many brothers and sisters do you have?"
"What medication are you taking now?"
"Have you ever received counseling or therapy?"

Requests for Clarification

Requests for clarification can be used for soliciting information as well as for encouraging the client to elaborate about his or her feelings. It is important to keep in mind that such requests can be overused or underused. When overused, they can become distractors that repeatedly interrupt the client's train of thought. When they are underused, however, the counselor may have difficulty understanding what the client is saying. Sometimes, the counselor is reluctant to seek clarification because it might impede or distract the client from the topic. If you are simply unable to follow the client's train of thought, it is more important to seek clarification than it is to allow the client to proceed. Here are some examples:

"Could you go over that again for me?"

"Could you explain that relationship to me again?"

"What did you mean a while ago when you said your parents were pretty indifferent?"

Intake-Interview Content

We have described the intake as an information-gathering interview, but we have not indicated what that information should be. This section presents a suggested outline of topics to cover and the rationale for their importance. Morrison (1995) has written a helpful guide for the first interview.

An assumption behind the intake interview is that the client is coming to counseling for more than one interview and intends to address problems or concerns that involve other people, other settings, and the future, as well as the present. Most counselors try to limit intake interviews to an hour. In order to do this, you must assume responsibility and control over the interview. The following is a suggested outline. Variations in this outline will occur, depending on the setting and on certain client variables such as age, gender, race, class, and ethnicity.

I. **Identifying Data**
   A. Client's name, address, and telephone number at which client can be reached. This information is important in the event the counselor needs to contact the client between sessions. The client's address also gives some hint about the conditions under which the client lives (large apartment complex, student dormitory, private home, etc.).
   B. Age, gender, ethnic origin, race, marital status, occupational status, and educational status. Again, this is information that can be important. It lets you know when the client is still legally a minor and it provides a basis for understanding information that will come out in later sessions.

II. **Presenting Problems, Both Primary and Secondary**
   It is best when these are presented in exactly the way the client reported them. If the problem has behavioral components, these should be recorded, as well. The following questions can help reveal this type of information:
   A. How much does the problem interfere with the client's everyday functioning?
   B. How does the problem manifest itself? What are the thoughts, feelings, and so on that are associated with it? What observable behavior is associated with it?
   C. How often does the problem arise? How long has the problem existed?
   D. Can the client identify a pattern of events that surround the problem? When does it occur? With whom? What happens before and after its occurrence?
   E. What caused the client to decide to enter counseling at this time?

III. **Client's Current Life Setting**
   How does the client spend a typical day or week? What social and religious activities, recreational activities, and so on are present? What is the nature of the client's vocational and/or educational situation? What is the client's living environment like? What are the client's most important current relationships?

IV. Family History

A. Father's and mother's ages, occupations, descriptions of their personalities, and relationships of each to the other and each to the client and other siblings.

B. Names, ages, and order of brothers and sisters, and relationship between the client and siblings.

C. Is there any history of emotional disturbance and/or substance abuse in the family?

D. Descriptions of family stability, including number of jobs held, number of family moves, significant losses, and so on. This information provides insights in later sessions when issues related to client stability and/or relationships emerge.

V. Personal History

A. Medical history: any unusual or relevant illness or injury from prenatal period to present, including hospitalizations, surgeries, or substance use.

B. Educational history: academic progress through grade school, high school, and post-high school. This includes extracurricular interests and relationships with peers.

C. Military service record.

D. Vocational history: Where has the client worked, at what types of jobs, for what duration, and what were the relationships with fellow workers?

E. Sexual relationship history: Where did the client receive sexual information? What was the client's dating history? Any engagements and/or marriages? Other serious emotional involvements prior to the present? Reasons that previous relationships terminated? What was the courtship like with present partner? What were the reasons (partner's characteristics, personal thoughts) that led to marriage? What has been the relationship with partner since marriage? Are there any children? Separations? Divorces? Be careful not to assume that the client's sexual orientation is heterosexual.

F. What experience has the client had with counseling and what were the client's reactions? Who referred the client?

G. Traumatic experiences: Has client encountered neglect, or physical, emotional, or sexual abuse? Medical traumas or accidents? Natural disasters?

VI. Description of the Client during the Interview

Here, you might want to indicate the client's physical appearance, including height and weight, dress, posture, gestures, facial expressions, voice quality, and tensions; how the client seemed to relate to you in the session; the client's readiness of response, motivation, warmth, distance, and passivity; and so on. Does there appear to be any perceptual or sensory functions that intrude on the interaction? (Document with your observations.) What was the general level of information, vocabulary, judgment, and abstraction abilities displayed by the client? What is the client's first language and second language? What is the stream of thought, regularity, and rate of talking? Are the client's remarks logical? Connected to one another?

What information have you gathered about the client's race, ethnicity, and general cultural affiliations?

VII. **Summary and Recommendations**

Here, you will want to acknowledge any connections that appear to exist between the client's statement of a problem and other information collected in this session. What is your understanding of the problem? What are the anticipated outcomes of counseling for this person? What type of counseling do you think would best fit this client? If you are to be this client's counselor, which of your characteristics might be particularly helpful? Which might be particularly unhelpful? How realistic are the client's goals for counseling? How long do you think counseling might continue? Is there anything in the client's history that seems like a "red flag" to you?

In writing up the intake interview, there are a few cautions to be made. First, avoid psychological jargon. It is not as understandable as you might think! Avoid elaborate inferences. Remember, an inference is a guess—sometimes an educated guess. An inference can also be wrong. Try to prevent your own biases from entering the report.

Using Intake-Interview Information

Following the intake interview, but preceding the second session, you will want to review the write-up of the intake interview. Counselors develop different approaches to using this information. Some counselors look primarily for patterns of behavior. For example, one counselor noted that her client had a pattern of incompletions in life; for example, he received a general discharge from the army prior to completing his enlistment, dropped out of college twice, and had a long history of broken relationships. This observation provided food for thought. What happens to this person as he becomes involved in a commitment? What has he come to think of himself as a result of this history? How does he anticipate future commitments?

Another counselor uses the intake information to look for signals that suggest how he might enter the counseling relationship. Is there anything to indicate how the client might relate to females? Is there something in the client's life at present that common sense would suggest is a potential area for counseling attention; for example, is the client in the midst of a divorce? Is the client at a critical developmental stage? The main caution is to avoid reading too much into the intake information. It is far too early for you to begin making interpretations about your client.

Opening Subsequent Interviews

If your first interview was used to collect information about the client, it will be important to focus on developing a therapeutic relationship in subsequent sessions. We refer you to the beginning of this chapter and to Chapter 2 for ways to develop this goal. Once you have established a relationship or rapport with your client, subsequent interviews will require that you reinstate the relationship that has developed.

Reinstating the relationship usually amounts to acknowledging the client's absence since the last interview. This includes being sensitive to how your client's world may have changed since your last contact and your reactions in seeing the client again. This can be done with a few short statements, such as, "Hello, Marvel. It's nice to see you again." This might be followed by some observation about the client's appearance: "You look a little hassled today" or "You're looking more energetic today." Or you might begin by asking, "How are you feeling today?" These types of questions focus on the client's current or immediate condition and reduce the likelihood that the client will spend the major part of the session recounting how the week has gone. If your client needs a bit of small talk to get started, it probably means that he or she needs time to make the transition into the role of help seeker or help taker.

The important point is that you probably will not need to go to the same lengths in establishing rapport as was necessary when counseling was first initiated. Keep in mind, however, that some degree of relationship building occurs in each and every session.

Terminating the Interview

The beginning counselor is often unsure about *when* to terminate the interview, and may feel ready to conclude either before or after the client is ready. A general rule of thumb is to limit the interview to a certain amount of time, such as 45 or 50 minutes. Rarely does a counseling interview need to exceed an hour in length, as both client and counselor have a saturation point. With children, sessions may only be 20 to 40 minutes in duration and some part of this time may be spent in play therapy.

There is also a minimal amount of time required for counseling to take place. Interviews that continue for no more than 10 or 15 minutes make it very difficult for the counselor to know enough about the client's concern to react appropriately. Indeed, counselors sometimes require 5 to 10 minutes just to reorient themselves and to change their frame of reference from their preceding attention-involving activity to the present activity of counseling.

Acceptance of time limits is especially important when the client has a series of interviews. Research has shown that clients, like everyone else, tend to postpone talking about their concerns as long as possible. Without time limits, the presumed one-hour interview may extend well beyond an hour as a result of this postponing tendency. It is the one instance in which the client can easily manipulate the counselor.

Sommers-Flanagan and Sommers-Flanagan (1994) have identified two factors basic to the closing process of the interview:

1. Both the client and the counselor need to be aware that the interview is "winding down."
2. Terminating a session involves what has already occurred, so no additional information should be sought or discussed during the last few minutes. (p. 170)

If the client introduces a new topic near the end of a session, the counselor can suggest discussing it at the outset of the next session. The rare exception to this would be when the client presents a truly urgent and immediate concern.

There are five tasks to accomplish in closing an interview, as cited by Sommers-Flanagan and Sommers-Flanagan (1994, p. 171): supporting the client, summarizing crucial themes and issues, instilling hope, empowering the client, and tying up loose ends. Some ways to accomplish these tasks are discussed next.

Other Termination Strategies

Often a brief and *to-the-point statement* by the counselor will suffice for closing the interview:

> "It looks as if our time is up for today."
> "Well, I think it's time to stop for today."

This type of statement may be preceded by a pause or by a concluding kind of remark made by the client.

Another effective way is to use *summarization*. Summarization provides continuity to the interview, is an active kind of counselor response, and often helps the client to hear what he or she has been saying. It is essentially a series of statements in which the counselor ties together the main points of the interview. It should be brief, to the point, and without interpretation. An example of a counselor's use of summarization at the end of an interview is the following:

> "Essentially, you have indicated that your main concern is with your family—and we have discussed how you might handle your strivings for independence without their interpreting this as rejection."

Another possible termination strategy is to *ask the client to summarize* or to state how he or she understood what has been going on in the interview, as in the following example:

> "As we're ending the session today, I'm wondering what you're taking with you; if you could summarize this, I think it would be helpful to both of us."

Mutual feedback involving both the client and counselor is another possible tool for termination of an interview. If plans and decisions have been made, it is often useful for both the counselor and client to clarify and verify the progress of the interview, as in the following example:

"I guess that's it for today; I'll also be thinking about the decision you're facing. As you understand it, what things do you want to do before our next session?"

EXERCISE **5.2**

Opening and Terminating the Interview

Use the following triadic exercise to review styles of opening and terminating the interview. With one class member as the speaker, another as the respondent, and the third as observer, complete the following tasks by using the Observer Rating Charts (Figures 5.1 and 5.2).

FIGURE 5.1   Observer Rating Chart: Opening the Interview

Counselor Response	Order
Unstructured invitation	
Restatement	
Reflection of feeling	
Summarization of feeling	
Request for clarification	
Acknowledgment of nonverbal behavior	

Opening the Interview

SPEAKER: Talk about yourself; share a concern with the listener.

LISTENER: Respond to the speaker as if you were opening an interview. Try out the responses mentioned in the chapter: unstructured invitation, restatement, reflection and summarization of feelings, and so on.

OBSERVER: Observe the kinds of responses made by the listener. Keep a frequency count of the types of responses made. Share your report with the listener.

RECYCLING: If, as the listener, you did not use at least two of the four response classes in your interaction with the speaker, complete the interaction again.

ROLE REVERSAL: Reverse the roles and follow the same process.

FIGURE 5.2   **Observer Rating Chart: Terminating the Interview**

Counselor Response	Order
Time limits	
Summarization of feelings	
Mutual feedback	
Structuring next session (time, date, etc.)	

Terminating the Interview

SPEAKER: Continue to explore the same topic you introduced in the preceding interaction.

LISTENER: Respond to the speaker as if you were terminating an interview. Try out at least one of the procedures mentioned in the section as approaches for termination of the interview (acknowledgment of time limits, summarization, or mutual feedback).

OBSERVER: Observe the procedure for termination used by the listener. Share your report with the listener.

RECYCLING: If, as the listener, you did not use any of the termination procedures, or if, for some reason, termination did not occur with your speaker, complete the interaction again.

ROLE REVERSAL: Reverse the roles and follow the same process.

Record the order and frequency of responses used. If the counselor's first response was an unstructured invitation, place a 1 in the space provided in the Observer Rating Charts. If the second counselor response was a restatement, place a 2 in the appropriate space, and so forth.

Terminating the Counseling Relationship

The process of terminating a counseling relationship can evoke various and even conflicting reactions for the counselor. Some may think of it as a loss experience if the relationship has been highly meaningful, or certainly as a "letting go" (Kramer, 1990). Others may consider termination to be an index of the counselor's success. From the client's point of view, termination may be a symbol of success or it may be a "recapitulation of the multiple preceding goodbyes in life"

(Hansen, Rossberg, & Cramer, 1994, p. 242). Whatever the interpretation, it is apparent that termination possesses an emotional dimension that can be intense.

Perhaps the most useful way to conceptualize termination is to think of it as a transition rather than an event (Hackney & Cormier, 1996). As the counseling relationship develops and as the client is able to address and resolve the issues that necessitated counseling, the prospect of termination becomes a therapeutic stage in the process. More often than not, the counselor becomes aware of the approaching termination first. Concerns related to the timing of termination, the preparation for termination, and the anticipation of therapeutic problems related to termination become dominant in the counselor's mind.

When Should Termination Occur?

Some counseling theories provide guidelines for the timing of termination. These include such possibilities as letting the client determine the timing or having the counselor establish the date of termination at the outset of counseling (Hackney & Cormier, 1996). Such issues will be dependent on your own theoretical orientation. However, there are some pragmatic factors that contribute to the question of timing. Hackney and Cormier (1996) have summarized these pragmatic considerations as follows:

1. When counseling has been predicated on a behavioral or other form of contract, progress toward the goals or conditions of the contract presents a clear picture of when counseling should end.
2. When clients feel that their goals have been accomplished, they may initiate termination.
3. When the relationship appears not to be helpful, either to the counselor or client, termination is appropriate.
4. When contextual conditions change—for example, the client or counselor moves to a new location—termination must occur.

Preparing Clients for Termination

Clients should be made aware throughout the process of counseling that there will come a time when counseling is no longer appropriate. This does not mean that they will have worked out all their issues, nor will it mean that they have acquired all the tools and awareness necessary for a happy life. It does mean that they have grown to the point at which they have more to gain from being independent of the counseling relationship than they would gain from continuing the relationship. We believe that human beings are happier and more self-fulfilled when they are able to trust their own resources. Of course, healthy people rely on others, but they do so out of self-perceived choice rather than self-perceived necessity. As Kottler (1991) observed, "Effective therapists are skilled at trying to help their client end in a way, *any* way, that allows them to feel good about their work and continue to be their own therapist in the future" (p. 171).

Occasionally, you will know in the first session with your client that the relationship will last a certain length of time. For example, if your client is seeking premarital counseling and the wedding is to take place in two months, the time constraints are apparent. People going to university counseling centers may know that vacations dictate the amount of time allowed for counseling. In such cases, it is appropriate to acknowledge throughout the relationship that these time constraints exist.

When the relationship is more open ended and determined by the client's progress, the termination stage begins well before the final session. We believe that for any relationship that has existed more than three months, the topic should be raised three to four weeks prior to termination. This allows the client time to think about and discuss the ramifications of ending counseling with the counselor.

Cultural Variables and Termination

It is important to recognize that not all cultural groups share the same values and beliefs about the dimension of time, and this, too, can affect the termination process. For example, Euro-Americans generally have a highly structured and future-oriented view of time, but some clients from other cultural groups have a much more casual view of time (Ivey, Ivey, & Simek-Morgan, 1997). In cross-cultural counseling situations, the time element of termination needs to be discussed, negotiated, and understood from the client's perspective, as well.

Also, many clients of color terminate counseling at a much earlier time than other clients. Often, these clients are the decision makers as to when to stop counseling, presumably because it is not relevant enough to them and their experiences, particularly their culturally linked experiences (Sue & Sue, 1990). Therefore, it is presumptuous to assume that in all situations the "control" of the termination process is in the counselor's hands.

Introducing Termination

Termination need not be presented as a major event. In fact, it is probably better to play it down rather than to play it up. If your clients' reactions suggest that it is a major event for them, then you can respond to that. It is better to acknowledge it as a fact rather than as an experience. This can be done by saying something on the order of:

> "We've been dealing with a lot of issues and I believe you've made a lot of progress. One of our goals all along has been to reach the point where counseling is no longer needed. I think we're reaching that point, and probably in about three or four weeks, we'll be stopping."

You can anticipate that your clients will have any of several reactions to this. They may feel good about their progress, nervous about the prospect of being on their own, or sad to see a significant relationship ending, to name but a few reactions.

Occasionally, it is appropriate to terminate gradually. This can be done by spacing the time between interviews. If you have been seeing your client weekly, change the appointments to every other week or once a month. Or you may schedule a six-month check-in that gives your client the sense of an ongoing relationship, one that leaves the door open, should that be necessary. Even with these gradual transitions, you will still have as a major concern the transition of a significant relationship.

In all cases, it is important to emphasize the client's continued growth once counseling has ended. This includes summations of what the client has learned in counseling, discussions of other resources and support systems the client can make use of in her or his life, and the invitation for followup sessions as necessary. Kottler (1991) observed that "some people believe that therapy never ceases, that clients continue their dialogues with us (as they do with deceased parents) for the rest of their lives" (p. 173).

Finally, it occasionally happens that the ending of a counseling relationship has a character of finality. Perhaps you or your client is moving. Or you may be referring your client to another help provider. In such instances, there may be a grieving process connected with termination. It is appropriate to view this grieving process as necessary and therapeutic in its own right. It is as important for the counselor as for the client. Occasionally, a client may terminate simply by canceling the next appointment and there is no formal termination that occurs, yet the counselor may still feel some grief. It is a symbolic or ceremonious conclusion, an acknowledgment that the relationship had importance and that reality dictates that it end. In such cases, it is better not to hang on to it; that would only make the transition more difficult. If you are making a referral to another counselor, you must give up your role as helper for both ethical and practical reasons.

Summary

It is true that the experienced counselor has developed a style for managing the counseling session, but beginning counselors must experiment with a variety of behaviors before a style begins to emerge. The verbal interventions included in this chapter are one way to begin defining that style. It is not assumed that all strategies will be comfortable or appropriate to every counselor trainee. Along the way, the beginning counselor is often confronted by misconceptions about helping, about client behavior, and about expectations.

In Chapter 2, we introduced the notion of counselor intentionality as a dimension of the helping relationship. If you will recall, the intentional counselor is one who can function in the interview with alternative behaviors and can conceptualize from different vantage points with a diverse group of clients. These skills are particularly important in the initial interview and in opening subsequent interviews. In some counseling settings, an intake interview will be required. Although the intake procedure is well defined in terms of the type of information to be obtained, the counselor's skills in establishing rapport, soliciting relevant information, and reassuring the client require more than an outline of topics.

The skills of interview termination and case termination call also for a counselor who possesses a repertoire of counseling skills and strategies. If termination is viewed as a transition from one psychological condition to another, the counselor functions as the bridge between those two conditions. Developing termination skills that are both natural to your personal style and effective in helping clients to make necessary adjustments will require time and experience. For the moment, it will suffice for you to understand the dynamics of the process and begin to address the matter of skill building.

DISCUSSION QUESTIONS

1. Discuss what it might be like to be a client seeking help for the first time from an unknown counselor. Now discuss this as it applies to a cross-cultural dyad.

2. Discuss the positive perceptions that a client might have after going through an intake interview.

3. What do you think are the most important elements, from a counselor's perspective, in terminating a significant relationship? From the client's perspective?

4. Why is it not ethical to begin or to continue helping a client who is also receiving counseling from another therapist?

RECOMMENDED READINGS

Hackney, H., & Cormier, L. S. (1996). *The professional counselor* (3rd ed.). Boston: Allyn and Bacon.

Hansen, J., Rossberg, R., & Cramer, S. (1994). *Counseling: Theory and process* (5th ed.). Boston: Allyn and Bacon.

Kramer, S. (1990). *Positive endings in psychotherapy.* San Francisco: Jossey-Bass.

Morrison, J. (1995). *The first interview: A guide for clinicians.* New York: Guilford.

Sommers-Flanagan, J., & Sommers-Flanagan, R. (1994). *Foundations of therapeutic interviewing.* Boston: Allyn and Bacon.

CHAPTER

<h1>6 Responding to Cognitive Content</h1>

The counselor responds to the client in many ways, both verbally and nonverbally. Since your responses will have an impact on clients and the topics they discuss, it is necessary to be aware of the effect your responses will have. One very important effect deals with the changing pattern of the client's verbal behavior. As the verbal interaction and communication begin, topics arise; some topics are developed, some are modified, and some are diverted into new topics. As an active participant in the counseling process, you must be sure that your responses will influence the *direction* of topic development in such ways as choosing from among the topics that are to be discussed and the length of time allotted to the topics. Responding to client content suggests alternatives and conscious choices that you will have to make in the interview. Then, when one choice has been made, the effect of that choice will become the basis for further alternatives. The following example will illustrate the types of choices you, the counselor, will be making. Suppose your client says:

> **CLIENT:** "I've known what this operation would do to my plans for a long time."

Your choices for responding are several. You could (1) paraphrase the client's remarks; (2) accent the word *operation* or the words *your plans;* (3) ask the question, "What will it do?"; (4) say "mm-hmm"; or (5) present an ability-potential type of response such as, "You are able to anticipate the consequences of the operation."

Obviously, these five responses will produce different effects with clients. The client in the above example may proceed to talk about the operation, about plans, or about how she anticipates events. In any case, your response would shape or mold the topic development, and, as a result, influence the future matters the client discusses.

In this chapter, we will be working with content choices of a cognitive nature, as opposed to affective or feeling-type choices. In other words, the emphasis now is on your recognition and demonstrated ability to identify and respond to client thoughts or ideas dealing with *problems, situations, people,* or *things.*

Recognizing Alternatives

Each comment of the client presents alternatives to you in terms of content to which you may respond. How you respond to one alternative will shape the next remark of the client. Your task is to identify accurately the kinds of content presented by the client and the alternatives to which you, as the counselor, can respond.

EXERCISE **6.1**

Identifying Alternative Topics

To give you practice in identifying topic alternatives, read carefully the following client statements. Then identify and list all the different topics in each client response.

1. "I don't know just exactly how it does work, but you can take weekend trips in connection with the Air Force. It would be like duty because you have to qualify for it and you can travel all over the U.S."

   _____

   _____

   _____

   _____

2. "And I thought it was great. And I realize that some people have a bad opinion of women in the service but, uh, they shouldn't really, because a woman is going to be what she is, no matter where she is."

   _____

   _____

   _____

   _____

Feedback
The correct answers to the exercises above are as follows:

1. a. I don't know just exactly how it does work.
   b. You can sign up to take weekend trips in connection with the Air Force.
   c. It would be like duty.

d. You have to qualify for it.

e. You can travel all over the U.S.

2. a. I thought it was great.

b. I realize that some people have a bad opinion of women in the service.

c. They shouldn't really.

d. A woman is going to be what she is no matter where she is.

Responding to Alternatives

The process of selecting alternatives can best be illustrated by excerpts from actual interviews:

> CLIENT: "I like this type of a setup where you can talk directly to people and talk with them. Uh, I don't like big crowds where I don't know anybody and they don't know me."
>
> COUNSELOR: "You'd rather not be in big crowds."

In this example, the client's response contained two basic communications: (1) I like to talk directly to people and (2) I don't like big crowds in which individuals get lost. The counselor chose to respond to the second communication in the client's response. Had the counselor responded by saying, "You prefer situations that permit you to get to know people," the topic focus would have been on getting to know people and the necessary conditions for this. As it was, the response led to a topic focus on the ambiguity of not knowing people. This does not necessarily mean that one response was more appropriate than the other; it is used only to point out the available alternatives.

A study of counseling typescripts suggests that when the counselor has alternative communications to which he or she may respond, the tendency is to respond to the *final* component of the response. Perhaps this is because of the immediacy of the final part of the response; but if so, that is a poor criterion. It is more logical that the counselor respond to the part of the client's communication that has *greatest bearing* on the client's concern and is therefore most important.

The counselor may also be tempted to respond to that portion of the client's communication that he or she finds most interesting. In this case, the interview tends to center on those topics that the counselor may identify with or be dealing with personally. Again, the counselor must ensure that the choice of alternative topics reflects a decision about the client's needs rather than the counselor's. This is especially true in instances of cross-cultural counseling. If the counselor chooses to respond to the portion of the client's communication that is most interesting to the counselor, this may be a reflection of the counselor's personal and cultural biases and cultural world view, and may not be relevant to the client's culture. In cross-cultural counseling, there are often barriers or stumbling blocks to intercultural communication (Pedersen & Ivey, 1993). (They are not likely to be barriers for those *within* the same culture because of shared meaning.) Assuming similarities instead of differences in cross-cultural counseling is one such barrier. The counselor cannot safely assume that what he or she chooses to attend to is what is of most importance to the client from a different culture.

Verbal Responses to Cognitive Content

There are several types of responses you can use to focus on and elicit specific content expressed in the client's communication. The responses presented here can be used specifically to respond to the cognitive content of the client's communication; that is, ideas that deal with *problems, situations, people,* and *things.*

Although these are not the only possible ones, four stimulus responses will be identified here for this purpose: silence, minimal verbal activity, restatement, and open-ended questions. Emphasis will be directed toward the latter two. The use of silence and minimal verbal stimuli has already been noted in previous chapters. Their use as discriminator responses will be presented here briefly.

Silence

Silence affects the course of topic development by indicating that the counselor does not want to select or direct the topic at the given time it is used (see Chapter 4). Although the use of silence gives the counselor much less control over the direction that topic development takes, it serves to increase the power of other types of responses. Thus, after you have remained silent for several moments, your next verbal response will have more influence in shaping the direction of topic development.

Minimal Verbal Activity

Minimal verbal responses are those verbalizations and vocalizations that people use when they are listening to someone else. The most common are "mm-hmm," "mmm," "yes," "oh, " and "I see." They are unobtrusive utterances, but have a significant reinforcing value. That is to say, when an utterance such as "mm-hmm" is used consistently following a particular topic or word, the future occurrence of that particular topic or word usually increases.

Restatements

The restatement is the repetition of all or a selected portion of the client's previous communication, and it neither adds to nor detracts from the basic communication. It confirms for the client that the counselor has heard the communication. Operationally, the restatement may be defined as a simple, compound, complex, or fragmentary sentence that mirrors the client's previous communication. It is dependent in its grammatical structure on the grammatical structure of the client's previous response. The restatement can be used effectively so long as it is interspersed with other types of counselor responses. Otherwise, it can produce a parrotlike effect that has an adverse effect on clients.

Examples of restatements will help you understand this particular response:

CLIENT: "I'm hoping to get a good job this summer."
COUNSELOR: "You're hoping to get a good job." *(Restatement)*

CLIENT: "It doesn't look like we'll get a vacation this summer."
COUNSELOR: "No vacation this summer." *(Restatement)*

CLIENT: "I like people but I sure get tired of them."
COUNSELOR: "You like people but you also get tired of them." *(Restatement)*

Now, try your hand with a few restatements:

CLIENT: "This has been a really rough year for me."
YOU: "_____."

CLIENT: "Probably the worst class I have is literature."
YOU: "_____."

Discuss your responses with someone.

Open-Ended Questions

Open-ended questions require more than a minimal one-word answer by the client. They are introduced with *what, where, when,* or *how.* You will find that it is very difficult to ask questions that clearly place the focus on your client. Typically, when you start asking questions, the client will give a minimal answer and then wait for the next question. In other words, the client has not assumed responsibility for the content of the interview. One purpose of the open-ended question is to prevent the client from answering questions with a yes or no response. Open-ended questions also are useful for encouraging clients to elaborate and to give information. Some examples of open-ended questions include the following:

"What do you like about it?"
"What is keeping you from doing it?"
"How do you feel about it?"
"How is it helping you?"

"When do you feel that way?"
"Where does that occur for you?"
"Who enables you to keep doing this?"

Why questions are usually avoided because clients rarely know the answer and because they appear intrusive.

Open-ended questions can easily be overused in an interview. A beginning counselor often tends to bombard initial clients with questions. Extensive use of questions gives a ping-pong effect; the counselor asks, the client answers, and so on, thus the counseling resembles little more than an interrogation process.

When counselors overuse questions, they may be acting more out of their own needs rather than trying to help the client in the form of structuring, clarifying, expecting, or soliciting information. Examples of situations in which questions are used to meet the *counselor's* needs include:

Voyeurism—wanting to know certain things about the client to satisfy our own curiosity,

Narcissism—wanting to make ourselves look good or look like the expert by the kinds of questions we ask,

Sadism—bombarding the client with frequent or painful questions so much as to constitute harassment. (Kottler, 1991, p. 160)

Dillon (1990) recommended two issues a counselor can consider to use questions selectively and effectively:

1. What is the purpose of my question?
2. How is this purpose therapeutic—how does it help the client?

Occasionally, beginning counselors resort to questions simply because they feel more comfortable with this type of lead. This is a good example in which silence may be used in lieu of another question. Ultimately, learning a variety of alternative verbal leads will help prevent overuse of questions.

It is also important to note that clients may have very different reactions to questions. Some clients may construe counselor questions as a sign of interest on the counselor's part. Other clients may view questions as intrusive and react by withdrawing. Questions can be culturally insensitive and offensive, particularly if they are ones that seek very personal information from clients in initial sessions or if they suggest a cause-effect orientation (Sue & Sue, 1990). Asking questions of a very personal nature may be perceived as lacking in respect by some Asian American clients. Also, the world view of some clients from other cultural groups, such as American Indians, reflects an intuitive and harmonious approach rather than a cause-effect approach. As with all verbal responses, counselors need to monitor closely the effects of their verbal leads, particularly questions, on new clients.

Try a few open-ended questions for yourself:

CLIENT: "It's hard to admit, but I really have wondered whether college is for me."

YOU: "_____ ."

CLIENT: "I've gotten to the point where I can't do anything I'm supposed to do."

YOU: "_____ ."

Discuss your responses with someone.

EXERCISE 6.2

Identifying and Responding to Cognitive Content

A. Identifying Cognitive Content

To give further practice in identifying cognitive content—thoughts or ideas pertaining to problems, situations, people, or things—read carefully the following client statements. Then identify and list the different cognitive topics within each client response.

1. "I'm thinking about either going to graduate school or getting a job—whichever would be better experience is what I'll do."

   _____

   _____

   _____

2. "People can say whatever they want about it, but as far as I'm concerned, my place as a woman is in the home and it will not change."

   _____

   _____

   _____

Feedback

The answers to the preceding exercises are as follows:

1. a. I'm thinking about going to graduate school.
   b. I'm also thinking about getting a job.
   c. I'll do whatever provides the best experience.

2. a. People can say whatever they want to about a woman's place.
    b. I think my place as a woman is in the home.
    c. My opinion about this will not change.

B. Responding to Cognitive Content

The following exercise will give you practice in using restatements and open questions. Read each client statement and then respond with the type of response indicated in parentheses:

1. **CLIENT:** "Yes, I think that the best way to learn a language is to actually live with the people and learn it that way. Um, the first year that I was going back to Germany, I didn't learn very much at all."

    YOU: *(Restatement)* "_____

    _____."

2. **CLIENT:** "I'd like to know the language, but still I can't carry on a conversation because it isn't used that much in my classes."

    YOU: *(Open-ended question)* "_____

    _____."

3. **CLIENT:** "I wanted to go back to school mostly because of the fact that I thought that there would be someone to lead me because I just don't know which direction to go sometimes for a few things."

    YOU: *(Restatement)* "_____

    _____."

4. **CLIENT:** "Well, I know you're supposed to study every night, which I don't do, but I'm not the only one who hasn't studied this semester. A lot of other kids have lost interest too."

    YOU: *(Open-ended question)* "_____

    _____."

Discuss your responses with someone.

Differentiation and Selective Responding

The emphasis in this chapter has been on the selective responding to some client messages as opposed to others. When the client presents you with a multiple message, you can respond to all the messages or to only part of them. If you respond to only part of the client's messages, that part to which you do not respond may be dropped by the client in future communication, unless it is very important to the client. In this case, the client may attempt to initiate discussions of the topic once again.

Selective responding involves a covert process on the counselor's part known as *differentiation,* which is the process of identifying all the different parts of the client's communication and making an intentional decision about which part to respond to and how. It also involves paying attention to or monitoring the effects of your choices on subsequent client communication.

The effects of selective responding require you to be very attuned to yourself and your own issues, and ultimately to be comfortable with yourself, your issues, and your feelings. Effective responses to clients demand a sort of consciousness on your part about yourself. For example, if you are personally uncomfortable with issues such as sexuality, abortion, divorce, and so on, you may avoid responding to the mention of these topics by clients, or if the expression of anger scares you, you may avoid responding to anything that might indicate the client is feeling angry. A major way that counselors become and stay conscious of themselves and their impact on clients is through consultation with a supervisor. We discuss this in greater detail in Chapter 11.

Because clients vary along many dimensions, the effects of your responses with clients will also vary in impact—positive and negative. Thus, it is erroneous to assume that all of the responses and interventions presented in this book will work with all clients or will have the same meaning or results for all clients.

To summarize the discrimination process of selective responding, consider these two key points:

1. The counselor is able to generate a maximum number of ideas, words and responses to communicate with a diverse group of clients.
2. The counselor is able to observe the effects of the responses implemented in the session with a diverse group of clients and is flexible enough to modify these responses when the observations suggest they are not working.

EXERCISE **6.3**

Selective Responding

A. Anticipating Client Responses
Using your responses to the client in Part B of the previous exercise, write what you think would be the client's response to what you said. For example, with response 1, if you had said, "When were you in Germany?" the client might have responded, "I was there from 1989 through 1991."

1. Your response: _____

_____

Client's next response: _____

_____

2. Your response: _____

_____

Client's next response: _____

_____

3. Your response: _____

_____

Client's next response: _____

_____

4. Discuss with another person the effects of each of your responses on the client.

B. Observed Practice

One of you, designated as the speaker, will share a concern with the listener. As the speaker, make sure your initial statement contains several different ideas to which anyone could respond. For example, "I'm really having trouble in school. There's just so much work I can't keep up with it. I wonder if I can make good enough grades. I also need to keep my job to have enough money to pay for tuition, but I don't know if I'll continue to be able to work and study at the same time."

1. The respondent's task is to select *one* of the ideas or topics and respond to it by using either a *restatement* or an *open question*. After your initial response, allow the speaker to continue, then respond with either *silence* or a *minimal verbal utterance*.
2. The observer's task is to track the way in which the speaker develops the topic and the course of future topics depending on which part of the communication the listener chose to respond to.
3. After completing this in one triad, reverse the roles and complete the same process two more times.
4. At the end of three practices, discuss what you have noticed about how the listener's choice of responses and topics influences the path of the speaker's communication.

Summary

In this chapter, we have shown that the counselor has numerous response choices, and each choice has a corresponding effect on the client's following statement. In this reciprocal arrangement, both the counselor and the client influence the path that counseling will take in the session. Most therapists would acknowledge the importance of the client's choices, which reflect how the client conceptualizes problems and solutions, self and others, success and failure, and responsibility and control. However, they do not always acknowledge that the counselor similarly influences the session by choosing to respond to some messages rather than others, by exploring some issues rather than others—in short, by selecting what becomes the focus of the session.

These counselor choices are made in rather commonplace ways, including silence, minimal vocal utterances, restatements of the clients' message, and open-ended questions. The highly experienced counselor makes these choices almost intuitively; the inexperienced counselor must make these choices deliberately. If the inexperienced counselor relies on intuition, the possibility of making bad choices is about equal to the possibility of making good choices. But what is more important, the inexperienced counselor who is unaware of, and thus is not making intentional choices, is very likely to lack a sense of what is happening in the process of counseling.

We have also indicated throughout this chapter that the effects of your responses will not only affect the focus and direction of each interview but also will vary among clients of various cultural groups. The client's world view is an important determinant in this process.

DISCUSSION QUESTIONS

1. What are some of the conditions that might work against you as you try to recognize the different messages in a client statement?

2. How can a counselor shape or influence the topical direction of a session without even being aware that he or she is doing so?

3. Under what counseling conditions might you want to have your clients talking about problems, events, situations, or people, as opposed to feelings?

4. With yourself or a partner, discuss ideas, beliefs, topics, or issues that are uncomfortable for you to talk about. How might this affect the way in which you respond to clients who present these issues and beliefs?

5. How might your own cultural affiliation and world view affect what you focus on in an interview?

RECOMMENDED READINGS

Dillon, J. T. (1990). *The practice of questioning.* New York: Routledge.

Ivey, A. (1994). *Intentional interviewing and counseling* (3rd ed.). Pacific Grove, CA: Brooks/Cole.

Ivey, A. E., Ivey, M. B., & Simek-Morgan, L. (1997). *Counseling and psychotherapy* (4th ed.) Boston: Allyn and Bacon.

Johnson, D. W. (1997). *Reaching out: Interpersonal effectiveness and self actualization* (6th ed.). Boston: Allyn and Bacon.

Pedersen, P., & Ivey, A. (1993). *Culture-centered counseling and interviewing skills.* Westport, CT: Praeger.

7 Responding to Affective Content

What are some of the ways you communicate how you feel? When you are "down in the dumps," how does your voice sound? When you are angry, what is your face like? Your mouth? Your eyes? Your jaws? When you are afraid, what are some of the expressions you use to communicate this feeling? Human beings have many ways of communicating their internal states. The set jaw often is associated with determination. The glaring eyes speak for anger, even in the small child. The trembling voice, the soft voice, the downcast eyes—all have their meanings.

Clients use all of the verbal and nonverbal modes to tell the counselor their problems. The emotions that accompany the narrative enrich and modify the message. They give the counselor the events of the clients' world *and* the clients' reactions to those events. These cues are not always easy to read and can vary across cultures. Clenched teeth can mean more than one thing. The trembling voice only suggests the presence of an intense emotion. A part of being a counselor is putting together the pieces or cues of clients' messages in such a way that you can make reasonably good guesses about the underlying emotion.

As indicated earlier, a client's communication presents alternatives. In addition to alternative cognitive topics, you will find that you are faced with choices between cognitive topics and affective topics. This chapter focuses on the affective message, how to recognize it, and how to reinforce its exploration by clients. As Teyber (1997) observed, "Conflicted feelings lie at the heart of enduring and pervasive problems. . . . This affective unfolding is a pivotal point in therapy because it reveals the emotional basis of client's problems" (p. 123).*

To review briefly, client communications that deal primarily with people, events, or objects may be described as *cognitive* details. Communications that reflect feelings or emotions may be described as *affective* details. Many messages contain both cognitive and affective components. When this occurs, the affective message may not be obvious in the words of the client. Instead, the feelings may

---

*This and all other material from this source are from *Interpersonal Process in Psychotherapy: A Guide for Clinical Training,* 3/e, by E. Teyber. Copyright ©1997, 1992, 1989 Brooks/Cole Publishing Company, Pacific Grove, CA 93950, a division of International Thomson Publishing Inc. By permission of the publisher.

be expressed through nonverbal modes, such as vocal pitch, rapidity of speech, body position, and/or gestures.

The Importance of Responding to Affective Content

Affective content represents feelings or emotions held by clients. Clients are often either unaware of their feelings or afraid of them. Many people, including those who learn to be helpers, do not want to feel feelings because of the rules those individuals have made about feelings. In fact, a major rule in dysfunctional families is "Don't feel"—sometimes made more specific like "Don't feel angry" or "Don't feel sad." Little boys may hear "Don't feel sad or cry—you'll be a sissy"; little girls may hear "Be nice—be a good girl—don't say anything angry." Often, these rules have the effect of masking or interfering with how people truly feel. One of the most important functions in responding to client messages is to give clients permission to feel their feelings, to allow their feelings just to be, rather than stifling, controlling, or holding them back. Persons who, in fact, have held feelings for a long period of time may tend to hold the feeling in a particular musculature of the body, such as tight shoulders or neck, tense lower back, churning gut, and so on (Kelley, 1974).

When clients are given permission to reveal and release feelings, often their energy and well-being are also increased. This occurs because all of the deep primary feelings have a survival value (Kelley, 1979). For example, anger allows an individual to protect his or her rights and establish personal boundaries or limits (Kelley, 1979). The capacity to recognize and express anger is the basis for healthy assertiveness. As Kelley (1979) observed, "The person who cannot become angry, whose anger is deeply repressed, is severely handicapped. . . . These persons' assertions lack conviction and they are often at the mercy of or emotionally dependent on those who are capable of becoming angry" (p. 25). Moreover, the expression of anger is useful in close relationships to "clear the air" and prevent chronic boredom and resentment from building up. Anger and disgust that are expressed and released prompt subsequent expression of love; pain and sadness that are expressed promote later expression of joy and pleasure; and fear that is discharged allows for greater trust (Kelley, 1974).

When a client's communication contains both cognitive and affective components, some therapists recommend the first priority is to acknowledge the affective pattern of the message. Teyber (1997), for one, noted that in all of the indices a therapist has about how to respond to a client, as a general guideline, the most productive response is to *respond to the feeling as the client is currently experiencing it.*

Teyber (1997) also noted that another important function of responding to affective content is to help clients *experience* rather than simply talk about feelings. "Little change occurs until clients are able to stop talking about their emotions in an intellectualized or objective manner, and actually experience their conflicted emotions in the presence of the therapist" (p. 129). One way to help clients experience their feelings involves modeling or reflecting the feelings, as we discuss later in this chapter. It is also important to do so when the clients are experiencing the full emotional impact of their issues, since change is most likely to occur at that time (Teyber, 1997).

Verbal and Nonverbal Cues Associated with Emotions

You may have wondered how you can identify another person's feelings. Although you cannot feel the client's feelings, you can infer what those feelings are and experience very similar feelings. That is to say, you may be able to know what it is like to feel a certain way. How do you do this? You draw from your own emotional experiences and recall that you, too, have experienced pain, anger, and joy, and remember how they felt. You must first recognize the feeling in your client before you can reproduce a similar feeling in yourself.

To do this, you may need to become more aware of, and sensitive to, certain verbal and nonverbal cues that are elements of the client's communication. Some of these cues are referred to as *leakage,* since they communicate messages the client did not deliberately intend to have communicated (Ekman & Friesen, 1969). Other cues, primarily verbal, are more deliberately intended and are more easily recognized and identified.

In the case of affective leakage, it is important to account for the inferences you draw. For example, when you say, "The client seems happy," that is an inference. If you say, instead, "The client is smiling, and that may mean that he is happy," then you have accounted for your inference.

The total impact of a client's message includes both verbal and nonverbal elements. The verbal impact means that there are certain nouns, adjectives, adverbs, and verbs that express the client's feelings about something or someone, as shown here:

"I am really *worried* about school."

The verbal element associated with the client's feelings in this example is the word *worried*. These kinds of words can be called *affect* words. They express some feeling that the client possesses. If an adverb such as *really* or *very* precedes the affect word, this indicates an even stronger intensity of emotion.

Nonverbal Cues to Affect

Nonverbal cues can be seen by observing the client's head and facial movement, position of body, quick movements and gestures, and voice quality. Although no single nonverbal cue can be interpreted accurately alone, each does have meaning as part of a larger pattern, or *gestalt*. Thus, there are relationships between nonverbal and verbal aspects of speech. In addition to the relationship between nonverbal and verbal parts of the message, nonverbal cues may also communicate specific information about the relationship of the people involved in the communicative process—in this case, the counselor and the client. Nonverbal cues convey information about the nature and intensity of emotions, sometimes more accurately than verbal cues. The *nature* of the emotion is communicated nonverbally primarily by *head* cues; the *intensity* of an emotion is communicated both by *head* cues and *body* cues (Ekman & Friesen, 1967).

Close observation of the client's body, nonverbal behavior, and facial expressions in particular can offer important information to the counselor about the nature and intensity of blocked feelings as well as feelings that are starting to emerge. For example, one of us recently saw a client who had been coming in weekly for the last few months. On this particular occasion, the counselor noted that shortly after the client sat down, her face became contorted. She then began to describe a situation that had recently occurred involving a loss of an important relationship. The counselor commented on her facial expression—the tightness of it—and inquired about what she might be holding back. She then immediately cried, and upon release of tears, her face softened and relaxed.

Culture and Nonverbal Affect Cues

It is very important not to assume the meaning of a nonverbal affect cue without checking it out with the client. In part, this is because the meaning may vary among persons and also among cultures. For example, there seem to be differences in cultures between *contact* and *noncontact* nonverbal behaviors such as eye contact, touch, and physical distance between the counselor and client (Watson, 1970). The one area of nonverbal expression that does *not* seem to vary among cultural groups involves facial expressions. The primary or basic emotions of anger, fear, sadness, and happiness do seem to be depicted in the same facial expressions across cultures, although the various norms of each culture may affect how much and how often these emotions are expressed (Mesquita & Frijda, 1992).

EXERCISE **7.1**

Identifying Behavior

Select a partner and interact with him or her for about five minutes. Then each of you, in turn, describe your partner, using the phrase:

"I'm observing that you are _____ ."

Be sure to describe what you *see*, not how you think the other person feels or what the nonverbal behavior means.

Types of Affective Messages

Although there are many different kinds of feelings, most feelings that are identified by words fit into one of four areas: affection, anger, fear, or sadness/depres-
sion. Although there are now many lists of affect words available, we continue to
use the one that we believe was the original of all such lists (shown on the next
few pages).

Positive Affect

Feelings of affection reflect positive or good feelings about oneself and others and
indicate positive feelings about interpersonal relationships. Many of them can be
identified by certain affect words. Affect word cues that communicate the general
feeling of well-being, affection, or satisfaction may be subclassified into five general areas:

Enjoyment	Competence	Love	Happiness	Hope
beautiful	able	close	cheerful	luck
enjoy	can	friendly	content	optimism
good	fulfill	love	delighted	try
nice	great	like	excited	guess
pretty	wonderful	need	happy	wish
satisfy	smart	care	laugh(ed)	want
terrific	respect	want	thrill	
tremendous	worth	choose	dig	

Source: T. J. Crowley, *The Conditionability of Positive and Negative Self-Reference Emotional Affect
Statements in a Counseling-Type Interview.* Unpublished doctoral dissertation. Amherst: University of Massachusetts, 1970. Reprinted by permission.

You can continue to add to this list of affect words related to affection. Can
you begin to get the feeling for the message implicit in the usage of words such as
these? Certain nonverbal cues often occur simultaneously with affection word
cues. The most obvious of these cues are facial ones. The corners of the mouth may
turn up to produce the hint of a smile. The eyes may widen slightly. Facial wrin-
kles disappear. Often, there is an absence of body tension. The arms and hands
may be moved in an open-palm gesture of acceptance, or the communicator may
reach out and touch the object of the affection message. When the client is
describing feelings about an object or event, there may be increased animation of
the face and hands.

Anger

Anger represents an obstruction to be relieved or removed in some way. Different kinds of stimuli often elicit anger, such as *frustration, threat,* and *fear*. Conditions such as competition, jealously, and thwarted aspirations can become threats that elicit angry responses. Anger often represents negative feelings about oneself and/ or others. Many times, fear is concealed by an outburst of anger. In such cases, the anger becomes a defensive reaction because the person does not feel safe enough to express fear. Anger is also a cover-up for hurt. Beneath strong aggressive outbursts are often deep feelings of vulnerability and pain. Verbal cues that suggest anger may be classified into four general categories:

Attack	Grimness	Defensiveness	Quarrelsomeness
argue	dislike	against	angry
attack	hate	protect	fight
compete	nasty	resent	quarrel
criticize	disgust	guard	argue
fight	surly	prepared	take issue
hit	serious		reject
hurt			disagree
offend			

Source: T. J. Crowley, *The Conditionability of Positive and Negative Self-Reference Emotional Affect Statements in a Counseling-Type Interview.* Unpublished doctoral dissertation. Amherst: University of Massachusetts, 1970. Reprinted by permission.

You can continue to add to this list of affect words related to anger. Remember that anger covers a broad group of feelings and can be expressed in many ways. With the expression of anger, the body position may become rigid and tense, or it may be characterized by gross changes in body position or movement. Sometimes, anger toward another person or the self may be expressed by *hitting,* which consists of fault finding or petty remarks directed at the object of the anger. For example, in counseling a couple with relationship problems, one partner may express this sort of anger by continual verbal attacks on the other person or by incessant remarks of dissatisfaction with the partner. Hitting can also be expressed through nonverbal cues such as finger drumming or foot tapping.

Certain vocal qualities are also associated with anger. Many times, the voice will become much louder as the person becomes more rigid in what he or she is saying; if the anger is very intense, the person may even shout. In some instances of intense anger, the feeling may be accompanied by tears. Many times, the expression of anger will cause vocal pitch to become higher. With some people, however, the vocal pitch actually is lowered, becoming more controlled and measured. This often means that the person experiencing the anger is attempting to maintain a level of control over his or her feelings.

Fear

Fear represents a person's reaction to some kind of danger to be avoided. Often, this reaction is a withdrawal from a painful or stressful situation, from oneself or from other people and relationships. As such, the person experiencing the emotions of fear may also be isolated and sad or depressed. Fear can also be described as a negative set of feelings about something or someone that results in a need to protect oneself. Verbal cues that suggest fear may be classified into four general categories:

Fear	Doubt	Pain	Avoidance
anxious	failure	awful	flee
bothers	flunk	hurts	run from
concerns	undecided	intense	escape
lonely	mediocre	unpleasant	cut out
nervous	moody	uncomfortable	forget
scare	puzzled	aches	
tense	stupid	torn	
upset	unsure		

You can continue to add to this list of affect words suggesting fear. Remember that fear is a broad category of feelings and can be expressed in a variety of ways.

Several facial cues are associated with fear. The mouth may hang wide open as in shock or startlement; the eyes may also dilate. Fear may cause a furrow to appear between the eyebrows. Fear of the counselor or of the topic at hand may be reflected by the client's avoidance of direct, eye contact, although remember that the meaning and use of eye contact varies among cultures.

Body positions and movements are also associated with the expression of fear. At first, the person experiencing fear may appear to be still in body position or may draw back. However, after this initial period, body movements usually become greater as anxiety increases, resulting in jerky and trembling motions. Although parts of the body may shake, often the hands are tightly clasped, as if giving protection. Tension may also be indicated through actions such as leg swinging, foot tapping, finger tapping, or playing with a ring or other piece of jewelry.

Voice qualities are also indicators of the level of anxiety the client is experiencing. As the level of anxiety increases, the breathing rate becomes faster and breathing becomes more shallow. As anxiety and tension increase, the number of speech disturbances increases. This yields a greater number of cues, such as errors, repetitions, stutterings, and omissions of parts of words or sentences. The rate of speech also increases as anxiety mounts, so an anxious person may speak at a faster than usual rate. The intonation of a depressed person or one in the grip of fear is also a departure from the normal intonation. The voice quality may become more subdued with less inflection, so that the voice takes on more of a monotonal quality.

Sadness

Some of the more common conditions expressed by clients are feelings of sadness, loneliness, or depression. These emotions may be a response to a variety of client conditions, including unsatisfying personal relationships, environmental conditions such as disempowerment and oppression, physiological imbalances, or even nutrition. Verbal cues that suggest sadness, loneliness, or depression include the following:

Sadness	Loneliness	Depression
unhappy	alone	depressing
adrift	abandoned	depressed
sorrowful	isolated	disillusioned
distressed	missing	weary
grieved	missed	listless
heartsick		discouraged
		despondent
		gloomy

Source: T. J. Crowley, *The Conditionability of Positive and Negative Self-Reference Emotional Affect Statements in a Counseling-Type Interview.* Unpublished doctoral dissertation. Amherst: University of Massachusetts, 1970. Reprinted by permission.

It is important to recognize that sadness has different meanings among cultures. In fact, in some societies, depression is not even recognized as an illness or a sign of something being wrong but rather an indication of spiritual insight (Castillo, 1997). In another example, O'Neill (1993) found that among Native Americans living on reservations, sadness had positive connotations because "it signified maturity and recognition of the tremendous loss they experienced through domination by Angelo American society" (Castillo, 1997, p. 208). Grief is also a phenomenon that is embedded in sociocultural contexts. In Greece, for example, a widow grieves for five years after her partner's death (Kramer, 1993). Moreover, while sadness in Western society is often characterized by a *cognitive* feature such as self-talk, in many non-Western societies, it is represented more by *somatic* symptoms (Castillo, 1997).

EXERCISE 7.2

Identifying Affect Cues

To give you practice in identifying nonverbal and verbal affect cues, complete the following exercises:

A. Identifying Nonverbal Affect Cues
Select a partner. One of you will be the speaker; the other will be the respondent. The speaker should select a feeling from the following list:

> Contentment or happiness
> Puzzlement or confusion
> Anger
> Discouragement

Do not tell the respondent which feeling you have selected. Portray the feeling through nonverbal expressions only. The respondent must accurately identify the behaviors you use to communicate the feeling and should infer the feeling you are portraying. After he or she has done so, choose another and repeat the process. When you have portrayed each feeling, reverse roles and repeat the exercise.

B. Linking Body Cues and Emotions
Many emotions are expressed graphically by descriptions about the body. Smith (1985) has provided an excellent list of some of these. We recommend his exercise, which is to enact each of them with your own body and note the feeling and body sensations that accompany each enactment.

He holds his head high.	He puts his best foot forward.
He has a tight jaw.	He drags his heels.
He does not hold his head straight.	He puts his finger on it.
His head is cocked.	He meets one with open arms.
He looks down his nose.	He is tight-fisted.
He keeps a stiff upper lip.	He waved me away.
He does not look one in the eye.	He is shady.
He is down in the mouth.	His shoulders are square.
He turns away.	He stoops low.
He has shifty eyes.	He sits tall.
He has a stiff neck.	He sits straight.
He sticks his chest out.	He is tied up in a knot.
His shoulders are stooped.	He is backward.
His arms are outstretched.	He is forward.
He is heavy-handed.	He leans on people.

| He wants to sit on it. | He is weak in the knees. |
| He puts his foot down. | He is a high stepper. (pp. 60–61)* |

C. Identifying Verbal Affect Cues

The speaker should select a feeling from the following list:

Surprise
Elation or thrill
Anxiety or tension
Sadness or depression
Seriousness or intensity
Irritation or anger

Do not inform the respondent which feeling you have selected. Verbally express the feeling in one or two sentences. Be certain to include the word itself. The respondent should accurately identify the feeling in two ways:

1. Restate the feeling using the same affect word as the speaker.
2. Restate the feeling using a different affect word but one that reflects the same feeling.

Here is an example:

> **SPEAKER:** "I feel *good* about being here."
>
> **RESPONDENT:** "You feel *good?*"
>
>   or
>
> "You're *glad* to be here."

Choose another feeling and complete the same process. When you have expressed each feeling, reverse roles and repeat the exercise.

D. Identifying Affective Components

Read the following client statements taken from actual interview typescripts and identify the affective component(s) in each statement by writing first-person sentences and by underlining the affect word of each client's communication. Here is an example:

> **CLIENT:** "I'm not the type that would like to do research or, uh, things that don't have any contact directly with people. I <u>like</u> to be with people, you know—I feel at home and secure with people."

---

*This and all other quotations from this source are from *The Body in Psychotherapy* by Edward W. L. Smith. Copyright © 1985 by McFarland & Co., Jefferson NC 28640. Reprinted by permission.

In this statement the affect word *like* is identified and the following affective components are identified by written sentences using the first person:

1. I enjoy being with people.
2. People help me feel secure.

If there is more than one affective component within a given client communication, place an asterisk (*) next to the one that you feel has the greatest bearing on the client's concern. In the preceding example, asterisk either 1 or 2, depending on which has the greater bearing in your opinion.

Client Statements
1. "Well, uh, I'm happy just being with people and having them know me."
2. "And, and, uh, you know, they always say that you know some people don't like to be called by a number; well I don't either."
3. "In speech I'm, uh, well, in speech I'm not doing good because I'm afraid to talk in front of a bunch of people."
4. "I can't afford to lose my place on the honor roll and bring shame to my family."

Verbal Responses to Affective Content

It is too simplistic to say that the counselor communicates understanding of client feelings through attitudes such as empathy and positive regard. Although empathy and positive regard are necessary to the counseling relationship, the means for communicating these conditions also must be identified. Two primary reasons why the counselor may not respond to client feelings are (1) the counselor does not know what would be appropriate ways of responding and/or (2) the counselor "blocks" upon recognizing the client's feelings. Knowing how to respond to client feeling with empathy and positive regard takes more than the possession of these attitudes. The counselor must make sure that these attitudes are communicated through words, statements, and timing.

Teyber (1997) has observed how important it is for clients to receive from counselors a more satisfying response to their feelings than they have gotten from other persons in their past. In order to do so, when working with affective content from clients, counselors must be able to provide a safe and supportive atmosphere, often referred to as a *holding environment* (Teyber, 1997). A holding environment simply means that the counselor is able to allow and stay with or "hold" the client's feelings instead of moving away or distancing from the feelings or the client. In doing this, the counselor acts as a container; that is, the counselor's comfort in exploring and allowing the emergence of client feelings provides the support to help the client contain or hold various feelings that are often viewed by the client as unsafe.

This holding environment is usually dramatically different from what either the young client is experiencing or what an adult client experienced while growing up. If the child was sad or hurt, often the parent responded by withdrawing from the child, shaming the child for feeling that way, or denying the client's feeling (Teyber, 1997, p. 143). In all of these parental reactions, the child's feeling was not heard, validated, or "contained"; as a result, the child learned, over time, to deny or avoid these feelings. Children are developmentally unable to experience and manage feelings on their own without the presence of another person who can be emotionally present for them and receive and even welcome their feelings. If the parent was unable to help the child "hold" feelings in this manner, it will be up to the counselor to do so. Counselors do this by verbal responses that convey understanding of the client's feelings and by nonverbal responses that convey support and compassion. In this way, the counselor allows clients to know that he or she is "not overwhelmed or threatened by their feelings, is not judgmental or rejecting of them, does not need to move away from them in any way, and is still fully committed to the relationship" (Teyber, 1997, p. 146).

Blocking refers to the counselor's reaction to client feelings in ways that reduce or restrict his or her helpfulness. For example, the counselor may accurately identify the client's feelings of anger but avoid responding to these feelings for several reasons. The counselor might be afraid that the client will leave if the interaction gets too intense, or the counselor might not trust his or her own judgment and be afraid of turning the client off with an inaccurate response, or the counselor might fear that acknowledging the feeling would produce a flood of more intense feelings in the client that would be difficult to handle, or the counselor might have similar feelings that might be aroused. Client feelings related to sex, self-worth, and achievement are also potential blocks.

As mentioned earlier, the primary problem with blocking is that the counselor does not respond to the client's feelings in a more helpful way than the client received in the past. Teyber (1997) has listed a variety of ways in which counselors may block dealing with client affect appropriately:

Become anxious and change the topic

Fall silent and emotionally withdraw

Become directive and tell the client what to do

Interpret what the feelings mean and intentionally distance themselves

Self-disclose or move into their own feelings

Reassure and explain that everything will be all right

Diminish the client by trying to rescue him or her

Become overidentified with the client and insist that the client make some decision or take some action to manage the feelings. (p. 144)

When you find yourself responding in one of these ways, note what is happening to you and how you are feeling. This is another example of useful topics to talk over with your supervisor (see also Chapter 11).

It is possible to identify certain counselor responses that will assist you to discriminate among affective contents and communicate your understanding of the client's feelings at the same time. Two such responses are reflection of feelings and summarization of feeling.

Reflection of Feelings

The reflection-of-feelings response is distinctly different from the restatement response, but the two are often confused. As indicated earlier, the restatement is a paraphrase by the counselor of all or a portion of the *cognitive* content in a client's response, whereas the reflection is a paraphrase of the *affective* portion. When the client's response contains both cognitive and affective components, the counselor must differentiate between the two (see Chapter 8) in order to reflect the affective content.

Reflection of feelings accomplishes precisely what its name indicates: a mirroring of the feeling or emotion present in the client's message. This response helps clients to own and express feelings. The value in this is helping clients to recognize their feelings and to accept those feelings rather than fear them. Initially, clients may defend against feelings because they seem dangerous. People who feel sad may do everything in their power to avoid feeling sad or blue. Ultimately, the client needs to learn to trust his or her feelings; it is the experiencing and expressing the sadness rather than the blocking or numbing out of it that is healing (Brammer, Shostrom, & Abrego, 1992).

The reflection-of-feelings response can occur at different levels. At the most obvious level, the counselor may reflect only the surface feeling of the client. At a deeper level, the counselor may reflect an implied feeling with greater intensity than that originally expressed by the client. The more obvious level occurs when the counselor reflects an affect message that is *overtly* present in the client's message by using a *different* affect word but one that captures the same feeling and intensity expressed by the client, as in the following example:

> **CLIENT:** "I feel really mad that you interrupted me."
>
> **COUNSELOR:** "You're very angry about being interrupted."

The second kind of reflection occurs at a deeper level. This one mirrors an affect message that is only *covertly* expressed or implied in the client's message. Consider, for instance, the implied affect message in "I think we have a really neat relationship." The feeling inherent in the words refers to a positive affect message of *like, enjoy, pleased,* and so forth. Thus, a reflection that picks up on the implied feeling in this communication might be among the following:

"Our relationship is important to you."

"Some good things are in it for you."

"You're *pleased* with the relationship."

This reflection that occurs at a deeper level not only mirrors the *covert* feeling but also must at least match the intensity of the client's feeling and perhaps even reflect greater intensity of feeling. Furthermore, the most effective reflection is one that emphasizes what it is the client *anticipates*—in other words, one that acknowledges the *implied admission* of the client's message. Consider this sort of reflection in the following example. Note that the counselor reflects back the covertly implied feeling with a greater intensity of affect and acknowledges the implied admission—that is, what the client would *like* to do or feel, as shown here:

> CLIENT: "I feel like I have to be so responsible all the time."
>
> COUNSELOR: "Sometimes you'd feel relieved just to forget all that responsibility—to say 'to hell with it'—and really let go."

Although empathy and understanding of feelings are not themselves a panacea, they do serve some useful functions in the counseling process. For one thing, empathy enhances emotional proximity, creating an atmosphere of closeness and generating warmth. Also, empathy contributes to a sense of self-acceptance. When one person feels really understood by another, there is often a feeling of relief—"Gee, I'm not so confused and/or mixed up after all"—and a sense of acceptance about oneself—"This other person has understood me without condemning the way I think or feel."

Summarization of Feelings

Summarization of feelings is very similar to reflection of feelings in that it is a response that discriminates between different affective components of the client's communication and communicates understanding of the client's feelings by the counselor. The basic difference in the two responses is one of *number*, or quantity. The reflection of feelings responds to only *one* portion of the client's communication, whereas the summarization of feelings is an integration of several affective components of the client's communication. Thus, summarization of feelings is really an extension of reflection of feelings. In this response, the counselor is attending to a broader class of client response and must have the skill to bring together seemingly diverse elements into a meaningful gestalt (Ivey, Ivey, & Simek-Morgan, 1997).

Like the reflection of feelings, summarization of feelings involves reflecting the feelings of the client in your own words. Again, this encompasses not just one feeling but a bringing together of several feelings into a significant pattern.

Although there are some instances in which clients present one predominant feeling, there are other instances in which clients have several feelings going on at the same time. Teyber (1997) noted that two common affective constructions with mixed components include anger-sadness-shame and sadness-anger-guilt. In the first sequence, the primary feeling is often anger but it is a negative response to hurt or sadness. Often, the experiencing of the anger and sadness provokes shame. In the second sequence, the predominant feeling is sadness but it is often connected to anger that has been denied because the expression of it produces guilt. These affective sequences are typically acquired in childhood and are a result of both family of origin rules and culture. The summarization-of-feelings response can identify the various affective states the client describes or experiences. Consider the following examples:

> **CLIENT:** "I'm so pissed off at my mother and my wife. They're always on my back, telling me what to do, where to go, how to think—planning my whole life for me. It's been this way for years. I wish I could do something different but I just feel hopeless about it. I wish for once I could be a man and stand up to them but I just keep giving in and giving in."

> **COUNSELOR:** "You seem to be feeling several things in this situation—first, you're obviously *angry* about their behavior. Also, you feel *sad* and perhaps *ashamed* about your powerlessness to effect any change—is that accurate?"

> **CLIENT:** "I'm really feeling down and out about my job. It's so hard to find the energy to keep going in day after day. I don't really mind the work but over the years the people there have been so nasty that I don't want to be around them. I know if I weren't the nice person that I am I would probably really tell them a thing or two."

> **COUNSELOR:** "You're feeling *discouraged* about your job. It also sounds like you're feeling pretty *angry* and *fed up* with your co-workers but, because of your own niceness, you feel a little *guilty* or *reluctant* to express your irritation with them."

Summarization of feelings is often used instead of reflection of feelings when a client's communication contains many different affective elements rather than just one or two. It can also be used effectively when the interview appears to be bogged down. For example, when one topic has been covered repeatedly or when a dead silence occurs during an interview, summarization can increase the interview pace. By tying together various feelings, summarization can identify a central theme. It also provides direction for the interview, and may thus furnish the needed initiative to get the interview going again.

In using both the reflection-of-feelings and the summarization-of-feelings responses, be careful to heed our earlier caution about the suitability of these two responses for diverse groups of clients, especially in initial sessions. Ivey, Gluckstern, and Ivey (1993) noted:

> In White, North American and other cultures, men are expected to hold back their feelings. You aren't a "real man" if you allow yourself to feel emotion. While many

men can and do express their feelings in the helping interview, some should not be pushed too hard in this area in the first phases of counseling. Later, with trust, exploration of feelings becomes more acceptable.

In general, women in all cultures are more in touch with and more willing to share feelings than men. Nonetheless, this will vary with the cultural group. Some cultures (for example, Asian, Native Americans) at times pride themselves on their ability to control emotions. However, this may also be true with those of British and Irish extraction.

African Americans and other minorities have learned over time that it may not be safe to share themselves openly with White Americans. In cross-cultural counseling situations, trust needs to be built before you can expect in-depth discussion of emotions. (pp. 73–74)

EXERCISE **7.3**

Responses to Affective Components

A. *Responses to Client Statements*
For the following counselor-client interactions, please observe the following directions:

1. Read each interaction carefully.
2. For each client statement, identify, by writing sentences, the various affective components of the communication.
3. For each client statement, write your own response to the affective portion(s). Use both a reflection of feelings and a summarization of feelings for each client statement.

> CLIENT: "Uh, I'm unsure why I'm having such a hard time letting my family and friends know I'm gay. I mean I watch TV now and I see a whole sort of cultural revolution going on there. But when it comes to me, I feel very hesitant."

Affective components: _____

_____

_____

Reflection of feelings: _____

_____

Summarization of feelings: _____

_____

CLIENT: "My daddy won't want to meet you because you're Black and I'm half Black. And he treats my mom and me like dirt. And he thinks only White people deserve to be treated well. I just wish I had a dad who was good to me and my mom. I miss that."

Affective components: _____

_____

_____

Reflection of feelings: _____

_____

Summarization of feelings: _____

_____

B. Observed Practice
Complete the following exercise with two other people:

1. One of you, designated as the speaker, should share a personal concern with the respondent.
2. The respondent's task is to respond *only* to affective topics using only the two responses covered in the chapter: reflection of feelings and summarization of feelings.
3. The observer will use the Observer Rating Chart (Figure 7.1, page 106) to keep track of the number and kinds of responses used by the listener. This feedback should then be given to the listener.
4. After interacting for approximately 10 minutes, reverse the roles.

Summary

The expression and development of affect is naturally assumed to be part of the process of counseling. However, this does not mean that the beginning counselor will be either comfortable with or sensitive to affective messages. Sometimes, affect is implicitly expressed in the client's communication. At other times, one type of affect masks a different and perhaps more significant affect, such as anger masking fear. When these conditions exist, it is easy to miss the affective message.

In this chapter, we have introduced verbal and nonverbal cues that suggest the presence of affect, the nature of affect, and how to respond selectively to affect. We have also emphasized that the meaning of affect cues varies among clients and cultures. The development of these counseling responses is closely related to the

FIGURE 7.1 Observer Rating Chart

Counselor Response	Type of Counselor Response	
	Reflection of Feelings	*Summarization of Feelings*
1.		
2.		
3.		
4.		
5.		
6.		
7.		
8.		
9.		
10.		
11.		
12.		
13.		
14.		
15.		
16.		
17.		
18.		
19.		
20.		

client's perception of counselor empathy. In other words, as you become more accomplished at recognizing affect accurately and responding to it, your behavior will be perceived as increasingly empathic. Reflecting and summarizing client feelings are two particularly helpful counseling responses in communicating your understanding to clients. This is not to suggest that you would want to respond to every perceived feeling. In Chapter 8, we shall consider the process of selective responding to affective or cognitive messages and the effect of your choices on the progress of the interview.

DISCUSSION QUESTIONS

1. When a client's message contains both cognitive and affective components, what conditions might lead you to respond to the affective element? How might this be affected by the client's culture?

2. Although the reflection of feelings and the summarization of feelings were mentioned specifically as appropriate responses to affect, they are not the only appropriate responses. What other responses might be appropriate? How?

3. Often, clients are less aware of their feelings than of their thoughts. How might you assist clients to become more aware of their feelings by the way you choose to respond?

4. One of the things we discussed in this chapter is the issue of *counselor blocks*—that is, ways in which a counselor may deliberately or inadvertently avoid responding to client affect. Considering the primary emotions of anger, fear, sadness, and happiness, what affect area do you think you would be most likely to block? How does your history contribute to this?

RECOMMENDED READINGS

Castillo, R. J. (1997). *Culture and mental illness.* Pacific Grove, CA: Brooks/Cole.

Cormier, W. H., & Cormier, L. S. (1998). *Interviewing strategies for helpers* (4th ed.). Pacific Grove, CA: Brooks/Cole.

Knapp, M. L., & Hall, J. (1992). *Nonverbal communication in human interaction* (3rd ed.). Orlando, FL: Holt, Rinehart and Winston.

Mesquita, B., & Frijda, N. (1992). Cultural variations in emotions: A review. *Psychological Bulletin, 112,* 179–204.

Smith, E. (1985). *The body in psychotherapy.* Jefferson, NC: McFarland & Co.

Teyber, E. (1997). *Interpersonal process in psychotherapy* (3rd ed.). Pacific Grove, CA: Brooks/Cole.

CHAPTER 8

Differentiating between Cognitive and Affective Messages

You have seen in Chapters 6 and 7 that there are many ways of responding to any client statement. Since your responses greatly influence the nature of topic development, you will be faced with the decision of which kind of content to respond to and, thus, emphasize. Very often, the client's particular response contains *both* a cognitive message and an affect message. Typically, in early interviews the affect message is disguised. The disguises may be thin but nonetheless necessary to the clients. It is their way of protecting themselves until they can determine what kinds of things you are willing to listen to. Once you are able to hear the affect message (and this comes with practice), you will have to make some decisions. It is important that you respond to that portion of the client's communication that you think is most significantly related to the client's concerns. The process of choosing between client cognitive and affective topics is called *differentiation*. Whether you choose to respond to the cognitive portion or the affect portion depends largely on what is happening in the interaction at that moment and on what the client needs. In other words, choosing to respond to the cognitive content serves one objective, whereas choosing to respond to the affect content serves another objective.

Some approaches (e.g., the phenomenological) favor almost an exclusive emphasis on affect, whereas others (e.g., rational-emotive, reality therapy) suggest that the primary emphasis should be on the cognitive process. Of course, there are many variables influencing this sort of emphasis. In working with one client who intellectualizes frequently, the counselor may focus primarily on affect in an effort to get the client to recognize and accept his or her feelings. However, the same counselor, with another client who intellectualizes, may choose to emphasize cognitive elements if the counseling time is too limited for the client to feel comfortable with emotions. There are certainly times when emphasis on the affective takes precedence over the cognitive area and vice versa. Generally, though, during the interview process it is important to respond to *both* affective and cognitive topics. This is because, for all clients, there are times when feelings govern thoughts and times when thoughts and their consequences govern or influence feelings. The important point is not which comes first, but which type of counselor intervention is likely to be the most effective for each particular client.

Setting the Stage for Affect

In earlier chapters, we noted that, at the outset, it is important to get clients to talk. Clients must be able to talk about themselves, identify and express feelings, identify their own behaviors, and relate to the immediate present. Strong feelings of vulnerability on the part of clients may prevent them from doing anything other than responding to their need for defending and protecting themselves. Reduction of these feelings can release energy previously used by clients for preserving their own image and make that energy available for growth and change. It is *only* at this point that clients can talk about themselves and identify and own their feelings and behaviors.

Thus, your initial objective, or first *process goal,* is to reduce the client's initial anxiety. Therefore, your first strategy with every client is an exploratory one; you must determine the effect your behavior has on the client by the client's initial responses to you.

Responding to affect early in the counseling process often can be the best strategy for reducing client anxiety. This communicates your acceptance and understanding of these feelings to the client. However, with some clients, your response to their affect message may only induce greater anxiety. With this kind of client, you will have to modify the strategy and respond to cognitive topics in order to find out how the client thinks and what kind of ideas he or she has.

Counselors who always emphasize feelings to the exclusion of cognitive content impose certain limitations on the counseling process. Some of the limitations of responding only to feelings include the following:

1. Responding only to feelings is unrealistic and therefore reduces the possibility of the client's ability to generalize aspects of the counseling relationship to other relationships. For most clients, it is highly unlikely that any of their friends or family would take only their feelings into account.
2. Responding only to feelings fosters an internal focus to the exclusion of the world around the client. Clients may become so preoccupied with themselves that the level of their other relationships deteriorates even more. Also, as we mentioned in Chapter 7, responding to an internal focus reflects a Euro-American world view that will not be compatible with the world view of some clients from other cultural groups.
3. Responding to affect induces catharsis—the ventilation of pent-up feelings and concerns. For some clients, this may be all that is necessary. For other clients, this is not a sufficient goal. With catharsis, there is a greater possibility of reinforcing "victim mythology"; that is, the counselor's responses to feelings may only generate more client negative self-referent statements.

On the other hand, responding primarily to cognitive content presents the following limitations:

1. It may reinforce the intellectualization process; that is, it may encourage the client to continue to abstract and deny feelings that are actually influencing his or her behavior.
2. It may not provide the opportunity that the client needs to share and express feelings in a nonjudgmental setting. The counseling relationship may be the only one in which a client can feel that his or her emotions (and consequently, the self) will not be misunderstood.
3. It may continue to repeat a pattern similar to the rules in the client's family of origin in which "feeling talk" is not allowed, encouraged, or explored.

Again, it must be stressed that the initial strategy in the differentiation process is an *exploratory* one. All clients will respond differently to your emphasis on feelings or on cognitive content.

Types of Differentiating Responses for Cognitive and Affective Content

Several counselor responses are useful as discriminators for either cognitive or affective portions of the client's message. There are responses that can place emphasis on one component of the message, to the exclusion of other parts of the client's response. Three particularly useful responses are the accent, the ability-potential response, and the confrontation.

The Accent

The *accent* is a one- or two-word restatement that emphasizes a very small portion of the client's communication. Its effect is that of a question or a request for clarification or elaboration, such as:

> **CLIENT:** "I'm having a hard time deciding which college to attend. Uh, I'm not used to making decisions, so it's really perplexing to me."
>
> **COUNSELOR:** "Perplexing?" *(Accents an affect word.)*

What other words could the counselor have accented in this client response?

1. _____ , which would emphasize: cognitive   affective
2. _____ , which would emphasize: cognitive   affective

Model Answers
1. "Hard time?"
2. "To you?"

Choosing "hard time?" would have emphasized the affective portion, but accenting "to you?" would have emphasized the cognitive part of the communication.

The use of the accent places emphasis on a particular thought or feeling. Usually, it encourages clients to clarify or expand on their previous statement, since it suggests that the counselor does not fully understand the client. It is used most appropriately to highlight a word that seems vague and abstract. Hence, it elicits specificity from the client.

The accent may be used to respond to either the affect or the cognitive message. The client must have used an emotionally laden word in his or her message in order for the counselor to accent the affect. This is one limitation of the accent. Here is an example:

CLIENT: "I don't think I will make the grades to stay here."

The counselor has no affect word to accent in this statement. However, the cognitive portion could be accented by saying, "Here?" However, if the client said:

CLIENT: "I'm afraid I won't make the grades to stay here."

Then the counselor could respond with "Afraid?" The word *afraid,* which is an affect-type word, can be accented or emphasized, thus inviting the client to elaborate on his or her emotional reaction to the possibility of not doing well enough to stay in school. Try your skill with the accent in the following client statements:

1. CLIENT: "Things seem pretty bad now."

    YOU: "_____ ." *(Emphasizing cognitive or affective?)*

2. CLIENT: "I don't know what to do about it."

    YOU: "_____ ." *(Emphasizing cognitive or affective?)*

The Ability-Potential Response

The *ability-potential response* is one in which the counselor suggests to clients that they have the ability or potential to engage in a specified form of activity. It can be used either as a response to some cognitive portion or to some feeling expressed in the clients' communication. It not only reinforces the clients' sense of control and management of their own lives and affairs but it also communicates the counselor's faith in the clients' ability to act independently. The ability-potential response is a useful tool for fostering the client's sense of self-efficacy—that is, the client's personal beliefs about capability, empowerment, and confidence (Ozer & Bandura, 1990). As Cormier and Cormier (1998) noted, "Perceived self-efficacy is a major determinant in whether people engage in a task, the amount of effort they exert if they do engage, and how long they will persevere with the task if they encounter adverse circumstances" (p. 565). Clients with low self-efficacy may exhibit a greater degree of "learned helplessness" and pessimism (Seligman, 1990). The ability potential can be used to suggest a course of action that is potentially beneficial to the clients, as in the following exchange:

> **CLIENT:** "I don't know where I'm going to get the money to pay that bill."
>
> **YOU:** "You could work for a semester and earn the money."

In other words, you are suggesting that the client has the ability or the potential to pay the bill, should he or she work for a semester and earn the money. Typically, the ability-potential response begins with "you could" or "you can." Like all of the other types of counselor responses that you have been learning, it can be overused. When that happens, it begins to sound unreal, hollow, and meaningless. It is used effectively as a means of identifying alternatives available to the client. It is misused when, in oversimplification, the counselor attempts to suggest or prescribe something as a panacea. The effect of this is to negate or hide the client's feelings of concern.

Make two ability-potential responses in the following client statements:

> **CLIENT:** "I don't know what he'd do; I'm just hanging in thin air because I don't know how he feels about it."
>
> **YOU:** "_____
> _____."

> **CLIENT:** "I think I'd like to teach, but I don't know what the requirements and qualifications are."
>
> **YOU:** "_____
> _____."

The Confrontation

One of the most useful counselor responses is the *confrontation*. The word itself has acquired some excess emotional meanings. The confrontation is sometimes misconstrued to mean lecturing, judging, or acting in some punitive or hostile manner. Egan (1998) refers to the confrontation as a *challenging* response. A more accurate notion is to regard the confrontation as a response that enables clients to face what they want or feel they need to avoid. The avoidance might be a resistance to the client's own feelings or to another person, including the counselor and counseling relationship. The avoidance is usually expressed as one part of a discrepancy present in the client's behavior. Thus, the confrontation helps the client to identify a contradiction, a rationalization or excuse, a misinterpretation, or some sort of dissonance.

The discrepancy or contradiction is usually one of the following types:

1. A discrepancy between what clients say and how they behave (e.g., the client who says he is a quiet type but who talks freely in the interview)
2. A contradiction between how clients say they feel and how their behaviors suggest they are feeling (e.g., the client who says she is comfortable but who continues to fidget)
3. A discrepancy between two verbal messages of the client (e.g., the client who says he wants to change his behavior but who in the next breath places all blame for his behavior on his parents or on others)

The confrontation is a statement that establishes a "you said/but look" condition. In other words, the first part of the compound sentence is the "you said" portion. It repeats a message of the client. The second part of the compound sentence presents the contradiction or discrepancy—the "but look" of the client message. Here are examples:

"You say school isn't very satisfying, but your grades are excellent."

"You keep putting that job off, and eventually you're going to be back in the same trap of being mad at yourself."

The first part, or the "you said" portion, need not be stated by the counselor. Instead, it may be implied if the client's discrepancy is obvious, such as:

CLIENT: "I just can't talk to people I don't know."

COUNSELOR: "[You say . . . (implied part)] But you don't know me."

Using the confrontation suggests doing just what the word implies and *no more*. The confrontation *describes* client messages, *observes* client behavior, and *presents* evidence. However, the confrontation should *not* contain an accusation, evaluation, or problem solution.

The confrontation serves several important purposes:

1. It assists in the client's achievement of *congruency*—that is, a state in which what the client says and how the client behaves correspond.
2. Its use establishes the counselor as a role model for direct and *open communication*. If the counselor is not afraid to confront these contradictions, perhaps the client can be less afraid of them.
3. It is an action-oriented stimulus. Unlike the reflection stimulus that mirrors the client's *feelings*, the confrontation mirrors the client's *behavior*. It is very useful in initiating action plans and behavior change on the client's part, since it is often the avoidance that maintains the client's problematic behavior.

Patterson and Welfel (1994) observed that all confrontations run the risk of threatening a client, particularly those who focus on myths the clients have believed about themselves and/or their families. For this reason, the use of confrontation must be judicious and timely. Since a confrontation is likely to be better received in the presence of high levels of empathy and positive regard, it is often not used in initial or early interviews. Usually, it is a more effective tool once the safety of the relationship has been well established and the client's anxiety level is lowered (Cormier & Cormier, 1998). It is also useful to phrase a confrontation in a tentative manner and at a point in the session where there is ample time left to discuss the client's reactions to the confrontation. As with any response, it is important to ensure that the counselor is confronting as a way to help the client grow rather than as an indirect way of venting one's own anger or frustration (Egan, 1998).

In some instances, such as with clients addicted to substances, the confrontation is used in a very direct, firm, and repetitive way in order to break through the addict's continued use of denial and rationalization. Confrontation may be especially useful for manipulative and acting-out Euro-American male clients (Ivey, 1994). Caution needs to be exercised in using this response with some clients of color, as some Asian American, Latino American, and Native American clients may view being confronted as lacking in respect and sensitivity (Sue & Sue, 1990).

Try out the confrontation in these client statements:

CLIENT: "Just because I have five or so drinks every day doesn't make me an alcoholic. I still go to work every day."

YOU: "_____

_____."

CLIENT: "I'm not really angry at my father; he's been doing this to me all my life."

YOU: "_____

_____."

Discuss your responses with someone.

EXERCISE 8.1
Differentiating Responses

A. Responding to Client Statements
In the following client statements, identify the *affective* and *cognitive* components of each, differentiate between the alternatives, then write an appropriate counselor response for each. Limit your responses to accent, ability potential, and confrontation. The type of response to use for each client state-

ment is specified in parentheses. Tell whether you responded to the affective or cognitive portion. Give your rationale for doing so.

> **CLIENT 1:** "I'm having misgivings about whether or not to go back to the reservation."
>
> **YOU:** *(Accent)* "_____."
>
> **CLIENT 2:** "It's pretty tough being in the minority here at school. I don't know how to react."
>
> **YOU:** *(Ability potential)* "_____."
>
> **CLIENT 3:** "I don't know why my wife is always on my back about my drinking. Hell, I hear that in Russia they drink a half a bottle of vodka a day—so what makes me different?"
>
> **YOU:** *(Confrontation)* "_____."
>
> **CLIENT 4:** "I really do want to come out but I just don't know how. I can't seem to take the first step."
>
> **YOU:** (1) *(Ability potential)* "_____."
>
> (2) *(Confrontation)* "_____."

B. Observed Practice
Complete the following exercise with two other people:

1. One of you, designated as the speaker, should talk about yourself with the respondent.
2. The respondent's task is to:
   a. Identify cognitive and affective topics present in the speaker's communication.
   b. Choose which topic you will respond to.
   c. Respond using only the three responses covered in the chapter: accent, ability potential, and confrontation.
3. The observer will use the Observer Rating Chart (Figure 8.1) to keep track of the number and kinds of responses used by the respondent.
4. After approximately 10 minutes of interaction, reverse the roles.

FIGURE 8.1 **Observer Rating Chart**

Counselor Response	Type of Counselor Response		
	Accent	*Ability Potential*	*Confrontation*
1.			
2.			
3.			
4.			
5.			
6.			
7.			
8.			
9.			
10.			
11.			
12.			
13.			
14.			
15.			
16.			
17.			
18.			
19.			
20.			

Effects of Responding to Affective Content

The importance of responding to client feelings as an anxiety-reduction tool has already been mentioned. Generally speaking, responding to affect diminishes the intensity of feelings. For instance, responding to (accepting) strong feelings of anger expressed by the client will reduce their intensity and assist the client in gaining control of them.

The expression of feelings may be an important goal for some clients. Some people have had so little opportunity to express their feelings openly that to find an acceptant listener provides highly beneficial relief.

Responding to affect with acceptance and understanding can also assist clients in incorporating personal feelings and perceptions into their self-image. In other words, the counselor's acceptance of feelings that have been previously denied and labeled as "bad" by the clients suggests that they may have mislabeled these feelings, and thus themselves.

Finally, responding to affect often is the best way to communicate your warmth and involvement with clients. That is, responding to client feelings establishes a high level of trust between you and your clients. It is precisely this kind of trust that enables clients to own their feelings, behaviors, and commitment to behavior change.

Effects of Responding to Cognitive Content

We have already noted that responding to cognitive content can be an anxiety-reduction tool for clients easily threatened by feelings. Thus, there are times when rapport with clients is established more quickly by discovering how they think before wondering how they feel.

It is also important to realize that behavior incorporates both feelings and thoughts. In order to solve problems and make decisions effectively, clients have to be able to think as well as to feel. Responding to cognitive content assists clients in developing and expressing those thought processes involved in problem solving and decision making.

Because behavior is governed by thoughts as well as feelings, clients need to examine not only what they feel but how they think. Behavior rigidity is often maintained by the kinds of thought patterns present in the clients' repertoires. These may need to be discussed and explored before any behavior change can occur.

Although exploration of feelings is useful to most clients, it is often not sufficient for goal achievement. Once the counseling goals have been established, action plans must be developed to produce goal attainment. Responding to cognitive content goes one step further than responding to affect in that it focuses directly on behavior change.

The Differentiation Process in Cross-Cultural Counseling

The differentiation process and selective responding is particularly challenging in cross-cultural counseling. The temptation is to respond to the content or the affect of client messages in a way that is consistent with your own culture and yet may be inconsistent with the client's culture. Although it is important for counselors to "keep track of the salient cultural perspective" of clients and the shifts in these perspectives over time, "the counselor and client are typically bound by different rules of behavior and learned expectations in multicultural settings.... Culture-centered counselors not only need to focus on the client's salient culture, but also dare not be distracted by their own contrasting (cultural) salience" (Pedersen & Ivey, 1993, p. 188).

Summary

The first seven chapters focused on skills that are basic to the helping relationship. In this chapter, we introduced the process by which the counselor makes discriminations—sometimes subtle discriminations—that affect the outcome of a session. Choosing to respond to the cognitive dimension of a client's problems leads the session in one direction. Choosing, instead, to respond to the affective dimension leads in a quite different direction. The cultural affiliations of both counselor and client help to shape this process.

Once your exploratory objective has been achieved and you have chosen when to emphasize affective content and when to emphasize cognitive content, it is time to develop and implement strategies for each of these areas. There are some strategies that are more effectively used in working with affective material. Other strategies are best implemented when the focus is on behavior and cognitions rather than feelings. These strategies are presented in the following chapters.

DISCUSSION QUESTIONS

1. Every counselor has a natural inclination toward feelings or thoughts. That is, when given an option, the counselor will respond to feelings (or choose to respond to thoughts) without thinking about goals. Which would be your natural inclination? What is it about your life, childhood, current wants, and so on, that leads you to this inclination?

2. What do you think you will have to do in order to overcome your natural inclination? What are the conditions in counseling that would justify your responding to feelings, if your natural inclination was to respond to thoughts (or vice versa)?

3. If you were a client, would you prefer a counselor whose natural inclinations were toward feelings or toward rational thinking? What would be the advantages for you if you had the counselor you preferred? What would be the disadvantages to you with such a counselor?

RECOMMENDED READINGS

Cormier, S., & Cormier, B. (1998). *Interviewing strategies for helpers* (4th ed.). Pacific Grove, CA: Brooks/Cole.

Egan, G. (1998). *The skilled helper* (6th ed.). Pacific Grove, CA: Brooks/Cole.

Hutchins, D., & Cole-Vaught, C. (1997). *Helping relationships and strategies* (3rd ed.). Pacific Grove, CA: Brooks/Cole.

Pedersen, P., & Ivey, A. (1993). *Culture-centered counseling and interviewing skills.* Westport, CT: Praeger.

Conceptualizing Problems and Setting Goals

It is appropriate now to consider some of the larger issues of counseling—namely, the nature of client problems and the establishment of goals that are realistic antecedents to the solution of those problems. There are philosophical questions that underlie these issues, since there is no one way of conceptualizing human problems. We will not be able to resolve the philosophical problems for you. In fact, it may require the greater part of your career to do that. But we will present a viewpoint that represents our stand at this time. We find it useful because it focuses not only on our clients but also on the world that they return to after each counseling session—a world in which the problems are real.

The Client's World

What brings clients to counseling? The answer to this, more than any other question, will reveal your role as counselor. It is a disarmingly simple question, but not one to be taken lightly. We begin with this response:

1. Clients enter counseling when they experience needs that they, alone, are unable to understand or to meet, or when their particular coping strategies to meet needs no longer work.

That is only the beginning of an answer, however. Three processes have been identified and require further elaboration. These are *to recognize a need, to understand that need,* and *to meet that need.*

First, what does it mean to *need* something? It suggests that something is missing, that there is a hole, an emptiness. This condition reflects a dissatisfaction or incompleteness with the status quo. Something other than the status quo is required in order that the need diminish. Since any movement from the status quo involves *change,* implicit in the meeting of a need is a solution involving change.

This brings us to our second response to the original question:

2. The experience of *needing* is a natural part of the process of living and is the means by which people facilitate and enhance that process.

All human beings share certain basic needs. These include the need for security, nourishment, survival, affiliation, love, and self-esteem. In a classic article, Jourard (1963, pp. 33–38) has conceptualized these needs in a way that is useful for counseling. They include the following:

1. *Survival needs:* All people are concerned with self-preservation and safety. This includes psychological safety as well as physical safety. Although people may not always recognize threats to their psychological safety, they do recognize their responses to those threats—namely, increased anxiety, inaccurate or restricted perceptions of the world, and increasingly inappropriate behavior.

2. *Physical needs:* These include the need for nourishment, shelter, income, freedom from pain, rest, and replenishment of energy. When these needs go unmet or become distorted (e.g., overeating or migraine headaches), people's responses may inhibit the satisfaction of still other needs (e.g., the migraine sufferer finds it difficult to achieve love and sex needs).

3. *Love and sex needs:* These are the needs to become involved in a close personal way with another human being. People grow in their development of these needs and often recognize their intensity only when they have suddenly experienced the loss of a close personal relationship. When these needs are unmet, people question their potential to love and be loved, to be in an extended relationship, or to be able to give to or take from another person.

4. *Status, success, and self-esteem needs:* These are the needs that motivate people to achieve in the eyes of their peers and to gain respect, confidence, or admiration. When these needs are unmet, people lack self-respect and self-confidence, or overreact with excessive and manufactured self-respect and self-confidence.

5. *Mental health needs:* When these needs are met, people feel like functional human beings. When they are unmet, people are incongruent, disillusioned, disoriented, and vulnerable to despair.

6. *Freedom needs:* These are the needs to feel autonomous, free to make personal choices, or free not to choose. When these needs go unmet, people feel restricted, undervalued, or unappreciated.

7. *Challenge needs:* These are the needs for activity, future orientation, and opportunity. When they are missing, people are vulnerable to boredom, meaninglessness, or emptiness.

8. *Cognitive-clarity needs:* These needs reflect the drive to resolve the conflicts in values, ideas, and commitments that exist in people's lives and the need to live one's life with honor and integrity.

Perhaps you would add to or take away from this list, according to your view of human beings. The point, however, is that all human beings experience needs as a part of living. To experience a need does not set a person apart as unusual, inadequate, or in some other way lacking. On the other hand, human beings are not always adept at recognizing (comprehending) experienced needs, nor do they necessarily possess the skills required to meet needs once the needs are recognized. To recognize and meet one's needs is not necessarily a natural part of the process of living; it must be learned.

The place where people learn or do not learn what their needs are and how to get them met is in their family of origin. This is where needs are either affirmed and met or shamed and rejected. Teyber noted:

> Many enduring psychological problems begin when basic childhood developmental needs are not met . . . and once the need gets consistently or repetitively blocked, the child in growing up will either block the need in the same way his or her environment blocked it to avoid reexperiencing the need or will to try to rise above the need to have it met indirectly or to partially gratify it by a particular style of coping. . . .
>
> Childrens' unmet childhood needs do not dissipate or go away as they grow up. The need may be repressed or defended against, but it continues to seek expression. As a result, clients do not give up trying to have the need met. At the same time, the unmet need remains too anxiety-arousing to be expressed directly. So clients try to rise above the unmet need and indirectly, fulfill it by adopting . . . a particular interpersonal coping style. (1997, pp. 195–199)

For example, an adult client whose early needs for affection were shamed may block current needs for affection and claim, "I don't need anybody's love. I can make it on my own." Yet, at some level, the unmet need for affection will still try to seek expression, and when it does, the client will try to cope with it in a particular way, but usually in an unsatisfying or troublesome way.

In addition to this intrapsychic view of needs, we also need to recognize the role of external stressors and environmental events in creating needs. For example, clients also experience needs in terms of current life events and may enter therapy when various life stressors or developmental issues become too hard to handle. Consider, for instance, an adult woman is coping well with her marriage and her job. But as her aging father unexpectedly develops Alzheimer's disease, her world starts to fall apart and she experiences needs now that were either not there or not apparent to her before this event.

Current life events and environmental stressors are particularly important in shaping needs of clients who feel marginalized because of race, gender, sexual orientation, and socioeconomic status and who experience the effects of stereotyping, discrimination, and oppression on a frequent and repetitive basis. In these situations, emotional distress resulting from current needs often is more the result of a lack of both real and perceived power in a client's everyday, current life rather than unmet developmental childhood needs (Brown & Ballou, 1992). For example, consider the situation of a financially challenged African American woman who is raising her three children single-handedly. She has no living parents to help her in child rearing and her two brothers were shot and killed in an urban gang fight. She has a part-time job with no benefits and is in danger of losing it because she has needed to take days off to care for her sick children. Furthermore, in riding the subway to her place of work, she is met with racial taunts. Clearly, the context of her current world is a major factor in her presenting needs.

Thus far, we have drawn a picture of the client as a person who is (1) continually experiencing needs, (2) not always understanding or even recognizing some of those needs, and (3) seeking your assistance when unrecognized and unmet needs become the bigger issue of living. Though this may be an adequate description of the person entering counseling, it fails to embrace the total situation of the client. Any description of clients must also include the world in which they live, including significant others, employment or the setting in which they spend the major portion of the day, expectations for self and others, habits and routines, dreams and fantasies of the future, attitudes toward the past, values and the meanings of life, and methods developed for survival (survival of responsibilities, tensions, disappointments, expectations of others, dashed hopes, etc.). You may wish to refer to our discussion of the initial interview in Chapter 5 for a review of all of these components, as conceptualizing client problems begins in the initial session.

The Role of the Counselor

Based on what we have said about the client who is entering counseling, it follows that you would have some fairly clear responsibilities. These responsibilities are above and beyond creating a favorable climate for counseling—even beyond being a good and caring listener. It is your role to hear the unmet needs as clients describe their problems and to help them hear those needs, as well. Next, it is your role to help clients formulate goals that will help meet the needs. From these goals, plans of action may be constructed, implemented, and evaluated. Finally, you must help clients recognize that they are making progress. When clients have lived with problems too long, it is difficult to trust any progress.

The counseling process may often be viewed as an unfolding process in which the outer, more obvious problems precede the more subtle, less obvious problems. As an example, consider an Asian American man who comes to counseling with an obvious problem: He cannot fall asleep at night. He has a *physical need* to sleep. After the insomnia problem has been addressed and the goals and strategies have been formulated to help with this, focus is then directed toward those pressures that led to the insomnia in the first place. Often, this may be the result of old wounds or unmet needs that have become recently reactivated. For instance, he recently lost his job as a result of layoffs; he may now feel lacking in self-respect and self-confidence and have *esteem needs*, wanting to be respected, valued, and appreciated by himself and by others. He does not want to "lose face" among his family and culture. These may be carry-over needs from family and culture that are now being felt again because of a major loss. He may also have *survival* needs related to loss of income in his current life.

As you attempt to conceptualize or understand problem states, it is important that you keep in mind the client responses that can further complicate and add to the problem. These responses may be above and beyond the client's attempt to solve the problem. They include the following:

1. *Beliefs:* The client may already have that contribute to the problem, impede the solution, or become the problem
2. *Feelings:* The emotional responses to the problem that often exaggerate the problem, impede the comprehension of the problem, or become the problem
3. *Behavior:* The habits and routines that are inappropriate responses, and perhaps contributors to the problem
4. *Interaction patterns:* Those established ways of reacting to familiar others, including the miscommunication channels, expectations, self-fulfilling prophesies, coping styles, and so on
5. *Contextual factors:* Time, place, concurrent events, and cultural and sociopolitical issues.

Problem conceptualization does not come quickly. It comes progressively. After your first session with clients, you will begin to have some hunches about them, their world (and how they view it), and their problems (and how they view them). In subsequent sessions, these initial hunches will be modified as you understand your clients better and as your clients understand and report their world to you. There will be mistaken hunches along the way. These are to be accepted as part of the process, too. Acknowledge and discard them. The remainder of this chapter is an extension of the conceptualizing process—that is, conceptualizing the client's goals.

Process and Outcome Goals

The counseling process involves two types of goals: process goals and outcome goals. *Process goals* are related to the establishment of therapeutic conditions necessary for client change. These are general goals, such as establishing rapport, providing a nonthreatening setting, and possessing and communicating accurate empathy and unconditional regard. They can be generalized to all client relationships and can be considered universal goals. Process goals are your primary responsibility; you cannot expect your clients to help you establish and communicate something like unconditional regard.

Unlike process goals, *outcome goals* will be different for each client. They are the goals directly related to your clients' changes, to be made as a result of counseling. As you are able to help your clients understand their concerns, you will want to help them understand how counseling can be used to respond to these concerns. The two of you will begin to formulate tentative outcome goals together. As counseling continues, the original goals may be modified through better understanding of the problems and through the development of new attitudes and behaviors that will eliminate or reduce problems. Goal setting should be viewed as a flexible process, always subject to modification and refinement. Most importantly, outcome goals are *shared* goals, goals that *both you and your clients* agree to work toward achieving.

Outcome goals that are visible or observable are more useful, since they allow you to know when they have been achieved. Not all outcome goals are stated as visible goals, however. For example, consider these two outcome goals:

1. To help your client develop more fully his or her self-actualizing potential
2. To increase the frequency of positive self-statements at home and at work by 50 percent over the next six weeks

Both of these could be considered to be outcome goals. They might even be so closely related as to be the same in terms of outcomes. Your clients may be much more attracted to such goals as developing their self-actualizing potential. You may want to view the development of self-actualizing potential as a composite of many smaller and more specific goals. To state it a little differently, self-actualizing is a hypothetical state that cannot be observed. It can only be inferred through certain visible and audible behaviors. Using this goal, you have no way of knowing the types of activity that your clients will enter into while proceeding toward the goals. As a result, you and your clients will know very little about what they could be doing in the relationship, and you will have no way of assessing progress toward the desired results. Consequently, the first goal listed is not as satisfactory as the second, in that it does not provide you or your clients with specific guidelines for change.

When outcome goals are stated precisely, both you and your clients have a better understanding of what is to be accomplished. This better understanding permits you to work more directly with your clients' problems or concerns, and reduces tangential efforts. Equally important are the benefits you are able to realize in working with specific behavioral goals. You are able to enlist the cooperation of your clients more directly, since they are more likely to understand what is to be done. In addition, you are in a better position to select viable techniques and strategies when your clients have specific objectives. Finally, both you and your clients are in a better position to recognize progress—a rewarding experience in its own right. It is also important to realize that specific observable statements of outcome are required now as part of treatment planning by almost all counseling agencies that receive both state and federal funding because they are clues to client progress and effectiveness of the counselor's strategies and interventions.

Culturally Appropriate Counseling Goals

Counselors who expect clients who feel marginalized from the mainstream culture to develop long-range goals based on a variety of mental health needs may find that their services are irrelevant. Clients faced with financial challenges, discrimination, and disempowerment may be far more concerned with survival and physical needs and short-term goals that are oriented toward resolution of current life issues (Rosado & Elias, 1993).

Sue and Sue (1990) noted that "closely linked to the actual process of counseling are certain implicit or explicit goals . . . and that different cultural and subculture groups may require different counseling processes and goals" (p. 162). It is important for counselors to identify their own cultural biases and values and to ensure that they do not steer clients in a direction that disavows the beliefs and values of the *client's* culture.

EXERCISE 9.1

Goal Setting

Maria is a young Latina woman who is a junior in college. She initially comes to the student counseling center for career counseling, but after the fourth session, she discloses that she was sexually molested on one occasion at a family gathering by her 21-year-old cousin when she was 11 years old. She breaks down and cries when describing this situation. She has never told anyone about this before. She would like to tell her mother but her cousin is adored and revered within her family structure and she is not sure her mother will believe her.

Identify a few goals that you think might be appropriate in working with Maria, given that you know very little about her, so far.

_____

_____

_____

_____

_____

Are your goals specific or vague? How would you and Maria know when you had achieved these goals? Are your goals process or outcome goals? If they are outcome goals, how would achieving them affect Maria? Are your goals consistent with Maria's cultural affiliation?

Three Elements of Good Outcome Goals

Perhaps you have noticed from our previous examples that outcome goals are different from process goals in several respects. A well-stated outcome goal includes the following elements: the *behavior* to be changed, the *conditions* under which the change will occur, and the *level* or amount of change. These elements apply to any outcome goal, whether it is to modify eating patterns, reduce negative self-appraisal, or increase saying no to unreasonable requests.

The first element of an outcome goal specifies in behavioral terms what the client will do differently as a result of counseling. In other words, determine what unmet needs will become the targets of change and in what specific ways.

The second element of an outcome goal indicates the conditions under which the desired change will occur. It is important to weigh carefully the situations or settings in which the client will attempt a new behavior. You would not want to set your client up to fail by identifying settings in which there was little hope for success. The client might agree to modify eating habits at home during the evening, but not to attempt to modify eating habits at the company dinner on Saturday night.

The third element of outcome goals involves the choice of a suitable and realistic level or amount of the new behavior. That is to say, *how much* of the new behavior will the client attempt? Some clients enter diets with the expectation that they will reduce their consumption from 3,000 calories per day to 900 calories per day. A more realistic goal might be to reduce to 1,500 calories. This brings us to another thought about goals. As you modify goals, you come increasingly closer to the ultimate goals of the client. Each time you set a goal, it is a closer approximation of the results. Successive approximations are very important. They allow the client to set more attainable goals, experience success more often, and make what might be dramatic changes in lifestyle.

EXERCISE 9.2

Outcome Goals

In the following exercise, examples of client outcome goals are presented. Determine which of the three elements of an outcome goal—behavior, condition, or level—may be missing. After each example, list the missing parts, using B for behavior, C for condition, and L for level. Feedback will be provided to you at the end of the exercise.

The following example is provided as an illustration: to increase job placement (behavior) of clients with physical challenges seen in a rehabilitation agency (condition) by 30 percent in a one-year time period (level).

Identify the missing parts in the following six outcome goals:

1. To decrease temper tantrums
2. To increase exercise to two times a week over a six-week period
3. To decrease the number of nightly arguments at home with your (the client's) partner
4. To decrease tardiness
5. To reduce aggressive behavior with a sibling by 50 percent

6. To make three positive comments about the strengths of each member of your (the client's) family during a one-week period

Feedback

1. The missing elements are the condition *(C)* and level *(L)* of the goal.
2. This goal specifies the behavior and the level; the condition *(C)* is missing.
3. The level *(L)* of the goal is missing.
4. This goal specifies the behavior; the condition *(C)* and level *(L)* are missing.
5. The behavior *(B)* is missing; "aggressive behavior" is a label and does not specify what the person would reduce.
6. This is a complete outcome goal! "Making positive comments" is the behavior; "three of them in one week" is the level; "to each family member" is the condition.

Translating Vague Concerns into Specific Goals

Rarely does a client begin by requesting assistance in achieving specific behavior changes. Instead of saying, "I want to be able to talk to people without getting nervous," the client is likely to say, "I am shy." In other words, a personal characteristic has been described rather than the ways in which the characteristic is experienced. It then becomes the counselor's job to help the client describe the ways in which the characteristic could be changed.

Taking nonspecific concerns and translating them into specific goal statements is no easy task for the counselor. You must understand the nature of the client's problem and the conditions under which it occurs before the translation can begin. Even then, there are difficulties. Egan (1998) has suggested the use of certain future-oriented questions to help guide clients in the goal-setting process:

What would this problem situation look like if I were managing it better?

What changes in my present lifestyle would make sense?

What would I be doing differently with the people in my life?

What patterns of behavior would be in place that are not currently in place?

What current patterns of behavior would be eliminated?

What would be happening that is not happening now?

What would I have that I don't have now?

What accomplishments would be in place that are not in place now?

What would this opportunity look like if I developed it? (p. 232)

What can you expect of yourself and your clients in terms of setting specific goals? First, the goals that are set can never be more specific than your understanding and the client's understanding of the problem. This means that at the outset of counseling, goals are likely to be nonspecific and nonbehavioral. *But nonspecific goals are better than no goals at all.*

As you and your client explore the nature of a particular problem, the type of goal(s) appropriate to the problem should become increasingly clear. This clarification will permit both of you to move in the direction of identifying specific behaviors that, if changed, would alter the problem in a positive way. These specific behaviors can then be formulated into goal statements; as you discuss the client's problems in more detail, you can gradually add the circumstances in which to perform the behaviors and how much or how often the target behaviors might be altered.

After you and your client have established the desired outcome goal together, you can identify some action steps that might help the client achieve the overall goal or target. These action steps can be thought of as *subgoals*. Subgoals consist of a series of smaller or intermediate steps or tasks that help the client perform the desired behaviors gradually. When several subgoals are identified, these are usually arranged in a sequence or hierarchy. The client completes one subgoal successfully before moving on to another one. By gradually completing the activities represented by subgoals in a successful manner, the client's motivation and energy to change may be reinforced and maintained. Successful completion of subgoals also may reduce potential failure experiences by giving the client a greater sense of control and empowerment.

EXERCISE 9.3

Outlining Goals

Assume that Brent has come to you for counseling, complaining of insomnia. As you and Brent probe the facets of his concerns, you can consider the specific changes Brent would like to make. Gradually, these changes can be developed into an outline of desired goals. We refer to this as an *outline* because the major headings (I and II) represent the two overall or primary outcome goals for Brent; the subheadings reflect the subgoals or activities Brent might perform to achieve the overall goal gradually. Remember that goal setting is a flexible process, and that the goals listed in this outline might change as counseling with Brent progresses.

Outcome Goal I: To be able to go to sleep within an hour of going to bed at least four nights of the week at home.

A. To identify in writing all of his prior solutions for trying to go to sleep (counting sheep, daydreaming, eating a snack, etc.).

B. To substitute these "trying to go to sleep" activities with "trying to stay awake" activities.

Outcome Goal II: To double (50 percent increase) Brent's positive feelings and thoughts about himself over the time in which he receives counseling.

Complete the goal outline for this second outcome goal listed above. You might begin by establishing the criteria that Brent would consider important. You might also consider having Brent describe some of the situations in which he feels good about himself. You may also want to explore how he felt about growing up as a young boy in his family and his cultural referent group. What could Brent do to achieve his short- and long-term directions? From this kind of information and using your own imagination, construct the specific types of subgoals that would help Brent implement this second outcome goal. Continue this process for outcome goals II and III for Brent.

Outcome Goal II: _____

A. _____

_____

B. _____

_____

C. _____

_____

D. _____

_____

Outcome Goal III: To acquire another job at a higher salary range within the next year.

A. _____

_____

B. _____

_____

C. _____

_____

D. _____

_____

Notice the process by which outcome goals are established:

1. They begin as overall goals that are directly related to the client's specific or general concerns or descriptions of a set of problems and that are consistent with the client's culture.
2. Specific and observable subgoals are established which, if achieved, permit the realization of the overall goals.

Thus, goal setting moves from general to specific goals; the specific goals are directly related to the general goal, and the general goal is a reflection of the problems and needs presented to the counselor.

Client Resistance to Goal Setting

Occasionally, a client may be hesitant about setting goals or reluctant to work toward change. For instance, upon completing a counseling session with her client, a counselor said, "This was the fourth interview, and I still cannot get him to talk about goals." When this happens, the counselor must deal with the question, What is the client resisting?

In working with clients who are resistant to goals, it is helpful to realize that such behavior is purposeful. That is, what the client does or avoids doing achieves some desirable result for the client. Consequently, you may find that the client who resists setting goals may be protecting the behavior that is in need of modification because that behavior is doing something desirable. An example is the chronic smoker. Although an individual may recognize the negative consequences of smoking, he or she also clings to the habit, believing that it is a helpful way to deal with a tense situation, that it is relaxing, that it increases enjoyment of a good meal, and so forth.

It becomes your task to get clients to identify what they gain from their current behavior. In so doing, you may determine whether that gain or outcome can be achieved in more desirable ways. For example, a young student may throw paper airplanes out the school window in order to receive attention from peers. Gaining attention may be a desirable outcome. It is the method that is the problem. Therefore, you and your client may consider more appropriate means for gaining increased attention, other than throwing airplanes out the school window.

Sometimes, clients resist attempts to establish goals because they feel that the counselor (either overtly or subtly) is pushing them in a certain direction. As we mentioned earlier, this may be a particular issue with clients who feel marginalized. Unless clients can determine some *personal* goals of counseling, the probability of any change is minimal. You can avoid creating client resistance to goals by encouraging active participation by clients in the goal-setting process.

Client Participation in Goal Setting

Often, goal setting is construed to mean that you listen to the client, make a mental assessment of the problem, and prescribe a solution or goal. In fact, such a procedure is doomed to failure. The nature of counseling is such that the client must be involved in the establishment of goals. Otherwise, the client's participation is directionless at best and interferes with counseling at worst.

An example will illustrate this idea. A beginning counselor was seeing a client who was overweight, self-conscious about her appearance, reluctant to enter into social relationships with others because of this self-consciousness, and very lonely. The counselor informed the client that one goal would be for her (the client) to lose one to three pounds per week, under a doctor's supervision. With this, the client became highly defensive and rejected the counselor's goal, saying, "You sound just like my mother."

Goal setting is highly personal. It requires a great deal of effort and commitment on the client's part. Therefore, the client must select goals that are important to the client. In the preceding example, the client's resistance could have been prevented if the counselor had moved more slowly, permitting the client to identify for herself the significance of her weight and the importance of potential weight loss for herself. At this point, both the counselor and client could then work together to determine the specific goals and subgoals that, when achieved, might alleviate the client's concerns.

Again, we stress the importance of the client's cultural beliefs and values in deciding what goals to pursue for counseling. In the preceding example, consider the fact that most White girls and women in the United States are preoccupied with weight and body image in a way that many men and girls and women of color are not. It is up to the client, not the counselor in the mainstream culture, to decide what goals are relevant and appropriate.

Summary

In this chapter, we have entered into the therapeutically active portion of the counseling process. In addition to the interactive process that takes place between counselor and client, the counselor begins to establish an internal analytical process in which the client's world is studied. That *study* is both within the client's context and in the larger context of healthy, productive living. Clients will become involved in this study, often quite naturally, as they unfold their experiences, feelings, and thoughts about themselves, others, and their current world. Interwoven in this process is an emerging awareness of a different or perhaps better set of conditions, which become translated into *goals*. Some of these goals are related to the counseling relationship. Others are more related to the client's world. Through the recognition and establishment of these goals, the counselor begins to understand the direction counseling will take and can begin to help the client reach that same awareness. We will continue this exploration of the higher-order skills of counseling in Chapter 10.

DISCUSSION QUESTIONS

1. Both the client and the counselor bring their worlds into the counseling session. We indicated that goal setting evolves out of an understanding of the client's world. How might the counselor's world affect that process of goal setting? Should the counselor be concerned about this issue? Why?

2. With yourself or with a roleplaying partner, identify a current problem in your life. Consider the list of Egan's nine questions found in this chapter. How do these questions help you (or your partner) develop goals and future scenarios for this concern?

3. In the beginning of this chapter, we discussed how unmet childhood needs can be reactivated in adult life. As an exercise, first for yourself and then with a client, consider completing the following questions posed by Steinem (1992): "Write down on [a piece of paper] . . . the things you wish you had received in your childhood and did not" (pp. 104–105). When you have completed this exercise, you have discovered what your needs for yourself are now.

4. How might the needs of a financially challenged low-income client differ from the needs of a client with a high-paying and secure job? What about the needs of a company manager who was recently laid off due to downsizing? How would these needs affect the goals for counseling?

RECOMMENDED READINGS

Bisman, C. (1994). *Social work practice*. Pacific Grove, CA: Brooks/Cole.

Brown, L. S., & Ballou, M. (1992). *Personality and psychopathology: Feminist reappraisals*. New York: Guilford.

Egan, G. (1998). *The skilled helper* (6th ed.). Pacific Grove, CA: Brooks/Cole.

Prochaska, J. O., DiClemente, C., & Norcross, J. (1992). In search of how people change. *American Psychologist, 47,* 1102–1114.

Rosado, J. W., Jr., & Elias, M. J. (1993). Ecological and psychocultural mediators in the delivery of services for urban, culturally diverse Hispanic clients. *Professional Psychology, 24,* 450–459.

Satterfield, W. A., Buelow, S. A., Lyddon, W. J., & Johnson, T. J. (1995). Client stages of change and expectations about counseling. *Journal of Counseling Psychology, 42,* 476–478.

Using Counseling Strategies and Interventions

In the previous chapter, we mentioned a variety of factors that contribute to the problems that clients bring to counseling, including feelings, beliefs, behaviors, interactional patterns, and the complexity and multidimensionality of the presenting problems. To deal effectively with such complex issues, counselors need to equip themselves with a variety of strategies and interventions designed to work with all the various ways in which the problem is manifested.

In this chapter, we examine a number of helping strategies or interventions. Those that are presented here have been selected because they are used by counselors of varying theoretical orientations and because, when used in conjunction with each other, they treat the *whole* person. The strategies we describe are used to help clients (1) work through feelings, (2) work with belief systems and attitudes, (3) work with behaviors, (4) work with interactional patterns and relationships, and (5) work with social systems.

Working with Client Feelings

As we mentioned in Chapter 7, clients will be unable to change unless counselors respond to their feelings in a different way than has happened in the past. In this section, we describe several ways of working with client feelings to provide a more satisfying response to clients than they have received before.

Permission to Feel

Clients need the support and acceptance of the therapist to be able to feel their feelings. You can use *verbal leads* similar to the following to convey your own acceptance of the client's feelings. However, your acceptance must be genuine; otherwise, clients are likely to sense your own discomfort. Examples of leads to convey permission to feel include:

> "It's important to feel this now."
> "It's OK to feel just what you are feeling now."
> "Allow yourself to feel whatever comes up as we talk."

"It's OK for you to feel sad (angry, etc.)."
"You can show me how painful (irritating, etc.) this is."
"I accept your anger (sadness, etc.)."

At another level, you may wish to have clients give themselves permission to feel by suggesting *permission phrases* that they say or repeat after you, such as:

"It's OK for me to feel this way."
"I can accept my own feelings."
"I can face my sadness (anger, etc.)."
"I can show you how I feel."
"It's OK for me to feel sad (angry, etc.) with you."

Eliciting Feelings

Another strategy is to encourage clients to identify feelings, to acknowledge them, and to allow them to come to full expression. This is often and simply accomplished by using verbal leads or open-ended questions that focus on client feelings and help clients elicit different facets of their emotions. The following examples are particularly helpful:

Can you bring that feeling to life for me and help me understand what it is like for you when you are feeling that?

Do you have an image that captures that feeling, or is there a fantasy that goes along with it for you?

Is there a particular place in your body where you experience that feeling?

Is this a familiar or old feeling? When is the first time you can remember having it? Where were you? Who were you with? How did the other person respond to you?

How old do you feel that you are when you experience that feeling? Can you attach an age to it, such as being 7 years old or 13 years old?

Does this feeling have its own sound or movement? Can you make a sound that would let me hear what it's like or a gesture that would help me see it? (Teyber, 1997, p. 129)

Increasing Body Awareness

Clients can also learn to get in touch with their feelings through the use of strategies that encourage greater awareness of what is occurring within one's body. When a person feels tense, it is usually seen or experienced in the contraction of a muscle or group of muscles. Continued tension results in pain such as a headache or numbness, which occurs from nerve pressure accumulated from the tension. Smith (1985) has recommended the following invitation to help clients acquire body awareness:

> Close your eyes and just relax for a few moments. Breathe comfortably. (Pause) (Repeat the directions to relax and the pauses until the client seems to be involved in the exercise.) Check out your body to see what you find. Note anything in your body which calls attention to itself. Just monitor your body, inch by inch, from the tips of your toes to the top of your head and down to the tips of your fingers. In particular, note any hot spots, cold spots, tight or tense muscles, pains, tingling, or anything happening in your body. Don't try to edit or change anything, just be aware and note what is happening. (Pause for a minute or two.) Take your time. When you are finished, open your eyes. (Wait until client opens her or his eyes.) (p. 107)

Following this, the counselor asks the client to describe whatever he or she noticed.

Clients also can identify and express feelings by being asked to exaggerate a particular body action (Perls, 1973; Smith, 1985). This strategy is useful because people often make bodily movements that suggest an action that reflects a current and present emotion; it is considered a "slip of the body," much in the way a person says something unintended yet meaningful, as in a verbal "slip of the tongue." As Smith (1985) noted, by inviting the client to repeat the action in an exaggerated form, the meaning of the body action usually becomes apparent. Smith gave the following illustration:

> An example of this is the patient who, while talking about her ex-lover, begins slightly swinging her leg which is crossed over the other leg, knee on knee. The therapist asks her to be aware of her leg and she says, "Oh, I'm just nervous today." So the therapist asks her to exaggerate the movement. She swings her leg in a larger arc, with more force, and declares, "I must want to kick him. But I didn't know I was angry today. Oh, I just remembered what he said last week. I am mad at him!" (p. 110)

By asking the client to exaggerate the body movement, the counselor helps the client see that she has both repressed and inhibited a feeling of anger. When a client's movement is directed toward oneself—for instance, if she has been chewing her cheek—the exaggeration of this would also illustrate how she had taken the feeling of anger toward the ex-lover and directed it back toward herself.

Breathing

Another way to help clients get in touch with and express feelings is through work on breathing. According to Lowen (1965), every emotional problem is manifested in some sort of disturbance in breathing. Perls (1969), the founder of gestalt therapy, connected shallow breathing and sighing with depression, yawning with boredom, and restricted breath with anxiety. Smith (1985) observed that effective breathing is necessary for vitality; that insufficient breathing leaves the person in a state like "a fire with an inadequate draft" (p. 119). Healthy breathing involves the entire body (p. 120).

There are numerous ways to work with breathing. The first is to note to the client the occasions in which he or she holds a breath or breathes in a shallow or constricted manner. For some clients, it may be useful to teach them the art of deep breathing, in which the breath is started (inhaled) in the abdomen, moves up through the chest, and is released thoroughly in the exhalation, often with the aid of a vocal sound. When clients can breathe deeply and do not hold back or interrupt the breathing cycle, they are more likely to experience what they feel.

Another way to increase breathing awareness is to instruct the client to count the in-breath and the out-breath (Gilligan, 1997). For example, you might say, "As the breath comes in through the nostrils, filling up the lower diaphragm, say silently, 'breathing in, one.' As the breath goes out, say silently, 'breathing out, one'" (Gilligan, 1997, p. 76). The next breath is counted as two, then three, and so on. Other clients may use word mantras with their breath such as *let* on the in breath and *go* on the out breath.

Gilligan (1997) noted that the restriction of breathing is often such a chronic activity that it becomes unconscious or without awareness. He has suggested asking clients to recall an "antagonistic image, thought, or a feeling" and whether they sense it "inside" or "outside" their breath (p. 76). He observed that usually "difficult processes are experienced *outside* the breath" (p. 76). When the difficult experience is brought inside the breath, an important shift in relationship to the troubling experience usually occurs.

One of the advantages of breathing interventions is that breathing is a universal phenomenon. All people—regardless of differences in race, gender, age, class, sexual orientation and so on—breathe! Many have learned, over time, to shut down their breathing, resulting in a variety of somatic and emotional symptoms.

Incomplete Sentences

Another possibility to help clients elicit and express feelings is with the use of incomplete sentences. Usually, after some work has been done on breathing, the counselor "feeds" the client with an incomplete sentence stem and the client finishes the sentence with the first thing that comes to mind, continuing to say the same root of that sentence with different completions until there is a point at which the client seems finished. Then another sentence stem is "fed" by the counselor.

Examples of incomplete sentences developed by Branden (1971) to elicit feelings include:

> Something I'm feeling is . . .
> When I look at you, I feel . . .
> As you look at me, I feel . . .
> If I felt mad (or scared or shy or happy, etc.), I . . .
> One of the things that I do when I feel mad is . . .
> One of the things that might make me feel mad is . . .

One of the ways that feeling mad helps me is . . .
A good thing about feeling mad is . . .
A bad thing about feeling mad is . . .
The rule we had in my family about feeling mad was . . .

In using interventions to work with client feelings, it is important to recall the cautions we mentioned in Chapter 7 regarding culture. Some clients from some cultural groups may feel uncomfortable with these kinds of strategies because their cultural group does not focus on feelings or on revealing feelings to a nonfamily member. Other clients may be much more concerned with survival, class, and social issues, and so focusing on affect seems trivial and irrelevant to them.

Working with Client Beliefs and Attitudes

Beliefs and attitudes represent meanings, interpretations, or thoughts a client has about a situation—sometimes referred to as *cognitions*. Beliefs are potent because they affect clients' perceptions about themselves, others, and their lives.

Clients encounter all sorts of difficulty based on their beliefs and attitudes because they may be distorted and based on incomplete information. For instance, clients who are depressed or highly anxious tend to view themselves, others, and the world in a negative way (A. T. Beck, 1976; J. S. Beck, 1995). A major focus of these interventions is on changing the way the client thinks. In this section of the chapter, we describe two related but somewhat different ways of working with client feelings: the A-B-C-D-E analysis and cognitive restructuring.

A-B-C-D-E Analysis

The A-B-C-D-E analysis is an intervention strategy based on a cognitive counseling approach known as *rational-emotive therapy,* developed by a psychotherapist named Albert Ellis. According to Ellis, emotional distress is created by faulty, illogical, or irrational thoughts. In other words, if someone feels emotionally upset, it is not a person or a situation that creates the emotional upset but rather the individual's beliefs or thoughts about the situation. Reduction in emotional distress is created when the individual's irrational thinking is changed to rational thinking, through interventions such as the A-B-C-D-E analysis.

In the first part of this strategy, the client learns to recognize the *activating event (A),* usually a situation or person that the client finds upsetting. The activating event is often what prompts the client to seek counseling ("My relationship is on the rocks," "I lost my job," "My partner is a jerk," "I don't have any friends," "Why don't boys like me?" "I got passed over for the team," etc.). The most important aspect of this part of the strategy is to refocus clients from attributing their distress to this activating event to their thoughts about it. For example, the counselor might respond, "I realize it is upsetting to you not to make the team; however, it is not this situation in and of itself that is making you feel so bad but rather your thinking about this situation."

In the next part of the strategy, the client's specific thoughts or *beliefs (B)* about the activating event are explored and identified. The client may have both rational and irrational thoughts, but it is the irrational thoughts that contribute to the emotional distress and that need to be targeted for change. Rational thoughts are ones that are consistent with reality, are supported by data, and result in *moderate* levels of emotional upset (e.g., "I didn't play as well as other people in the tryouts and they got picked and I didn't"). Irrational thoughts are not based on facts or evidence and lead to high levels of emotional distress (e.g., "Because I didn't make the team I am a jerk"). Irrational beliefs often take the form of either catastrophization ("It will be awful when...") or "musturbation" ("I must...," "I should...," "I have to...").

The counselor then links the irrational beliefs with the resulting emotional and behavioral *consequences (C)*—that is, what clients feel and how they act as a result (e.g., "I feel so bad. I just can't seem to snap out of it. I didn't want to go back to school because I'm so ashamed of not making the team"). The counselor shows the client how his or her specific irrational beliefs led to these consequences. For instance, the therapist might respond, "You are feeling awful and staying away from school because you now view yourself as a nobody—it is not that you got passed up that is making you feel and act this way, it is the way you're now thinking about yourself."

The real work of the strategy comes next in the *disputation (D)* phase. Disputation involves disputing or challenging the client's irrational beliefs with the intent of eliminating them and helping the client acquire more rational thinking. The counselor uses questions to dispute the client's irrational beliefs. Some examples of questions suggested for cognitive disputation by Walen, DiGiuseppe, and Wessler (1992) include:

> Is that true? Why not?
>
> Can you prove it?
>
> How do you know?
>
> Why is that an overgeneralization?
>
> Why is that a bad term to use?
>
> How would you talk a friend out of such an idea?
>
> What would happen if—?
>
> If that's true, what's the worst that can happen?
>
> So what if that happens?
>
> How would that be so terrible?
>
> Where's the evidence?
>
> How is a disadvantage awful?

Ask yourself, can I still find happiness?

What good things can happen if X occurs?

Can you be happy even if you don't get what you want?

What might happen?

How terrible would that be?

Why would you be done in by that?

What is the probability of a bad consequence?

How will your world be destroyed if X happens?

As long as you believe that, how will you feel?

"Whatever I want, I must get." Where will that get you?

Is it worth it? (pp. 97–99)

When the disputation process has been effective, it will be apparent in new *effects (E)*, such as lessened emotional distress and changes in behavior (e.g., "I still don't like the fact I didn't make the team but I know I am not a jerk just because of that"). It is important for the counselor to help clients recognize when these emotional and behavioral shifts in effects occur.

Cognitive Restructuring

Cognitive or rational restructuring involves not only helping clients learn to recognize and stop self-defeating thoughts but also to substitute these thoughts with positive, self-enhancing, or coping thoughts. In the first part of cognitive restructuring, clients learn to stop obsessive, illogical, or negative thoughts as they occur. This involves discrimination training in which they are made aware of what "they tell themselves" before, during, and after problem situations. Clients might be instructed to note and record their negative thoughts before, during, and after stressful or depressing situations for one or two weeks.

After they are aware of the nature and types of their self-defeating thoughts, the counselor helps them work toward identifying more positive or coping thoughts that can replace the negative ones. These coping thoughts are considered to be incompatible with the self-defeating thoughts.

Coping thoughts are designed to help clients picture dealing with problem situations effectively, although not perfectly. In this way, they are considered better than mastery thoughts, which focus on perfection "because they sensitize the clients to possible mistakes and prepare them to recover from errors they may make in real life" (McMullin, 1986, p. 18). It is best to personalize these coping thoughts for each client. Clients also need to learn coping thoughts to use before, during, and after problem situations. For example, a client who fails tests due to anxiety might concentrate on thoughts such as "I will be calm" or "Keep your mind on your studies" before an exam. During an exam, clients learn to concentrate on the exam and to stay calm instead of worrying about flunking or thinking about their nervousness. After using some coping thoughts, clients can be taught to reward or congratulate themselves for coping—instead of punishing themselves for worrying.

When clients have identified some possible alternative coping thoughts to use, they can practice applying these thoughts through overt (roleplay) and covert (imaginary) rehearsal. The rehearsal may take the form of a dialogue or a script and may be read aloud by the client or put on index cards or audiotape. McMullin (1986) observed that for most clients, a period of at least six weeks is necessary for the practice of coping thoughts.

A sample cognitive restructuring dialogue used for rehearsal by a high school client who feared competitive situations is provided by Cormier and Cormier (1998):

> OK. I'm sitting here waiting for my turn to try out for cheerleader. Ooh, I can feel myself getting very nervous. (anxious feeling) Now, wait, what am I so nervous about? I'm afraid I'm going to make a fool of myself. (self-defeating thought) Hey, that doesn't help. (cue to cope) It will take only a few minutes, and it will be over before I know it. Besides only the faculty sponsors are watching. It's not like the whole school. (coping thoughts) Well, the person before me is just about finished. Oh, they're calling my name. Boy, do I feel tense. (anxious feelings) What if I don't execute my jumps? (self-defeating thought) OK, don't think about what I'm not going to do. OK, start out, it's my turn. Just think about my routine—the way I want it to go. (coping thoughts) (p. 383)

Identifying and internalizing coping thoughts seem to be crucial in order for clients to really benefit from cognitive restructuring. Gradually, clients should be able to apply their newly found coping skills to the in vivo situations as these occur. If cognitive restructuring is successful, clients can detect increased use of coping thoughts and decreased level of stress in their actual environment. In vivo practice seems crucial for the efficacy of this strategy in order to promote the clients' confidence in their newly learned beliefs (Meichenbaum, 1993).

The use of cognitive strategies with diverse groups of clients has received increased attention in the last few years. However, as Hays (1995) has pointed out, the values inherent in cognitive interventions reflect those of the mainstream culture. Kantrowitz and Ballou (1992) elaborated: "The rational thinking orientation of cognitive therapy and cognitive restructuring reinforces worldviews and cognitive processes that are stereotypically both Euro-American and masculine," running the risk that other, different world views and cognitions may be ignored or even rejected (p. 81). Also, as Brown (1994) asserted, there are instances for some clients where the supposedly irrational beliefs may be reasonable or even lifesaving, given the individual's life and environmental context (p. 61). Also, the process of challenging or disputing these beliefs may not fit with some clients from particular cultural groups. Therefore, a useful caveat is to cultivate awareness in using cognitive strategies. Be flexible in the way you implement these strategies and be sensitive to the client's reaction.

Working with Client Behaviors

There are a variety of strategies designed to help clients modify their behavior. Behavioral interventions are based on the assumption that behavior is learned; therefore, inappropriate or maladaptive behavior can be unlearned while more adaptive behavior can be acquired (Wilson, 1995). In this section, we describe three strategies designed to work with client behaviors: social modeling, behavioral rehearsal, and self-management.

Social Modeling

Social modeling, based on observational learning, refers to a process familiar to all human beings. If people are nothing else, they are observers. From earliest childhood, humans watch and imitate. Through this vicarious experience is acquired a great amount of knowledge and skills. The limitations to observational learning include a person's ability to observe, the attractiveness of the model, and the generalizability of the event to be learned.

As a helping strategy, *modeling* is used to help a client acquire desired responses or to extinguish fears—through observing the behavior of another person, the model. This observation can be presented in a live modeling demonstration by the counselor or in symbolic form through written and media-taped models.

Live Modeling

Live models can include the counselor, who demonstrates the desired behavior, or teachers or peers of the client. Usually, you will provide a modeled demonstration by a roleplay activity in which you take the part of the client and show a way to respond or behave. Live modeling is particularly useful in instances in which the client does not have response alternatives available. The modeled demonstration provides cues that the client can use to acquire new responses. For instance, a client who wishes to acquire self-expression skills may benefit from seeing you or a peer demonstrate such skills in roleplayed situations.

Symbolic Modeling

Although live models have much impact on the client, they are often difficult to use because of the lack of control in ensuring their systematic demonstration of the desired behavior. To correct for this, many counselors make use of symbolic models through audiotapes, videotapes, or films in which a desired behavior is introduced and presented. For example, symbolic models could be used with clients who want to improve their study habits. Reading about effective study habits of successful people and their scholastic efforts is a first step in helping clients specify those behaviors involved. Next, clients can listen to an audiotape or watch a videotape that describes effective study behaviors.

Characteristics of Models

In selecting models, it is best to maximize model-client similarity. Clients are more likely to learn from someone whom they perceive as similar to themselves. Such characteristics as age, gender, race, and ethnic background should be considered in selecting effective models.

A coping model may be more helpful to some clients than a mastery model. A client may be able to identify more with a model who shows some fear or some struggle in performing than someone who comes across perfectly. For example, a very shy, timid person could be overwhelmed by a very assertive model. This could be especially true if the client is from a cultural group that does not sanction individual expressiveness and assertiveness. This client may respond more quickly if he or she is exposed to a model who starts quietly and gradually increases assertive behaviors. Clients also may learn more from modeling when exposed to more than one model. Multiple models may have more impact on a client, because the client can draw on the strengths and styles of several different people. Multiple models are especially useful with bicultural and biracial clients.

When modeling fails to contribute to desired client changes, reassess the characteristics of the selected model(s) and the mode and format of the modeled presentation. In many cases, modeling can provide sufficient cues for the client to learn new responses or to extinguish fears. In other instances, modeling may have more effects when accompanied by practices of the target response. Such practices can occur through roleplay and rehearsal strategies, as described in the next section.

Behavior Rehearsal

The strategy of *behavior rehearsal* uses roleplay and practice attempts to help people acquire new skills and behave more effectively under threatening or anxiety-producing conditions. Behavior rehearsal is used primarily in three instances:

1. The client does not have and needs to learn the necessary skills to handle a situation *(response acquisition)*.
2. The client needs to learn to discriminate between positive and negative application of the skills or between inappropriate and appropriate times and places to use the skills *(response facilitation)*.
3. The client's anxiety about the situation needs to be sufficiently reduced so that the client can use skills already learned, even though they are currently inhibited by anxiety *(response disinhibition)*.

For example, if a client wants to increase self-disclosive behavior, but does not know what self-disclosure is or has not learned the skills involved in self-disclosing, the client has a deficient repertoire in self-disclosure and needs to acquire certain skills (response acquisition). On the other hand, there are times when the skills already are in the client's repertoire, but the client needs clarification or discrimination training in when and how to employ the skills (response facilitation). Many times, people have self-disclosure skills but use the skills inappropriately. A person may self-disclose too much to someone who is disinterested and withhold personal information from a significant other. In another case, the client's anxiety perhaps has inhibited the skills (response disinhibition). In other words, a client may have learned the skills of appropriate self-disclosure but avoids self-disclosing because of anxiety the client feels in certain self-disclosive situations. In selecting response targets for behavior rehearsal, remember that the behaviors need to be consistent with the values of the client's gender and cultural socialization patterns.

The practicalities of behavior rehearsal consist of a series of graduated practice attempts in which the client rehearses the desired behaviors, starting with a situation that is manageable and is not likely to backfire. The rehearsal attempts may be arranged in a hierarchy according to level of difficulty or stress of different situations. Adequate practice of one situation is required before moving on to another scene. The practice of each scene should be very similar to the situations that occur in the client's environment. To simulate these situations realistically, use any necessary props and portray the other person involved with the client as accurately as possible. This portrayal should include acting out the probable response of this person to the client's new or different behavior.

Behavior rehearsal can be overt or covert. In *covert* behavior rehearsal, clients practice the target behavior by *imagining* themselves performing the response in certain situations. For instance, clients might imagine themselves successfully presenting an important speech or initiating a discussion with a friend or a boss. In *overt* rehearsal, the client *acts out* the target responses in roleplayed scenarios. Both covert and overt rehearsal seem to be quite effective (Kazdin, 1982). A client could probably benefit from engaging in both of these forms of behavioral rehearsal. Initially, the client might practice covertly and later act out the responses in roleplayed enactments. Covert rehearsal also can be used easily by clients as homework, since imaginary practice does not require the presence of another person.

Feedback is an important part of roleplay and rehearsal strategies. It is a way for the client to recognize both the problems and successes encountered in the practice attempts, as well as a way of observing and evaluating one's performance and of initiating corrective action. However, feedback should not be used indiscriminately. Feedback may be more effective if the client is willing to change, if the feedback given is adequate but not overwhelming, and if the feedback helps the client identify other alternatives.

Following rehearsal attempts, clients can be encouraged to evaluate their performances. You will be another important source of feedback. Remember to reinforce the client for gradual improvement. Feedback also can be supplied by videotaped and audiotaped playbacks of the client's practices. These taped playbacks may be more objective assessments of the client's performance. At first, you can go over the tapes together and point out the strengths and limitations apparent in the practice. Gradually, the client should be able to analyze the taped playback alone—providing self-analysis and self-reinforcement for the practice efforts.

Modeling, Rehearsal, and Feedback: Components of Skill Training

The strategies of modeling, rehearsal, and feedback can be combined as a skill-training package. These strategies often are used to teach clients problem-solving skills, decision-making skills, communication skills, and assertion skills. For example, in assertion training, you begin by having the client identify one situation in which he or she wants to be more assertive. Then specify what assertive behaviors are involved and what the client would like to say or do. The situation is modeled and roleplayed consistently in the interview until the client can be assertive without experiencing any anxiety. Following successful completion of the task outside the interview, assertion training can continue for other kinds of situations involving self-assertion by the client. Successes at assertiveness will soon generalize to other situations, as well; that is, it will become increasingly easier for clients to be assertive on their own without assistance and feedback. Again, remember that the skill training must be culturally relevant to the client.

As an illustration, suppose you are working with a student who reports a lack of assertive classroom behaviors. You and your client would first specify the desired assertive skills. The skills selected would be appropriate for the student's age, gender, race, and cultural background. You may need to observe the student in the classroom setting to identify these target behaviors. In counting the number of times the student engages in assertive classroom behavior (asking questions, voicing opinions, engaging in group discussion, giving reports, volunteering for chalkboard work, initiating conversations with the teacher, etc.), you can obtain an accurate idea of the kind of assertive behaviors that are most prevalent in the client's repertoire and the ones the student needs most to strengthen. You can provide either live or symbolic models of these specific assertive behaviors. After the client has seen, listened to, or read about these modeled behaviors, he or she can demonstrate and practice small steps of such assertive classroom behaviors in the interview. Following practice attempts in which the client is able to demonstrate repeated efforts of a given behavior within the interview, he or she should be encouraged to practice it on a daily basis in the classroom.

Self-Management

Many people are legitimately concerned about the long-term effects of helping. In an effort to promote enduring client changes, counselors have become more concerned with client self-directed change. This interest has led many counseling researchers and practitioners to explore the usefulness of a variety of helping strategies called *self-control* or *self-management* (Wilson, 1995).

The primary characteristic of a self-management strategy is that the client administers the strategy and directs the change efforts with minimal assistance from the counselor. Self-management strategies are very useful in dealing with a number of client problems and may promote generalization to life settings of what clients learn in the interview. Self-management strategies are among the best strategies designed to strengthen client investment in the helping process. Self-management may eliminate the counselor as a "middle" person and ensure greater chances of client success because of the investment made by the client in the strategies for change. Two of the most useful self-management strategies include self-monitoring and self-reward.

Self-Monitoring

Recent emphases in behavioral approaches suggest the efficacy of a number of self-control procedures, of which self-monitoring is primary. Self-monitoring involves having clients count and/or regulate given habits, thoughts, or feelings. Self-monitoring seems to interfere with the learned habit by breaking the stimulus-response association and by encouraging performance of the desired response, which is then often reinforced by the individual's sense of progress following its accomplishment.

There are two issues that affect the self-monitoring strategy—reactivity and reliability. *Reactivity* means that the process of noticing one's own behavior closely can cause the behavior to change. *Reliability* refers to the accuracy with which the client counts the behavior. For therapy purposes, you and your client should attempt to structure the self-monitoring in a way that maximizes the reactivity. Therefore, in implementing the procedure, you will need to consider what, how, and when to self-monitor.

What to Monitor. An initial step involves selecting the behavior to monitor. Usually, individuals will achieve better results with self-monitoring if they start by counting only one behavior—at least initially. Clients may, for example, count positive feelings about themselves or thoughts of competency. The counting encourages greater frequency of these kinds of thoughts and feelings. Clients may count the number of times they tell themselves to do well on a task, or they may count the number of behaviors related to goal achievement (e.g., the number of times they tell their partner "I love you," the number of times they initiate conversations or participate in class discussions, etc.). The important thing is that they monitor behaviors that *they* value and care to change and that are consistent with their culture.

How to Monitor. The particular method the client uses to count the target response will depend on the nature of the selected response. Generally, clients will count either the *frequency* or *duration* of a response. If they are interested in knowing how often the response occurs, they can use a frequency count to note—for example, the number of times they smoke, talk on the telephone, initiate social conversations, or think about themselves positively. Sometimes, it is more useful to know the amount of time the behavior occurs. A person can count the duration or length of a behavior in these cases. For example, clients might count how long they studied, how long they talked on the telephone, or the length of depressed periods of thought. Occasionally, clients may find it useful to record both the frequency and duration of a response. In choosing to count the occurrences of a behavior either by the number or by the amount of time, there is a simple rule of thumb recommended by Watson and Tharp (1997): They suggest using frequency counts if it is easy to count the number of separate times the behavior is performed, and duration counts if separate occasions are not easy to count or if the target behavior continues for several minutes at a time. Obviously, there are some times when a client may monitor both frequency and duration—for example, the number of cigarettes smoked in a day as well as the amount of time spent in smoking cigarettes in a day.

In some cases where the target response occurs very often or almost continuously, or when the onset and termination of the target responses are hard to detect, the frequency and duration methods of recording may not be too useful. In these instances, clients could record with an interval method. In the interval method of recording, they could divide the time for recording (8:00 A.M. to 8:00 P.M.) into time intervals such as 30 minutes, one hour, or two hours. During each time interval, they simply record the presence or absence of the behavior with a "yes" if the behavior occurred or a "no" if it did not.

Clients will need to record with the assistance of some recording device. These can range from simple devices—such as notecards, logs, and diaries for written recordings—to more mechanical devices—such as a golf wrist counter, a kitchen timer, a wristwatch, or a tape recorder. The device may increase the reactivity of self-monitoring if it is obtrusive; yet it should not be so noticeable that it is embarrassing or awkward for clients to use. The device should be simple to use, convenient, portable, and economical.

When to Monitor. The timing of self-monitoring can influence the change produced by this strategy. Generally, there are two times when clients can record: before the response (prebehavior monitoring) or after the response (postbehavior monitoring). In prebehavior monitoring, the client reveals the intention or urge to engage in the behavior before doing so. For instance, the client records times when she or he has an urge to eat a dessert or a snack but does not. In postbehavior monitoring, the client records after the behavior has occurred. For example, the client records after each time she or he exercises. The effects of self-monitoring may depend on the timing and on whether there are other factors competing for the client's attention at the time the response is recorded. Although Kanfer and Gaelick-Buys (1991) have stated that there are insufficient data to judge whether pre- or postmonitoring is most effective, we suggest the following two rules of thumb:

1. *To decrease the monitored behavior:* Since you want to decrease the number of cigarettes you smoke (or the number of self-critical thoughts you have), each time you have the urge to smoke but do not (or start to criticize yourself but refrain from doing so), then count this on your log.
2. *To increase a behavior:* Since you want to increase the number of times you verbally express your opinions to someone else (or the number of positive, self-enhancing thoughts), count and record on your log immediately after you express an opinion (or as soon as you are aware of thinking something positive about yourself or your accomplishments).

Counting, or quantifying, behaviors is the initial step in self-monitoring. The second and equally important step in self-monitoring is charting or plotting the behavior counts over a period of time. This permits clients to see progress that might not otherwise be apparent. It also permits clients to set daily goals that are more attainable than the overall goal. Clients can take weekly cumulative counts of self-monitored behaviors and chart them on a simple line graph. After graphing the data, the public display of the graph may set the occasion for both self- and external reinforcement.

To summarize, self-monitoring is most likely to produce desired behavioral changes when the following conditions exist (Cormier & Cormier, 1998):

1. The client is motivated to change the behavior to be monitored.
2. The client monitors a limited number of behaviors and these behaviors are discrete.
3. The monitoring act is closely related in time prior to or after the monitored behavior.
4. The client receives some feedback from the monitoring that is compared with the client's goals.

Self-Reward

Research suggests that the effects produced by self-monitoring may be greater and more permanent if self-monitoring is accompanied by other therapeutic strategies, such as self-reward (Kanfer & Gaelick-Buys, 1991). Self-monitoring can always be combined with other helping strategies as a way to collect data concerning the occurrence of goal behaviors. As we noted in the previous section, self-monitoring also can be used intentionally to induce therapeutic change. However, the therapeutic gains from self-monitoring may be maximized with the explicit use of other self-management strategies to increase or decrease a response.

Self-reward involves the self-presentation of rewards following the occurrence of a desired behavior. It is intended to strengthen a behavior. Self-reward functions like external reinforcement. A *reinforcer* is something that, when administered following a target response, tends to maintain or increase the probability of that response in the future.

There are two ways clients can use self-reward. First, they can give themselves rewards after engaging in specified behaviors. For example, clients could imagine being on a sailboat after doing daily exercises or could buy themselves treats after daily studying. Second, they could remove something negative after performing the desired behaviors. For instance, an overweight client could remove a "fat picture" from the wall after losing a certain number of pounds. In most cases, we recommend the first approach (self-presentation of a positive stimulus) because it is more positive than the second.

There are three major factors involved in helping a client use a self-reward strategy: what to use as rewards, how to administer the rewards, and when to administer the rewards.

Types of Rewards. First, you will want to help your clients select appropriate rewards. Clients should choose things that are truly reinforcing. There are different types of rewards to use. An example of a verbal-symbolic reward is self-praise, such as thinking, "I really did that well." Imaginal rewards involve visualizing or fantasizing scenes that produce pleasure and satisfaction. Material rewards include tangible events such as an enjoyable activity, a purchase, or tokens or points that can be exchanged for something. Rewards also can be current or potential. A current reward is something enjoyable that occurs on a daily basis, such as eating, reading, or getting the mail. A potential reward is something that could occur in the future that would be satisfying and enjoyable. Taking a trip and going out for a meal are examples of potential rewards.

Clients should be encouraged to select a variety of rewards, including both current and potential, material, imaginal, and verbal-symbolic. This may prevent one reward from losing its potency or impact. You can help clients select rewards by having them identify some ongoing and potentially satisfying thoughts and activities. An occasional client may have difficulty in identifying rewards. In lieu of using a very enjoyable activity as a reward, this client might choose a more mundane daily activity, such as answering the telephone or walking up or down stairs.

Using a frequently occurring activity as a reward is based on the *Premack principle,* which states that a high-probability behavior can be used to reinforce a low-probability behavior (Premack, 1965). For instance, something a student engages in frequently, such as getting up from the desk, can be made contingent on something the student does infrequently, such as completing assignments or work problems. The rewards used can be tailored to each client, since not all events or fantasies are reinforcing for all persons. The selected rewards should relate to the client's personal history, be acceptable to the client, and be something the client wants to do and is capable of doing (Kanfer & Gaelick-Buys, 1991). The rewards should also be *culturally* relevant to each client. What seems rewarding for one person may not be at all rewarding for another.

Delivery of Rewards. After selecting rewards, clients will need to work out ways to administer the rewards. They should know what has to be done in order to present themselves with a reward. You might encourage them to reward themselves for *gradual* progress toward the desired goal. Daily rewards for small steps are more effective than delayed rewards for a great improvement.

Timing of Rewards. Clients also need to present the rewards at certain times in order to maximize the self-reward strategy. The reward should come only *after* target behavior has been performed in order to have the most impact. Also, *immediate* rewards are more effective than delayed rewards.

Client Commitment to Self-Management
A critical problem in the effective use of any self-management strategy is having the client use the strategy regularly and consistently. Clients may be more likely to carry out self-management programs given the presence of certain conditions:

1. The use of the self-management program will provide enough advantages or positive consequences to be worth the cost to the client in terms of time and effort. The self-management program must do more than simply meet the status quo.
2. The client's use of the program may be strengthened by enlisting the support and assistance of other people—as long as their roles are positive, not punishing. Former clients, peers, or friends can aid the client in achieving the goals through reinforcement of the client's regular use of the self-management strategies.
3. The counselor maintains some minimal contact with the client during the time the self-management program is being carried out. Counselor reinforcement is quite important in successful implementation of self-management efforts.

You can provide reinforcement (anything that serves to increase the frequency of a desired response) easily through verbal approval ("That's great," "I like that") or by knowledge of progress ("You did very well," "You did the task so well," "You've done a great job in improving your study habits"). Have the client drop in or telephone during the course of the self-management program. This enables you to provide immediate encouragement to the client.

Many of the behavioral strategies have been used quite effectively with diverse groups of clients, perhaps because these strategies focus on action and change rather than insight and exploration (Sue & Sue, 1990). Still, it is important to remember that some of the notions underlying behavioral interventions are decidedly Eurocentric in that they focus on an internal locus of control and responsibility. As Casas (1988) noted, "As a result of life experiences associated with racism, discrimination, and poverty," some clients have developed a cognitive set of "an external locus of control and responsibility" that is antithetical to these strategies (pp. 109–110). Again, we stress the importance of considering the client's world view and of adapting the behavioral strategies to the client's gender and culture.

Working with Client Interactional Patterns and Relationships

With any individual client who seeks counseling, the client is part of a larger interpersonal network, sometimes referred to as an *interpersonal system*. In any interpersonal system such as a marriage, a family, a work department, or a peer group, all segments of the system are interrelated, and change in one part affects the entire system. In those interpersonal systems to which the client belongs, the client typically interacts in predictable patterns. These patterns can be seen within the context of the counseling system as well as within the various systems to which the client belongs. In other words, the counselor can see the client's typical interpersonal pattern not only in the kinds of interactions the client reports with other persons but also in the way this interpersonal pattern is reenacted within the counseling relationship. Thus, in working with interactional patterns of the client, the counselor can intervene at two different levels: use of interventions that deal directly with the counselor-client system and use of interventions that have an impact on the client's interactional style with other persons. We will describe both levels of these strategies in this portion of the chapter.

Reenactment of Interactional Patterns in Counseling

Clients begin to develop predictable interactional patterns in their family of origin. Interactional patterns are affected by many factors, including family construction and birth order (Adler, 1958), family rules and communication patterns (Watzlawick, Beavin, & Jackson, 1967), and general level of health or dysfunction of the family system (Miller, 1981; Haley, 1997). For many people who become clients, their family of origin experience was problematic in three major ways (Teyber, 1997):

1. There was a lack of a strong bond between the parents, sometimes referred to as a lack of a "primary parental coalition" (Minuchin, 1974).
2. There were disruptions or interruptions in the ways parents met children's developmental needs for nurturance, structure, separateness, and attachment.
3. There were child-rearing practices that were either too authoritarian or too permissive in nature.

To cope with this, children, as they grow older, develop a characteristic way of interacting with others. People who use an Adlerian counseling model refer to this as a "lifestyle" (Adler, 1958); those who use a transactional analysis model refer to this as a "script" (Woolams & Brown, 1979). We will talk about three characteristic interpersonal patterns from a developmental/dynamic model (see also Horney, 1970). Clients generally cope in interpersonal systems by (1) moving toward people, (2) moving away or withdrawing from people, or (3) moving against or resisting other people.

People who *move toward* others are likely to be perceived by others as understanding and accommodating. These sort of people are usually helpful and cooperative but have trouble being appropriately assertive, direct, and, above all, angry. This sort of lifestyle or interpersonal pattern is designed to elicit from others the support and nurturing that was missed as a child. With a client who behaves like this toward the counselor, the counselor must be careful not just to provide acceptance but also to focus on the general interpersonal style of the client—what the client has missed from his or her family and is trying to elicit from the counselor as well as, no doubt, from numerous other people.

Clients who characteristically *move away* or *withdraw from* people will demonstrate the same behavior in the counseling relationship. They may seek help but they will attempt to maintain as much emotional distance as possible and to remain emotionally unconnected from the counseling per se. Although at one level these clients are trying to push the counselor away, at another level they want desperately for the counselor to stay connected to them. These clients pose quite a challenge for counselors. To respond reflexively and give up on the client is nontherapeutic. At the same time, if the counselor attempts to become too emotionally connected, these clients will feel alarmed and anxious because this is so unfamiliar. The counselor will need to stay present and engaged at a pace that follows the client's lead, but above all, the counselor must not give up on these individuals.

Clients who *move against* people are likely to try to directly intimidate the counselor or to passively resist the counselor's efforts. They may behave in ways either to take control of the session or to "push the counselor's buttons" and make the counselor feel inadequate. These kinds of clients may be especially difficult for beginning counselors who may respond countertherapeutically with fear, competition, or counterhostility (Teyber, 1997). Again, as with the other instances we have described, it is important for the counselor not to respond reflexively and give these clients what they are trying to elicit. With these individuals, the counselor must avoid getting involved in a battle or power struggle and focus instead on what the clients may be trying to get and/or avoid with their interpersonal styles and the likely impact of such on their lives.

Why do clients act out their typical interactional pattern with counselors? Quite simply, it is a form of a test. They feel that the counselor will respond in the same old way as most everyone else, but they hope against hope that the counselor will provide a different and more helpful response. When the counselor does, they will not have to keep reenacting their same old pattern and can move beyond the point at which they become "stuck"—not only with the counselor but with other people, as well. Teyber (1997) presented the following brief illustration of this process.

> Suppose a compliant, dependent woman says to her male therapist, "Where should we start today?" The therapist will fail the test and reenact a familiar relational scenario if he says, "Tell me about _____ ." ... The therapist will pass the test and demonstrate that he is capable of engaging in a more egalitarian way than the client has been able to do with other male figures in her life when the therapist says, "I'd like to hear about what is most important to you. Let's begin with something that you would like to tell me about." (p. 234)

Teyber (1997) also noted, "The therapist can fail this test by responding in a way that reenacts old relational patterns, or the therapist can pass the test by behaviorally demonstrating that relationships can be different" (pp. 233–234).

Pattern Interventions

Another level at which the counselor can respond to in the interpersonal realm involves a change or modification in the patterns of interactions around the interpersonal problems the client reports. This is referred to as *pattern intervention* and comes from work on family therapy and Ericksonian hypnosis (Imber-Black, Roberts, & Whiting, 1988; O'Hanlon, 1987). In the previous section, we talked about a type of pattern intervention in which the counselor attempts to change the client's characteristic pattern by having the *counselor* respond in a new and more helpful way. In the pattern intervention, the *client* changes something about the way he or she interacts in a given situation with another person or group of persons.

In pattern intervention, the counselor looks for repetitive actions on the client's part in relationships with others that are observable enough to be modified in some way—something to the client's interpersonal pattern may be added, deleted, or in some way varied. Typically, modifications are made around three aspects of an interpersonal pattern: the behaviors, the situation or context, and the sequence of behaviors (Hudson & O'Hanlon, 1991). For example, suppose you are working with a teenaged girl whose presenting problem is that she has no friends. Upon exploring what patterns she uses in initiating and maintaining friendships, you describe that she has made a number of new friends in the past few years but that after several months, each friend has successively withdrawn from her, and all have told her the same thing—that she "bugs" them. When asking her what she thinks they mean by this, she rather openly states that she engages in a number of "smothering" behaviors once she makes a new friend. She follows her friends around at school, insists they eat lunch with her, and calls them frequently after school. Although she is supposedly trying to keep her friends close to her, her very actions are driving them away! In pattern interventions, you can work with helping this client modify her behaviors so that she gives her friends "space"—she requests having lunch with them only once in a while, not daily; she plans to call them perhaps once a week rather than several times a day; and so on. Of course, this is easier said than done—because with most teenagers, their primary motivation is to stay connected to their peers, no matter what!

In this example, you are helping the client modify the behaviors, the context, and the sequence of her behaviors that she engages in with her friends. Of course, it is also likely that aspects of this pattern will get reenacted with you, as well, so you will ultimately need to address the issue within your helping relationship as well as within her relationships with friends. The extent to which you do this, however, depends on the client's goals and the number of contacts or sessions that are available for working with her.

As with all of the other intervention strategies we have described in this chapter, there are also caveats to consider in working with clients' interpersonal patterns and systems. A noted Jungian therapist and author, James Hillman (1996), for example, argued that too much emphasis is placed on the role of parental influence, resulting in a reductive way in which counselors look at people. In his book, *The Soul's Code,* he has cited biographies of people who have had "bad" parenting and who, in response to some internal image or dream, have gone on to live productive and fulfilled lives.

The interventions associated with the systemic model have also been criticized by those who believe that these models are based on White, middle-class U.S. families, and, as a result, contain both covert gender and ethnicity bias (Hackney & Cormier, 1996; Enns, 1993; Stevenson & Renard, 1993). As an example of such difference, Berg and Jaya (1993, p. 32) observed that many middle-class White U.S. children seem to "fight" their way out of the family in order to individualize themselves, whereas for most Asian American children, being excluded from their family system is the worst imaginable consequence; "individuation" for these children is a foreign concept. Even the definition of what a "family system" is varies across cultural groups.

As a counselor, it is incumbent upon you to recognize the ways in which the values and patterns of your own interactional system may differ from your clients and to offer system interventions in a way that is syntonic with your clients' gender and culture. Toward this end, we recommend familiarizing yourself with the work of Boyd-Franklin (1989), Goldenberg and Goldenberg (1998), McGoldrick, Anderson, and Walsh (1989), and Midori Hanna and Brown (1995). (See also the recommended readings at the end of this chapter.) We also recommend consideration of some questions developed by Midori Hanna and Brown (1995) for implementing these strategies in gender and culturally sensitive ways (see Figure 10.1). In the following section of the chapter, we discuss interventions to use that more directly affect a client's environmental and cultural milieu—in other words, a client's social system.

Working with Client Social Systems

Almost all of the interventions we have presented in the preceding part of this chapter are drawn from counseling theories such as intrapersonal, self-in-relations, gestalt, rational-emotive, cognitive-behavioral, Ericksonian, and family systems. These theories have been developed by founding fathers and, as such, have been critiqued by multicultural theorists as reflecting an Eurocentric bias and value system and as being somewhat culturally irrelevant for clients who feel marginalized from the mainstream.

When issues of cultural salience such as race, gender, sexual orientation, and social class are considered, some of the more classic therapeutic interventions we have described may even be culturally contraindicated. According to Brown (1994), it is important to ask these questions in selecting a helping strategy:

1. Will this strategy oppress my client even more?
2. What does my strategy need to offer in working with a "multiply oppressed" client?

For those clients whose world views (i.e., basic perceptions and understanding of the world) do not reflect the "rugged individualism" of the Eurocentric tradition, other interventions that are more culturally appropriate are needed that address

FIGURE 10.1   Questions to Assess Gender, Racial, and Cultural Factors

1. Could role inflexibility regarding tasks be related to the problem?
2. Are communication styles disempowering to the females in the family?
3. Have generational coalitions developed as a result of disempowerment in the marriage?
4. Can disempowerment stereotypes ("nag," "passsive-aggressive") be relabeled to account for the context of powerlessness?
5. Can the female therapist model more egalitarian relationships with males in the family and can male therapists affirm female strength within the family?
6. What are family rules around females' personal development and autonomy outside the family?
7. What will each family member need from the therapist in order to feel understood and accepted?
8. How does your racial/cultural/religious heritage make your family different from other families you know?
9. Compared to other families in your cultural group, how is your family different?
10. What are the values that your family identified as being important parts of your heritage?
11. At this particular time in your (family's) development, are there issues related to your cultural heritage that are being questioned by anyone?
12. What is the hardest part about being a minority in this culture?
13. When you think of living in America versus the country of your heritage, what are the main differences?
14. What lesson did you learn about your people? About other peoples?
15. What did you learn about disloyalty?
16. What were people in your family really down on?
17. What might an outsider not understand about your racial/cultural/religious background?

Source: From *The Practice of Family Therapy: Key Elements across Models* by S. Hanna and J. H. Brown. Copyright © 1995 Brooks/Cole Publishing Company, Pacific Grove, CA 93950, a division of International Thomson Publishing Inc. By permission of the publisher.

group, community, and sociopolitical causes, as well as the individual causes the client presents. We describe five intervention strategies to work with, as suggested by the wonderful work of Lum (1996).* These are as follows:

> *Liberation* is the client's experience of release or freedom from oppressive barriers and control when change occurs. For some, it accompanies personal growth and decision-making: The client has decided no longer to submit to oppression. In other cases, liberation occurs under the influence of environmental change—for example, the introduction of a job-training program or the election of an ethnic mayor who makes policy, legislative, and program changes on behalf of people of color.

*From *Social Work Practice and People of Color: A Process-Stage Approach,* by Doman Lum. Copyright © 1996, 1992, 1986 Brooks/Cole Publishing Company, Pacific Grove, CA 93950, a division of International Thomson Publishing Inc. By permission of the publisher.

Empowerment is "a process whereby persons who belong to a stigmatized social category throughout their lives can be assisted to develop and increase skills in the exercise of interpersonal influence and the performance of valued social rules" (Solomon, 1976, p. 6). Claiming the human right to resources and well-being in society, individuals experience power by rising up and changing their situational predicament. The first step to empowerment is to obtain information about resources and rights. Then, choosing an appropriate path of action, the client participates in a situation in which his or her exercise of power confers palpable benefits. Practical avenues of empowerment include voting, influencing policy, or initiating legislation on the local level.

Parity relates to a sense of equality. For people of color, parity entails being of equal power, value, and rank with others in society and being treated accordingly. Its focal theme is fairness and the entitlement to certain rights. Parity is expressed in terms of resources that guarantee an adequate standard of living, such as entitlement programs (Social Security, Medicare), income maintenance, and medical care.

Maintenance of culture asserts the importance of the ideas, customs, skills, arts, and language of a people. By tracing the history of an ethnic group, worker and client can identify moments of crisis and challenge through which it survived and triumphed. Applying such lessons of history to the present inspires the client to overcome obstacles and provide a source of strength on which the client may draw. Maintenance of culture secures the client's identity as an ethnic individual.

Unique personhood is an intervention strategy by which stereotypes are transcended. Functional casework asserts the view that each person is unique in the helping relationship and that there is something extraordinary in each individual. When people of color act to gain freedom from social stereotypes, they assert their unique personhood and discover their humanity. (p. 115)

An important concept in using counseling strategies to effect change is that of *self-efficacy,* a cognitive process that mediates behavioral change (Bandura, 1989). When self-efficacy is high, clients feel a sense of personal agency, confidence, and empowerment. High self-efficacy not only influences feelings, beliefs, behaviors, and interactions, but also a person's biochemistry. Increasingly, self-efficacy is also being identified as a significant factor both in the use of prevention and risk programs and in the academic and career performance of diverse groups of clients (Cormier & Cormier, 1998). Self-efficacy seems to be an important factor in promoting change for female clients and for clients of color, especially when it is paired with some of the strategies proposed by Lum that focus on external social systems as well as an internal sense of confidence in oneself.

EXERCISE 10.1

Intervention Strategies

In this exercise, three hypothetical client cases are described. After reading over each case, describe what you believe the client's probable counseling goal would be and the related intervention strategies that could be used to help each client reach these goals. Consider goals and strategies for all of the five areas we discussed in this chapter: feelings, beliefs, behaviors, interactional patterns, and social systems. You may do this activity alone, with a partner, or in a small group discussion. You may wish to exchange your responses and ideas with other helpers or share your thoughts with your instructor.

A. Case 1

Asani is an Asian American at a large university; she is overwhelmed by the size of the university, having lived in a small town all her life. She is concerned about her shyness and feels it is preventing her from making friends. Asani reports being uncertain about how to reach out to people. She is also concerned about her performance on tests. Although she believes her study habits are adequate, she reports that she "blows" the tests because she gets so uptight about them. Asani believes her grades are a reflection of herself and her family. She is worried about bringing dishonor to her family if she gets low grades.

Probable Counseling Goals

1. _____

   _____

2. _____

   _____

3. _____

   _____

Possible Counseling Strategies

1. _____

   _____

   _____

2. _____

   _____

   _____

3. _____

   _____

   _____

B. Case 2

Mr. and Mrs. Yule have been married for seven years. Both are in their sixties, and this is their second marriage; their previous spouses died. Mr. and Mrs. Yule are concerned that they rushed into this second relationship without adequate thought. They report that they argue constantly about everything. They feel they have forgotten how to talk to each other in a civil manner. Mrs. Yule states that she realizes her constant nagging upsets Mr. Yule; Mr. Yule discloses that his spending a lot of time with his male buddies irritates Mrs. Yule.

Probable Counseling Goals

1. _____

_____

2. _____

_____

3. _____

_____

Possible Counseling Strategies

1. _____

_____

_____

_____

2. _____

_____

_____

_____

3. _____

_____

_____

_____

C. Case 3

Michael is a 13-year-old boy attending a middle school in an urban area. He is constantly starting fights and getting into trouble. He says he does not know how or why but suddenly he is punching other kids. Only after the fights does he realize his temper has gotten out of hand. He reports that he considers himself to be kind of "hot headed" and he likes that about himself. He reports spending a lot of time on the streets and he feels this greatly helps him survive. He says that although he is close to his mother, he rarely sees her, as she works two to three jobs to support the family. He has had no contact with his father since he was a young boy.

Probable Counseling Goals

1. _____
   _____

2. _____
   _____

3. _____
   _____

Possible Counseling Strategies

1. _____
   _____
   _____
   _____
   _____

2. _____
   _____
   _____
   _____
   _____

3. _____
   _____
   _____
   _____

Summary

In working with clients, all of whom present unique concerns and circumstances, you may find great use for the strategies described in this chapter. However, there are several cautions to consider in trying to use a counselor strategy effectively. The first caution in strategy implementation is to avoid oversimplification of the procedure. Although a procedure may seem relatively simple to implement, even with little experience, any therapeutic endeavor can be effective or ineffective, depending on how it is administered. Second, you must practice using strategies. You will not be an expert when you first start using them, but your skill will grow as you practice. Also remember that strategies are rarely used in isolation. Several different strategies or combinations of procedures may be necessary to deal with the complexity and range of concerns presented by a single client. As an example, suppose a counselor treats a client's alcoholism but ignores the anxiety for which alcohol is used as a tranquilizer. The strategies used to decrease the drinking behavior may not be too effective unless the counselor and client also use strategies to deal with the client's limited coping skills, self-defeating thoughts, and environmental issues that maintain the drinking.

Remember, too, that the effectiveness of counseling strategies depends, to some degree, on the strength and trust of the counseling relationship as well as the degree to which these strategies are used in a gender- and culture-friendly way. Responding to a client's social and environmental milieu is as important in strategy implementation as responding to a client's presenting feelings, beliefs, and behaviors.

Also, it is important to realize the limitations of counseling objectives and strategies and of counselors. One of the most frustrating experiences that counselors report is the experience of being thwarted in their attempts to help clients change and grow. Beginning counselors often approach the counseling process with a lot of zest, zeal, and unwavering idealism. Although a certain amount of this is useful, it can also lead to discouragement with oneself and with clients. Almost all clients will resist your attempts to help in some way. Some clients who see you at the request of someone else may be openly oppositional. Other clients may desire to change but because of biochemical imbalances may require medication for such things as depression or anxiety management. Clients with addictions may also find the process of recovery especially difficult. Clients from very dysfunctional family systems may find the weight of the system working against their own individual efforts to change. So, as you approach your growth and development and your own efforts in working with clients, it is important to remember that there are some limits to what happens in the counseling process and that almost all client resistance to change is about fear (Teyber, 1997). As clients become more able to trust themselves and you, your efforts and theirs will be rewarded.

DISCUSSION QUESTIONS

1. In this chapter, we discuss a variety of interventions to work with the *whole person* (e.g., the client's feelings, beliefs, behaviors, interactional patterns, and social systems). As you have read and worked with these interventions, which ones feel most natural and comfortable for you? Which ones do you believe you would have the most trouble with?

2. What places in your own body do you consistently hold in feelings? How do you become aware of these? What do you do to release them?

3. Can you identify situations for yourself in which your beliefs have affected the way you feel and act?

4. What persons have you used in your life for role models? What are their characteristics that appeal to you?

5. How do you apply self-management to everyday behaviors for yourself?

6. What is your characteristic interactional pattern? Can you trace it back to your family of origin? How do you think this pattern will affect the way you interact with your clients?

7. Refer to Figure 10.1 and, with a partner or in a small group, discuss these questions for yourself, your life, and your own history.

RECOMMENDED READINGS

Beck, J. S. (1995). *Cognitive therapy.* New York: Guilford.

Boyd-Franklin, N. (1989). *Black families in therapy: A multisystems approach.* New York: Guilford.

Brown, L. (1994). *Subversive dialogues: Theory in feminist therapy.* New York: Basic Books.

Cormier, S., & Cormier, B. (1998). *Interviewing strategies for helpers: Fundamental skills and cognitive-behavioral interventions* (4th ed.). Pacific Grove, CA: Brooks/Cole.

Corsini, R., & Wedding, D. (Eds.). (1995). *Current psychotherapies* (5th ed.). Itasca, IL: Peacock.

Enns, C. B. (1993). Twenty years of feminist counseling and therapy: From naming biases to implementing multifaceted practice. *The Counseling Psychologist, 21,* 3–87.

Gilligan, S. (1997). *The courage to love: Principles and practices of self-relations psychotherapy.* New York: Norton.

Goldenberg, H., & Goldenberg, I. (1998). *Counseling today's families* (3rd ed.). Pacific Grove, CA: Brooks/Cole.

Hays, P. A. (1995). Multicultural applications of cognitive-behavior therapy. *Professional Psychology, 26,* 309–315.

Hillman, J. (1996). *The soul's code: In search of character and calling.* New York: Random House.

Hudson, P. O., & O'Hanlon, W. H. (1991). *Rewriting love stories.* New York: Norton.

Kanfer, F. H., & Goldstein, A. P. (Eds.). (1991). *Helping people change* (4th ed.). New York: Pergamon.

Lum, D. (1996). *Social-work practice and people of color* (3rd ed.). Pacific Grove, CA: Brooks/Cole.

McGoldrick, M., Anderson, C., & Walsh, F. (Eds.). (1989). *Women and families: A framework for family therapy.* New York: Norton.

Midori Hanna, S., & Brown, J. (1995). *The practice of family therapy.* Pacific Grove, CA: Brooks/ Cole.

Smith, E. (1992). *The body in psychotherapy.* Jefferson, NC: McFarland.

Teyber, E. (1997). *Interpersonal processes in psychotherapy* (3rd ed.). Pacific Grove, CA: Brooks/Cole.

Watson, D. L., & Tharp, R. G. (1997). *Self-directed behavior: Self-modification for personal adjustment* (7th ed.). Pacific Grove, CA: Brooks/Cole.

Wolpe, J. (1990). *The practice of behavior therapy* (4th ed.). New York: Pergamon.

11 Receiving and Using Supervision

BY JANINE M. BERNARD

Thus far, this book has focused on the many facets of the relationship between the counselor and client and has outlined numerous ways to enhance that relationship. At this point, we will discuss another essential relationship in the process of helping—the relationship between the supervisor and the counselor. Our discussion cannot be all-inclusive because the supervision relationship has as many potential facets as the counseling relationship. Rather, this final chapter will provide a sketch of supervision parameters from the perspective of the consumer of supervision, with the hope that it will help you use supervision more quickly and more fully.

The Parameters of Supervision

In order to understand supervision, one must consider what happens in supervision, who provides the supervision, and in what context supervision occurs. It makes sense to start with a definition. Clinical supervision is

> an intervention that is provided by a senior member of a profession to a junior member or members of that same profession. This relationship is evaluative, extends over time, and has the simultaneous purposes of enhancing the professional functioning of the junior member(s), monitoring the quality of professional services offered to the clients she, he, or they see(s), and serving as a gatekeeper for those who are to enter the particular profession. (Bernard & Goodyear, 1998, p. 6)

We will now examine this definition more closely by looking at its parts:

1. *Supervision is an intervention.* Clinical supervision is different from counseling and teaching, though it is related to both. There are competencies and skills

Note: This chapter was written for this book by Janine M. Bernard, Ph.D., NCC, Professor of Counselor Education at Fairfield University, Fairfield, CT.

involved in supervision that allow the supervisor to help the supervisee* gain competence and insight into the dynamics of counseling. Supervision does not just happen—it is planned.

2. *Supervision is provided by a more advanced practitioner and involves evaluation.* A clinical supervisor is more advanced than the supervisee, at least on some important variables. At the same time, however, it is not always necessary that the supervisor be a highly seasoned counselor. Sometimes, a counselor who is developmentally only a couple of steps ahead of the supervisee can offer excellent feedback and direction. The important thing is that the supervisor be more advanced in the skill areas in which the supervisee needs help. Supervision also has an evaluative aspect. It is conducted, in part, to evaluate the counselor. This *summative evaluation* will occur after there has been enough supervision to expect a certain degree of competence. However, throughout the supervision experience, there is an evaluative component. When the supervisor suggests that a counselor go in a different direction with a client, that supervisor is making a judgment regarding what has transpired during counseling up to this point. This is called *formative evaluation* and is an intrinsic part of supervision. As will be seen later in this chapter, much of the difficulty within supervision centers on the evaluative role of the supervisor.

3. *Supervision extends over time.* An important aspect of supervision is establishing some clarity regarding the supervision contract. In other words, the relationship between counselor and supervisor will be different depending on how long the two will be working together and under what conditions. An assumption of supervision, however, is that the supervision relationship will last long enough to allow for some developmental progress for the supervisee. This is important because supervision includes an assumption that counseling competency shows itself in different ways, with different clients, and in different contexts over time. For example, a supervisor cannot assume after observing one counseling session that he or she knows the competence of the counselor. The supervisor might be able to evaluate the *counseling* that occurred after one session, but he or she cannot evaluate the competence of the *counselor*, at least not in any comprehensive way.

4. *The supervisor monitors and serves as a gatekeeper.* While conducting supervision, the supervisor is always aware that the supervisee represents only one level of the supervisor's responsibility. Ethically and legally, the supervisor also must monitor the quality of the counseling that is being delivered to the supervisee's clients. Judgments are always being made regarding the learning goals of the counselor in relationship to the counseling needs of the client(s). Beyond serving the counselor's immediate clients, the supervisor also serves as a gatekeeper for those who want to enter the counseling profession. In doing so, the supervisor accepts some responsibility for potential future clients as well as present ones.

---

*The terms *supervisee, trainee,* and *counselor* will be used interchangeably in this chapter.

Responsibilities of Supervisors and Supervisees

You and your supervisor have certain responsibilities to each other. These responsibilities include having formally scheduled contacts with one another on a regular basis, as well as access to supervision on an as-needed basis for crises or emergencies. Another responsibility involves providing each other with information about your cases, especially the management of difficult and problematic cases. You and your supervisor are ethically obligated to safeguard the communication of your clients in a confidential manner. Additionally, your supervisor is required to track your work with clients, monitor the quality of it, and provide you with regular and periodic feedback, including suggestions for improvement. Your supervisor also is ethically bound to restrict his or her relationship with you to just supervision. In other words, during the time you are being supervised, you do not have another kind of relationship with your supervisor that could compromise supervision. If a supervisor is also your close friend or counselor, this is what is referred to as a *dual relationship*, which is considered unethical by the American Counseling Association Code of Ethics (1995a).

The parameters of supervision go beyond the basic elements described in the definition of supervision. For example, who can be a supervisor and in what context does supervision occur? One answer to the first of these questions is that anyone who engages in supervision is a supervisor (assuming that the supervisor meets the criteria addressed in the definition of supervision). More specifically, a clinical supervisor can be a prepracticum or a practicum instructor, a doctoral student working with graduate student trainees, or a supervisor in a field setting who works with trainees as part of their graduate internship. Once a counselor has completed graduate training, the employer, supervisor, or senior counselor in an agency, school, or other work setting may be the clinical supervisor. More and more, however, a clinical supervisor is being asked to meet certain training criteria in the practice of supervision prior to assuming the role of supervisor (Borders, Bernard, Dye, Fong, Henderson, & Nance, 1991). This has occurred as the supervision training literature has become more sophisticated.

Beyond level of experience and training in supervision, it should be noted that part of becoming a supervisor involves a *decision* to supervise. In graduate training, this decision is implicit, if not explicit, in the structure of the training program. The practicum instructor has made a decision to supervise by teaching the course. Therefore, the counselor need not be concerned about whether supervision will occur. Later on, however, as counselors enter their first professional positions, supervision may or may not be forthcoming. In such a situation, it is often up to the counselor to request supervision.

Another important distinction is that between clinical supervision and administrative supervision. Your employer in a mental health center, for example, is your administrative supervisor, since this person has the power to hire and/or fire you, to increase your salary, to determine your job description, and so forth. However, this person is not automatically a clinical supervisor. A clinical supervisor must be working with you in some manner to improve your counseling ability.

Finally, *context* refers to more than the work or training setting in which supervision occurs; it refers also to larger social and political contexts. Your supervisor must share some values with you in order to be an effective supervisor. He or she must also help you appreciate that both counseling and supervision relationships are determined, in part, by the parameters reflected in a diverse society. Addressing these issues is an essential part of appreciating context within supervision (Leong, 1994).

The Focus of Supervision

What is your supervisor looking for? For beginning counselors or counselors who are working with a new supervisor, this is a common and legitimate question. In fact, *role ambiguity* (i.e., not knowing what is expected of you) has been documented as a common issue for novice counselors (Olk & Friedlander, 1992).

This section will describe the four major areas that supervisors focus on when evaluating counselor performance. Understanding the differences among these categories will help you not only to know what your supervisor will be looking for in your counseling but also to hear your supervisor's feedback with a more discriminating ear.

The four areas will be described as *skills* to imply that all four categories represent groups of behaviors that can be learned (to differing degrees for different people) and that can be refined. The four areas or categories are (1) intervention skills, (2) conceptualization skills, (3) personalization skills, and (4) professional skills (Bernard, 1979, 1997; Lanning, 1986).

Intervention Skills

Intervention skills are those overt behaviors that distinguish counseling from other social interactions. They are what you *do* in your sessions. Intervention skills include all *observable* counselor behaviors; therefore, the other three categories must often be inferred from the counselor's intervention skills. Greeting the client, requesting information, reflecting what you hear, confronting what seems to be a contradiction, structuring a roleplay, supporting a client in distress—all are intervention skills. Intervention skills range from simple (restatement) to sophisticated (paradoxical intervention), depending on the abilities of the counselor.

When a supervisor is focusing on a counselor's intervention skills, the feedback will sound something like this:

"I thought your initial question was a good one."

"You used a lot of questions in your session. I wonder if you could increase your use of reflections."

"Would you be willing to try a roleplay with the client?"

"Your nonverbal behavior communicated a lot of caring for the client."

Conceptualization Skills

As the term implies, *conceptualization skills* are thinking skills. Much of the covert activity of the counselor falls into this category. Conceptualization skills include identifying the major concern of the client, recognizing dominant themes in a counseling session, planning for future sessions, and choosing a particular helping response (or technique) with a certain goal in mind. Using a reflection of feeling in a counseling session is a process skill; choosing which client message to reflect is a conceptualization skill. Without adequate conceptualization skills, intervention skills are relatively useless because the counselor's responses, even if well executed, would be random or unrelated to what was happening in the session. Purposeful counseling occurs when the counselor conceptualizes accurately.

Supervisory statements that have as their focus the conceptualization skills of the counselor are as follows:

"When you asked about her mother, what were you looking for?"
"I thought you picked up all of the major themes in the session."
"Where are you going from here with this client?"
"Do you think your approach was sensitive to her cultural background?"
"Did that homework assignment accomplish what you hoped it would?"

Notice that four of the five examples of supervisor feedback were in the form of questions. This will often be the case for conceptualization skills and, similarly, for personalization skills. The supervisor can only infer what the counselor had in mind based on the intervention skills observed. In fact, the supervisor may not know where the counselor's skill deficit lies until such questions are answered. For example, the counselor may have asked a question when a reflection would have been far more helpful. But before the supervisor can be of help to the counselor, it must be determined whether the counselor (1) did not know how to phrase a helpful reflection (intervention skill deficit) or (2) did not know that a reflection was called for (conceptualization skill deficit).

Personalization Skills

The term *personalization skill* was originated to suggest that the counselor uses personal attributes, for better or for worse, in the therapeutic relationship (Bernard, 1979, 1997). The existence of such a category is an acknowledgment that counseling is indeed a very personal activity, and that it is impossible to separate your personal attributes and liabilities from your work entirely. Personalization also refers to the degree to which you have adapted to the role of helper. Therefore, personalization skills would include being comfortable with the professional responsibility of being a counselor, being able to separate your reactions to an issue from those of the client, allowing your sense of humor to emerge, not being defensive with an accusing client, being able to handle a range of emotions in yourself or when presented by the client, and being able to accept constructive criticism from your supervisor.

Possible supervisory comments that would address personalization skills are as follows:

> "You were able to keep your composure, even when the client became agitated. That's good."

> "It seemed to me that you almost apologized when giving the client a homework assignment, as if you didn't want to waste her time. That communicated a lack of confidence on your part. Is that how you felt?"

> "When your client stated his opinions about working women with small children, I thought you stepped out of your counselor role and started arguing with him. I wondered if he was baiting you and if you took the bait."

> "You're awfully quiet whenever I give you my feedback about your last counseling session. I've been wondering what that means."

Professional Skills

Professional skills have as much to do with performance outside the counseling relationship as within (Lanning, 1986). Perhaps these skills are less noticeable in initial training experiences and more evident in later experiences. They can overlap with personalization skills (e.g., being late for a counseling appointment because you are intimidated by the client) but remain a discreet category in and of themselves. These skills include turning in written reports on time, safeguarding confidentiality, behaving professionally in field placement, using others' professional titles when appropriate, dressing appropriately for counseling contacts, and related behaviors.

As you will note, some of the items listed here seem far more important than others. Safeguarding confidentiality is much more critical than not wearing jeans to see clients. On the other hand, what appears frivolous to some people may be very important to a client.

Cultural differences also play a part here; environment will carry meaning for clients, just as words do. If you remember that clients may be in an extremely vulnerable position in asking for help, you might be more receptive to the idea that the context within which that help is offered is intrinsically related to the help itself. For example, picture a client entering a counseling center to find three or four staff members laughing raucously. Assuming that the client is feeling somewhat ambivalent about seeking counseling, many negative thoughts could be stimulated by such a scene ("They're laughing about the client who just left"). Now assume that the counselor seeing this client is one of those jovial staff members. It is very unlikely that the counseling session that follows will be unrelated to the professional context that was presented to the client when he or she arrived.

Examples of supervisor comments that address professional skills are as follows:

"This might sound picky, but I don't think you should chew gum while you are counseling this client."

"I was pleased with how you handled the referral to the Family Counseling Center. Everything was in order."

"The last report you turned in had some grammatical errors and the use of slang. I've noted them on the report and would like you to rewrite it."

"What are you going to do if Elisabeth's teacher asks you about the content of your counseling with Elisabeth?"

Discriminating among Categories

Keeping the four categories in mind, it is important to realize that all four are present all the time in your work as a counselor. For example, as you begin a session with a new client, you will need intervention skills to proceed adequately; you will have thought about how you want the session to progress; you will be choosing your personal responses carefully; and you will be trying to present a professional appearance. Because all four areas are operating at all times, your supervisor is making some assumptions when choosing to focus on one category rather than the other three when giving you feedback. Perhaps an example will help make this point clearer.

In a supervision workshop conducted by the author, a videotape of a counseling session was shown in which the client teared up as she discussed a sensitive topic. When that happened, the counselor became very quiet and asked just one question for clarification. After the tape was viewed, a group of professional supervisors was asked to write down comments they would want to make to the counselor. Two of the supervisors focused on this particular segment of tape, but approached it from different angles. One said, "I wanted the counselor to say something to the client, to comfort her in some way." The other remarked, "I thought the counselor was threatened by the client's show of emotion. I would want to discuss this with her."

The first supervisor approached the issue as an intervention skill deficit (the counselor needed to do something that she did not do), and the second supervisor approached it as a personalization skill deficit (emotion may threaten this counselor). As you can see, the assumptions that were being made about the counselor were very different for the two supervisors.

In the situation just described, neither supervisor knew the counselor. It could make a big difference how a supervisor evaluates counseling behavior by knowing the counselor's strengths and weaknesses. On the other hand, supervisors have their own predispositions when observing counseling sessions; some are more likely to see events in intervention terms, whereas others are more likely to see them in conceptual terms. It is important for you to have some idea of the choices available to supervisors so that you can more fully appreciate the assumptions that go with those choices.

EXERCISE 11.1

The Focus of Supervision

For your own part, you can begin to determine the focus of your counseling sessions by asking four simple questions:

1. Did I know what to do in the session?
2. Did I know what I wanted to do?
3. Was I comfortable at that point?
4. Was my performance that of a professional counselor?

You can do this with roleplays or tapes of sessions.

Styles of Supervision

Now that you have a better idea of what supervisors look for in training and supervising counselors, we will discuss the choices supervisors make about their own behavior. As you will soon discover, if you have not already, different supervisors have different styles. Sometimes their style makes you feel confident and supported, and sometimes their style has a less positive effect on you (Berger & Buchholz, 1993). At least some of this has to do with the role they choose as they work with you (Bernard, 1979, 1997). By describing the different supervisory roles and their purposes, perhaps we can help you further understand the supervision process and its potential outcomes. Perhaps we can also encourage dialogue between you and your supervisor if the role being used in your supervision is giving you problems.

The Role of Teacher

The most common role for supervisors during the initial training of counselors is the *teacher role*. (For purposes of clarification, we shall use the word *instructor* to mean the person responsible for teaching a particular course, leaving the word *teacher* to mean a particular role or style the instructor may or may not wish to assume.) When in the teacher role, the supervisor takes responsibility for knowing what the counselor needs to do or learn. Therefore, the supervisor might instruct the counselor about a new technique, model a new intervention, or make other direct suggestions regarding the counselor's work. When the supervisor acknowledges the rightness or wrongness of a particular counselor strategy, the teacher role is being used. When a supervisor is in the teacher role, there is no question who is in charge.

Of the supervisor responses listed in the last section, several were in the teacher role. "Your nonverbal behavior communicated a lot of caring for the client" is an example of a supervisor in this role. The supervisor is taking full responsibility for knowing what is appropriate or inappropriate nonverbal behavior. Most instructional comments and evaluative comments are teacher comments.

The Role of Counselor

When supervisors focus on the interpersonal or intrapersonal dynamics of their counselors or trainees, they are most likely in the *counselor role*. The goal of the supervisor in this role is most often the personal growth of the counselor. Historically, this role has been widely used by supervisors, based on the assumption that the most legitimate way for counselors to grow professionally is to grow personally. Although the last two decades have offered differing opinions of this premise, there are times when the counselor role is the necessary and most desirable option for the supervisor to use. Furthermore, later in your career, supervisors are more likely to rely on the counselor role to stimulate your growth (Skovholt & Ronnestad, 1992). (It is important, however, for the supervisor to be careful to avoid a dual relationship and to suggest a referral to someone else if extensive counseling for personal issues is needed.)

Referring again to the supervisor statements listed earlier, the following is an example of a supervisor in the counselor role: "You're awfully quiet whenever I give you my feedback about your last counseling session. I've been wondering what that means." Another statement combined both teacher and counselor roles. See if you can identify the two roles in this comment: "It seemed to me that you almost apologized when giving your client a homework assignment, as if you didn't want to waste her time. That communicated a lack of confidence on your part. Is that how you felt?"

The Role of Consultant

When the goal of the supervisor is to encourage trainees to think on their own and to trust their own insights, the *consultant role* is most appropriate. When in this role, supervisors limit themselves to being a resource for their trainees. The authority for what will transpire in the supervisee's counseling is more equally shared. As a result, the consultant role conveys a degree of mutual trust and professional respect not necessarily found in the other two roles. On the other hand, respect is based on the expectation that the counselor can and will put forth the effort to use this role suitably.

A consultant comment from the preceding section is: "Did that homework assignment accomplish what you hoped it would?" This is a consultant response because the supervisor is not telling the counselor that the assignment did or did not succeed. However, if the counselor answers "Yes," and the supervisor responds, "Well, I don't agree," then the supervisor has very quickly changed from a consultant role to a teacher role.

The Need for Different Roles

One well-documented model of supervision is the *developmental model,* which describes counselor growth as advancing through sequential skill levels (Borders, 1986; McNeil, Stoltenberg, & Pierce, 1985; Stoltenberg & Delworth, 1987; Worthington, 1987). Depending on the developmental level of the counselor, different supervisor roles may be warranted.

Research indicates that trainees prefer their supervisors to be in the teacher role initially (e.g., Bear & Kivlighan, 1994; Rabinowitz, Heppner, & Roehlke, 1986; Stoltenberg, Pierce, & McNeil, 1987; Winter & Holloway, 1991). This is because novice counselors tend to be unsure of themselves, and the teacher role gives the structure and sense of security that they need at first. After they have received considerable training, they are more likely to prefer a consultant approach. When the supervisor is in this role, it allows the counselors to stretch their wings and use their supervisor primarily as a resource. Throughout training and beyond, the counselor role may be needed (if not welcome) because trainees occasionally hit personal snags that block their therapeutic efforts.

Supervisors' roles can be deliberate or the result of personal preference or habit. Some supervisors are natural teachers and have a difficult time altering their style, even when the situation calls for it. Other supervisors keep their identity as counselors foremost in their work and approach their trainees as they would approach their clients. Finally, some supervisors like to give all trainees the opportunity to go at their own pace and thus prefer the consultant role. Frequently, the use of role involves a trial-and-error process. If the consultant role does not work with one trainee, then the teacher role is tried, whether or not the supervisor is aware of this change.

In the example given at the end of the previous section, the supervisor switched from consultant to teacher when the consultant role did not produce the desired response. (The supervisor obviously wanted the trainee to say that the homework did not accomplish what had been hoped.) This was not a good use of the consultant role because the supervisor was not willing to go along with the trainee's judgment. A direct teacher statement, "I don't think the homework assignment worked as you had hoped," would have been better in the long run.

You might be asking, What if I don't like my supervisor's style? What can I do about it? First of all, you might determine if you encourage a certain role behavior. For example, if you approach supervision by asking a lot of questions, you are inviting your supervisor to assume the teacher role. If you try to convince your supervisor that you felt very anxious in your last session, you are (perhaps inadvertently) requesting the counselor role. When you make definitive statements about your work, you are encouraging a consultant role from your supervisor.

Second, if you believe that the problem is not in your approach but due to your supervisor's preference, you can ask if another role might be tried for a while. Again, knowing about the supervision process allows you to influence it. You might want to have your supervisor in the consultant role rather than the teacher or counselor role. One trainee approached her supervisor with this request. Her supervisor's reaction was, "I think that's a good idea. I agree that I've been too active in supervision. On the other hand, if it's going to work, I think you need to come to supervision more prepared. Perhaps you could review your tapes [audiotapes of counseling sessions] ahead of time and be prepared to identify segments that gave you difficulty and give your opinion of what went wrong." The trainee found this a reasonable plan. You might have noticed that the supervisor was *teaching* the counselor how to use him as a *consultant*. This kind of transition is often needed when a change of supervision role is to occur.

As a final note, we would like to mention that many, if not most, supervisors use all three styles in their work. It is not necessary that you be able to track your supervisor's style at all times. Rather, the issue of supervision role becomes relevant when you are trying to pinpoint why you are feeling stressed under supervision or why you do not think you are progressing as quickly as you would like. The supervisor's role may or may not be the problem, but it is one more important piece of the puzzle for you to consider.

Methods of Supervision

Now that we have discussed the different focal points in supervision and the different roles a supervisor can assume, we will comment on the methods available to supervisors to conduct supervision. This section describes several distinct ways that supervisors gain access to the trainee's counseling for the purpose of supervision.

Self-Report

Until the introduction of technology into most counselor training programs, the most frequent form of supervision was for the counselor to report to the supervisor, either in writing or verbally, what was transpiring in counseling, and for the supervisor to react to this information as presented. This method of supervision is called *self-report* because the counselor is in control of what he or she chooses to report about the counseling session or counseling relationship. Self-reporting is still used in supervision, though not as frequently as it once was and not as often in the initial stages of counselor training (prepracticum and practicum). When self-reporting is used, the focus is generally on conceptualization and personalization skills. A major disadvantage of self-reporting, and the reason for its decline in popularity, is that it does not allow the supervisor to help the counselor work on blind spots, as can be done when using more direct forms of supervision. Also, evidence shows that the recall rate of even seasoned psychotherapists when asked to report the principal themes of a counseling session is less than 50 percent (Wynne, Susman, Ries, Birringer, & Katz, 1994). Those supervisors who prefer self-report generally adhere theoretically to the assumption that the most salient aspect of supervision is the relationship between the supervisor and supervisee.

Audiotape, Videotape, and Live Observation

The use of audiotape, videotape, and live observation are combined here because they all involve a similar supervision approach—that of observing a trainee's counseling, followed by a supervision session based on what was heard and seen. Most training programs prefer this form of supervision, at least for the earlier stages of counselor training, and have some facility or laboratory for this purpose. The advantage of direct (live observation) or indirect (audiotape or videotape) observation is that it allows the supervisor to address the intervention skills that were apparent in the observed session. In addition, this method of supervision allows supervisors to compare their perceptions of what transpired in counseling with those of their counselors when the case is subsequently discussed.

Although technology can be a great aid to the supervision process, its advantages are akin to its disadvantages. For example, videotape is literally as clear as a picture, but this level of stark feedback can be either revealing or embarrassing to the supervisee. Audiotape is also a tremendous asset to learning, but when tapes are reviewed in a pro forma manner in the supervision session, the exercise can be fruitless. Therefore, there are two rules of thumb that are good for supervisors and supervisees to consider in using technology in supervision:

1. The vulnerability of the supervisee must be considered a part of the formula when audiotape, videotape, or live observation is used for the purpose of supervision. This does not mean that the supervisor should walk on eggshells, but it does mean that a certain level of trust and goodwill must be communicated to counter this vulnerability.
2. Case conferences using technology must be carefully planned, with taped segments carefully preselected either by the counselor or by the supervisor and with specific training goals in mind (Bernard & Goodyear, 1998; Goldberg, 1985; West, Bubenzer, Pinsoneault, & Holeman, 1993).

Live Supervision

Live supervision is different from live observation in that the former includes the active participation of the supervisor during counseling. Because live supervision is in some ways a team approach to counseling, it is typically reserved for advanced trainees. When using live supervision, the supervisor observes the session behind a one-way mirror and interrupts the session to give the counselor a suggestion. There are several ways to structure this type of supervision: (1) supervisors can phone in their suggestions using a closed-circuit phone intercommunication system; (2) supervisors can call the counselor out of the counseling room to discuss the progress of the session; (3) there can be a prearranged time (e.g., 20 minutes into the session) when the counselor will leave to discuss the session with the supervisor; or (4) the counselor can wear a small hearing device in the ear (referred to as a "bug in the ear") so the supervisor can make comments without interrupting the session (Bubenzer, Mahrle, & West, 1987).

Although this method of supervision has been criticized as interfering with the counselor-client relationship, it offers some distinct advantages. Because the supervisor is working closely with the counselor, difficult cases can be assigned to the trainee more quickly because, in effect, the trainee is not "alone" in the counseling room. In addition, the supervisor can redirect a session that is going poorly, rather than wait until later to give the counselor remedial feedback. As a result, there is more opportunity for success from the trainee's standpoint. To date, those supervisors and counselors using live supervision have found it to be a very satisfactory method of training and of accomplishing the goals of supervision.

Simulation

Not all supervision involves actual clients. Especially in the earlier phases of training, trainees may be asked to roleplay different counseling situations in order to gain some experience prior to taking on the responsibility of seeing actual clients. When simulating, trainees are asked either to share a real concern (although they are usually advised to share only issues that would be appropriate to reveal in a nonconfidential setting), or are given a role to play with which they may or may not have had any life experience. Simulation can be used in conjunction with any of the methods of supervision described earlier.

Individual versus Group Supervision

Supervision can occur individually (one supervisor with one counselor) or in a group of counselors. Typically, the trainee will receive some of both forms during a counselor education program. In individual supervision, the focus will be on the trainee exclusively, with the supervisor offering his or her expertise in ways that will benefit the individual trainee. Individual supervision is person centered. In a group, trainees usually take turns presenting one of their cases, and the group then discusses it. There is potentially more opportunity for different instructional techniques with group supervision, including roleplays (with feedback from the observers) for the purpose of practicing different approaches. Group supervision also allows the advantages of permitting trainees to learn from the cases of their peers, as well as their own cases. Therefore, while individual supervision is more focused and more efficient for a particular trainee, group supervision holds the possibility of vicarious learning and a more efficient use of the supervisor's time.

Avoiding Supervision

As we stated in the beginning of this chapter, supervision is evaluative in nature. Counseling is a very personal activity, and feedback about your counseling can be taken very personally, leaving you feeling highly anxious and threatened by the prospect of receiving supervision. It can be difficult to separate your value as a person from your success as a helper when your motivation to help is strong.

Therefore, we will address the issue of avoiding supervision. Most counselors who avoid supervision do so psychologically, not physically, though there are counselors who avoid supervision by missing or coming late to their supervision sessions.

Bauman (1972), in what now is considered a classic article, pointed out that counselors can play games to avoid dealing with their skill issues. He outlined some of the postures presented by supervisees that, in effect, help them to avoid supervision. Bauman's list of five "games" is as relevant today as it was when it was published, and includes such strategies as submission, turning the tables, "I'm no good," helplessness, and projection.

Submission

In the *submission* game, trainees yield immediately to the superior knowledge of the supervisor. Discussion is not warranted because the trainee begs out as a result of obvious inferior judgment. He or she accepts all feedback unquestioningly—almost, it seems, before hearing it. Under such conditions, the trainee communicates complete malleability and unaccountability.

Turning the Tables

We alluded to the game of *turning the tables* earlier when we discussed the counselor who solicits the teacher role from the supervisor through extensive questioning. The trainee approaches supervision with an infinite list of questions to solicit advice from the supervisor. The trainee, therefore, is in control of the supervision session and keeps the supervisor at arm's length.

"I'm No Good"

The game of *"I'm no good"* is more active than the submission strategy. Here, the trainee must convince the supervisor that he or she is on the verge of becoming a counselor casualty. The trainee magnifies counseling mistakes, placing the supervisor in the role of diminishing those self-deprecating remarks and assuring the trainee that there is hope. One possible consequence of this game is to invite the supervisor into a counselor role.

Helplessness

Yet another variation on the same theme, *helplessness* is a stance protesting lack of experience as a reason for the supervisor to take full responsibility for the direction of the trainee's counseling. The trainee's energy seems to be directed at convincing the supervisor that the case is too unique, too advanced, too vulnerable to legal ramifications, and so on, for the trainee to take primary responsibility.

Projection

Finally, a frequently used avoidance posture is to project the mistakes one has made in counseling onto the supervision process itself. The most salient example of *projection* is when the trainee protests that sessions that are observed by the supervisor are far more stilted and self-conscious than sessions that occur in the absence of the supervisor (or when the tape recorder is turned off). The message is that, for whatever reason, the supervisor never really sees the trainee's highly developed (or even adequate) counseling skills.

Liddle (1986) has asserted that trainee resistance stems from an attempt to avoid a perceived threat. She lists five possible sources of threat in supervision: (1) evaluation anxiety; (2) performance anxiety (living up to one's own standards of performance); (3) personal issues within the supervisee (such as having unresolved feelings about death when counseling a client who is mourning the loss of a loved one); (4) deficits in the supervisory relationship; and (5) anticipated consequences (resisting the learning of how to confront out of fear of client anger).

Does knowing about resistance help to avoid it? How do you overcome those things that threaten you in supervision? First of all, it is essential that you realize and accept that some anxiety in supervision is unavoidable (Yager, Witham, Williams, & Scheufler, 1981). It could even be said that feeling no anxiety is in itself a form of avoidance. Second, you must try to identify the sources of your anxiety if you are to resolve them. If you feel yourself avoiding supervision, you might discuss this with your supervisor. If that seems too threatening, you could find a peer you trust to help you uncover the motives or fears underlying your resistance. Finally, trainees need to find productive ways to handle their resistance rather than succumbing to a psychological avoidance of supervision. For example, pairing some of the ideas presented earlier, say that you are playing helpless with your supervisor out of a fear that learning to confront will cause client anger. Continuing to be helpless is inappropriate. However, it is highly appropriate to acknowledge your fear to your supervisor. Once you and your supervisor are dealing with the real issue, there are innumerable ways to conquer your fears. The point is to acknowledge that those fears are a normal and legitimate part of supervision (Liddle, 1986) and that avoiding them is counterproductive.

Putting Your Development
as a Counselor in Perspective

Although most counselors manage to resist the urge to sabotage their supervisors, why is it that this is a chronic temptation, especially early in training? Why are the fears so poignant at this juncture? At least one answer lies in an understanding of the development of the professional counselor.

A common frustration among novice trainees is that they feel they are getting worse, not better, during the initial phases of training. What once came naturally to them (i.e., being helpful to others) now seems a monumental challenge that causes humiliation and even shame. It can be very helpful to understand the development of counseling expertise to assuage some of this frustration. In their well-regarded book, Skovholt and Ronnestad (1992) described the eight stages of professional development for counselors from pretraining to retirement. The transition from stage one to stage two is most relevant to our discussion here.

In stage one, the future counselor is in the *conventional* stage—the stage of being a natural helper in his or her world. It is in this stage that you determine that counseling might be a good profession for you, from a combination of self-evaluation and feedback from friends and family. The next stage, called the *transition to professional training,* upsets the balance that you had as a natural helper. Where you once had confidence that you had some innate ability to be of help to others, you now feel enthused but insecure. Where you once relied on what you already knew and your common sense, now you are overwhelmed with new concepts that seem to be coming from several different sources. Feeling overwhelmed is included by Skovholt and Ronnestad as one of the major reactions to this stage. There are five more stages to follow, none as fraught with insecurity as this one. That's the good news. The bad news is that there is no way to get to these more advanced stages without working through this stage and its challenges. It also should be noted, however, that the transition stage includes the acquisition of knowledge and personal introspection that delights most students and serves to balance their discomfort. The point is that your first supervisory experiences may feel the most uncomfortable for developmental reasons alone. Once you have some experience (and some success!) under your belt, supervision should become safer and more rewarding.

Preparing for Supervision

The emphases on resisting an urge to avoid supervision and understanding the limits of your professional developmental stage might start to imply an adherence to Woody Allen's dictum that 90 percent of life is showing up! There is, however, more to your role in supervision than showing up.

Goodyear, Brinley, and Kivlighan (1997) studied the perceptions of both supervisors and relatively seasoned supervisees regarding the behaviors that characterized desired supervisee behavior. There was considerable agreement between supervisors and supervisees. Many of the behaviors that emerged were related to preparing for supervision, both in what one does between supervision sessions and how one communicates during supervision.

For example, the respondents felt that it was important for supervisees to arrive for supervision with samples of their counseling (e.g., audiotapes) that had already been reviewed and with questions based on those reviews. They felt that supervisees should be prepared to offer a summary of their work with each client as well as conceptualizations of each client, to have paperwork completed carefully, and to be able to articulate what he or she needed from supervision. Besides

these types of behaviors that displayed an investment in supervision, the participants of this study also mentioned several behaviors that communicated trust in
the supervisor and willingness to take risks. For example, it was perceived as
highly valuable if supervisees were willing to share personal biases that might
have an impact on their work with clients, feelings that might be aroused during
supervision, and fears and self-doubts that might affect their work. Additionally,
it was viewed as essential that the supervisees sought out the supervisor in unique
situations, including all crises and emergencies. Being prepared, therefore, seems
to translate into doing some *focused work* between supervision sessions, having an
openness during supervision that will allow you to explore your own issues and to
hear the feedback the supervisor is giving you, and *recognizing* when additional
supervision is required.

EXERCISE 11.2

Preparing for Supervision

In a small group, make a list of ways you can prepare for supervision. In a similar fashion, make a list of ways you can increase the likelihood of using the
supervision you receive in subsequent counseling sessions.

Using Supervision

Some of the results of the Goodyear, Brinley, and Kivlighan (1997) survey were
focused on using supervision. Obviously, supervision is not successful if it does not
result in direction for the supervisee. Therefore, the final category of supervisee
behaviors that were viewed as valuable have to do with a willingness to *act on* the
suggestions provided by your supervisor.

All things being equal, translating supervision to direction for the counselor
is a shared responsibility between the supervisor and the trainee. That is, the
supervisor should conduct the session so that it is clear how you are to implement
his or her suggestions. If, however, this is not clear, you should ask for clarification
before you are expected to perform again. This will avoid a common complaint
made by supervisors that certain trainees are enjoyable to work with, but they do
not seem to follow through on supervisory suggestions.

Even if it is clear how you are to use a supervisory suggestion, it is wise to
give yourself some time to review what was gleaned from supervision before your
next counseling session. What seems perfectly clear in a discussion with your
supervisor may become muddled or somehow out of reach during the counseling
session if you have not integrated the concepts into your own frame of reference
prior to the session. This failure to integrate is a common mistake made by train-

ees—one that causes them unnecessary feelings of discouragement and embarrassment. The key to maximizing supervision is to invest additional energy between supervision and subsequent counseling sessions. This will help you avoid having to expend energy after the session to recover from disappointment of lack of success.

Summary

Several components of supervision have been addressed. Clinical supervision exists, however, only when all these segments operate in union. Regardless of focus, role, or method, supervision is most often described as the most rewarding part of a counselor's training. Likewise, supervisors report a high degree of satisfaction in their work with supervisees. Both parties are reflecting the distinct pleasure of passing on and safeguarding the profession of counseling.

DISCUSSION QUESTIONS

1. Everyone approaches a new experience with certain expectations. List three things you hope to receive from supervision. List three things you know that you do not want from supervision. Discuss.

2. Looking over Bauman's list of five "games," which one do you think you are most likely to play? When you are playing this game, what should your supervisor do?

3. Most trainees receiving live supervision for the first time are nervous about how clients will react to this method. With a partner, roleplay an explanation of live supervision to a client. Give each other feedback.

4. If you were a supervisor, what trainee behavior(s) would most irritate you? What would you do about it?

5. Knowing yourself as you do, what issues should be a focus during one of your initial sessions with your supervisor?

RECOMMENDED READINGS

Bauman, W. F. (1972). Games counselor trainees play: Dealing with trainee resistance. *Counselor Education and Supervision, 11,* 251–256.

Bernard, J. M., & Goodyear, R. K. (1998). *Fundamentals of clinical supervision* (2nd ed.). Boston: Allyn and Bacon.

Leong, F. T. L. (1994). Emergence of the cultural dimension: The roles and impact of culture on counseling supervision. *Counselor Education and Supervision, 34,* 114–116.

Skovholt, T. M., & Ronnestad, M. H. (1992). *The evolving professional self: Stages and themes in therapist and counselor development.* New York: John Wiley & Sons.

Yager, G. G., & Beck, T. D. (1985). Beginning practicum: It only hurt until I laughed! *Counselor Education and Supervision, 25,* 149–157.

APPENDIX

Counseling Strategies Checklist

Most counselor trainees view the opportunity for supervision as a mixed blessing. They know that their performance has weaknesses that are more easily identified by an observer. On the other hand, they feel vulnerable at the prospect of having someone view and assess their interview behavior, particularly when they cannot see that person. There are no easy solutions to this problem. Learning to feel comfortable with your supervisor is uniquely a function of your own goals and the supervisor's awareness of your discomfort. Therefore, you must identify the implications of your counseling goals in terms of your own risk taking, and you must be prepared to communicate your fears to your supervisor.

The Counseling Strategies Checklist (CSC) is suggested as one means of assessing your performance. It is divided into categories that conform to the skills chapters in this text. The supervisor may want to use parts of the checklist for each interview, rather than attempt to complete the total checklist each time you are observed. The checklist provides a point of departure for you and your supervisor to discuss the progress of the interview, as well as your input and its effect on your client.

One further point might be made in reference to the use of the supervisor evaluation. It was mentioned in the text that the counselor often encounters *blocks* while attempting to respond to clients. The counselor may be able to identify quite accurately the feeling the client is describing but may not be able to respond to that feeling. This would probably be described by psychodynamic counselors as *countertransference*. When the client talks about a problem that is also a problem for the counselor, the counselor may feel unqualified to respond or may be overwhelmed by personal feelings and unable to respond. It is at this point that a supervisor can be most helpful in counseling the counselor, helping him or her to work through personal feelings and identifying ways to manage these feelings the next time the situation arises. To receive this assistance from your supervisor, you must acknowledge your own blockage.

How to Use the Counseling Strategies Checklist (CSC)

Each item in the CSC is scored by circling the most appropriate response. The items are worded so that desirable responses are "Yes." "No" is an undesirable response. Following each section of the CSC there is space for observer comments.

You can use this to record general impressions and specific observations. One way we like to use the CSC is to note to what degree the counselor's responses are culturally appropriate for each client. Specific assessment of multicultural competencies can be found in Part VII of the checklist.

After the supervisor has observed and rated the interview, the two of you should sit down and review the ratings. Where noticeable deficiencies exist, you and the supervisor should identify a goal or goals that will remedy the problem. Beyond this, you should list two or three action steps that permit you to achieve the goal. After three or four more interviews, have the supervisor evaluate you again, and compare the two sets of ratings to determine whether progress was evident.

Part I: Counselor Attending Behavior (Nonverbal)

1. The counselor maintained eye contact with the client.   Yes   No

2. The counselor displayed several different facial expressions during the interview.   Yes   No

3. The counselor's facial expressions reflected the mood of the client.   Yes   No

4. The counselor often responded to the client with facial animation and alertness.   Yes   No

5. The counselor displayed intermittent head movements (up-down, side-to-side).   Yes   No

6. The counselor refrained from head nodding when the client did not pursue goal-directed topics.   Yes   No

7. The counselor demonstrated a relaxed body position.   Yes   No

8. The counselor leaned forward as a means of encouraging the client to engage in some goal-directed behavior.   Yes   No

9. The counselor demonstrated some variation in voice   Yes   No
   pitch when talking.

10. The counselor's voice was easily heard by the client.   Yes   No

11. The counselor used intermittent one-word vocalizations   Yes   No
    ("mm-hmm") to reinforce the client's demonstration of
    goal-directed topics or behaviors.

Counselor Attending Behavior (Verbal)

12. The counselor usually spoke slowly enough so that each   Yes   No
    word was easily understood.

13. A majority (60 percent or more) of the counselor's   Yes   No
    responses could be categorized as complete sentences
    rather than monosyllabic phrases.

14. The counselor's verbal statements were concise and   Yes   No
    to the point.

15. The counselor refrained from repetition in verbal   Yes   No
    statements.

16. The counselor made verbal comments that pursued the   Yes   No
    topic introduced by the client.

17. The subject of the counselor's verbal statements usually   Yes   No
    referred to the client, either by name or the second-
    person pronoun, *you*.

18. A clear and sensible progression of topics was evident in the counselor's verbal behavior; the counselor avoided rambling.   Yes   No

Comments: _____

_____

Part II: Opening the Interview

1. In the first part of the interview, the counselor used several different nonverbal gestures (smiling, head nodding, hand movement, etc.) to help put the client at ease.   Yes   No

2. In starting the interview, the counselor remained silent or invited the client to talk about whatever he or she wanted, thus leaving the selection of initial topic up to the client.   Yes   No

3. After the first five minutes of the interview, the counselor refrained from encouraging social conversation.   Yes   No

4. After the first topic of discussion was exhausted, the counselor remained silent until the client identified a new topic.   Yes   No

5. The counselor provided structure (information about nature, purposes of counseling, time limits, etc.) when the client indicated uncertainty about the interview.   Yes   No

6. In beginning the *initial* interview, the counselor used at least one of the following structuring procedures:

   a. Provided information about taping and/or observation   Yes   No

   b. Commented on confidentiality   Yes   No

    c. Made remarks about the counselor's role and purpose   Yes   No
        of the interview

    d. Discussed with the client his or her expectations about   Yes   No
        counseling

Comments: _____

_____

Part III: Termination of the Interview

    1. The counselor informed the client before terminating that   Yes   No
        the interview was almost over.

    2. The counselor refrained from introducing new material   Yes   No
        (a different topic) at the termination phase of the interview.

    3. The counselor discouraged the client from pursuing new   Yes   No
        topics within the last five minutes of the interview by
        avoiding asking for further information about it.

    4. Only one attempt to terminate the interview was required   Yes   No
        before the termination was actually completed.

    5. The counselor initiated the termination of the interview   Yes   No
        through use of some closing strategy such as acknowledgment
        of time limits and/or summarization (by self or client).

    6. At the end of the interview, the counselor offered the   Yes   No
        client an opportunity to return for another interview.

Comments: _____

_____

Part IV: Goal Setting

1. The counselor asked the client to identify some of the conditions surrounding the occurrence of the client's problem ("When do you feel _____ ?").   Yes   No

2. The counselor asked the client to identify some of the consequences resulting from the client's behavior ("What happens when you _____ ?").   Yes   No

3. The counselor asked the client to state how he or she would like to change his or her behavior ("How would you like for things to be different?").   Yes   No

4. The counselor and client decided *together* on counseling goals.   Yes   No

5. The goals set in the interview were specific and observable.   Yes   No

6. The counselor asked the client to orally state a commitment to work for goal achievement.   Yes   No

7. If the client appeared resistant or unconcerned about achieving change, the counselor discussed this with the client.   Yes   No

8. The counselor asked the client to specify at least one action step he or she might take toward his or her goal.   Yes   No

9. The counselor suggested alternatives available to the client.   Yes   No

10. The counselor helped the client to develop action steps for goal attainment.   Yes   No

11. Action steps designated by counselor and client were specific   Yes   No
    and realistic in scope.

12. The counselor provided an opportunity within the interview   Yes   No
    for the client to practice or rehearse the action step.

13. The counselor provided feedback to the client concerning the   Yes   No
    execution of the action step.

14. The counselor encouraged the client to observe and   Yes   No
    evaluate the progress and outcomes of action steps taken
    outside the interview.

Comments: _____

_____

Part V: Counselor Differentiation

1. The counselor's responses were usually directed toward the   Yes   No
   most important component of *each* of the client's
   communications.

2. The counselor followed client topic changes by responding   Yes   No
   to the primary idea communicated by the client.

3. The counselor usually identified and responded to the   Yes   No
   feelings of the client.

4. The counselor usually identified and responded to the   Yes   No
   behaviors of the client.

5. The counselor verbally acknowledged several (at least two) nonverbal affect cues. Yes No

6. The counselor encouraged the client to talk about his or her feelings. Yes No

7. The counselor encouraged the client to identify and evaluate his or her actions. Yes No

8. The counselor discouraged the client from making and accepting excuses (rationalization) for his or her behavior. Yes No

9. The counselor asked questions that the client could not answer in a yes or no fashion (typically beginning with words such as *how, what, when, where, who,* etc.). Yes No

10. Several times (at least two) the counselor confronted the client with a discrepancy present in the client's communication and/or behavior. Yes No

11. Several times (at least two) the counselor used responses that supported or reinforced something the client said or did. Yes No

12. The counselor used several (at least two) responses that suggested a course of action the client had the potential for completing in the future. Yes No

13. Sometimes the counselor restated or clarified the client's previous communication. Yes No

14. The counselor used several (at least two) responses that summarized ambivalent and conflicting feelings of the client. Yes No

15. The counselor encouraged discussion of negative feelings   Yes   No
    (anger, fear) expressed by the client.

Comments: _____

_____

Part VI: The Process of Relating

1. The counselor made statements that reflected the client's   Yes   No
    feelings.

2. The counselor responded to the core of a long and   Yes   No
    ambivalent client statement.

3. The counselor verbally stated his or her desire and/or intent   Yes   No
    to understand.

4. The counselor made verbal statements that the client   Yes   No
    reaffirmed without qualifying or changing the
    counselor's previous response.

5. The counselor made attempts to verbally communicate   Yes   No
    his or her understanding of the client that elicited an
    affirmative client response ("Yes, that's exactly right," and
    so forth).

6. The counselor reflected the client's feelings at the same   Yes   No
    or a greater level of intensity than originally expressed
    by the client.

7. In communicating understanding of the client's feelings, the   Yes   No
    counselor verbalized the anticipation present in the client's
    communication (i.e., what the client would like to do or
    how the client would like to be).

8. When the counselor's nonverbal behavior suggested   Yes   No
    that he or she was uncertain or disagreeing, the counselor
    verbally acknowledged this to the client.

9. The counselor answered directly when the client asked about his or her opinion or reaction.　　Yes　No

10. The counselor encouraged discussion of statements made by the client that challenged the *counselor's* knowledge and beliefs.　　Yes　No

11. Several times (at least two) the counselor shared his or her own feelings with the client.　　Yes　No

12. The counselor encouraged the client to identify and discuss his or her feelings concerning the counselor and the interview.　　Yes　No

13. The counselor voluntarily shared his or her feelings about the client and the counseling relationship.　　Yes　No

14. The counselor expressed reactions about the client's strengths and/or potential.　　Yes　No

15. The counselor made responses that reflected his or her liking and appreciation of the client.　　Yes　No

Comments: _____

_____

Part VII: Multicultural Competencies*

1. The counselor displayed an awareness of his or her own racial and cultural identity development and its impact on the counseling process.　　Yes　No

*From *Pathways to Multicultural Counseling Competence: A Developmental Journey,* by B. Wehrly. Copyright © 1996 Brooks/Cole Publishing Company, Pacific Grove, CA 93950, a division of International Thomson Publishing Inc. By permission of the publisher.

2. The counselor was aware of his or her own values, biases, and assumptions about other racial and cultural groups and did not let these biases and assumptions impede the counseling process.   Yes   No

3. The counselor exhibited a respect for cultural differences among clients.   Yes   No

4. The counselor was aware of the cultural values of each client as well as of the uniqueness of each client within the client's racial and cultural group identification.   Yes   No

5. The counselor was sensitive to nonverbal and paralanguage crosscultural communication clues.   Yes   No

6. The counselor demonstrated the ability to assess the client's level of acculturation and to use this information in working with the client to implement culturally sensitive counseling.   Yes   No

7. The counselor displayed an understanding of how race, ethnicity, and culture influence the treatment, status, and life chances of clients.   Yes   No

8. The counselor was able to help the client sort out the degree to which the client's issues or problems are exacerbated by limits and regulations of the larger society.   Yes   No

9. The counselor was able to assess and identify the locus of the client's problem etiology.   Yes   No

10. The counselor was able to help the client deal with environmental frustration and oppression.   Yes   No

11. The counselor was able to recognize and work with   Yes   No
    the client dealing with multiple oppressions.

12. The counselor *worked with* the client to bring about   Yes   No
    change rather than *doing for* the client.

13. The counselor and client *worked together* to determine   Yes   No
    mutually acceptable and culturally sensitive goals.

Comments: _____

_____

REFERENCES

Adler, A. (1958). *What life should mean to you.* New York: Capricorn.

American Association for Marriage and Family Therapy. (1991). *Code of ethical principles for marriage and family therapists.* Washington, DC: Author.

American Counseling Association. (1995a). *Code of ethics.* Alexandria, VA: Author.

American Counseling Association. (1995b). Summit results in formation of spiritual competencies. *Counseling Today,* p. 30.

American Psychological Association. (1992). *Ethical principles of psychologists* (rev. ed.). Washington, DC: Author.

Axelson, J. (1993). *Counseling and development in a multicultural society.* Pacific Grove, CA: Brooks/Cole.

Baker, S. B. (1992). *School counseling for the twenty-first century.* New York: Macmillan.

Bandura, A. (1989). Human agency in social cognitive theory. *American Psychologist, 44,* 1175–1185.

Banikiotes, P. G., Kubinski, J. A., & Pursell, S. A. (1981). Sex role orientation, self-disclosure, and gender-related perceptions. *Journal of Counseling Psychology, 28,* 140–146.

Bauman, W. F. (1972). Games counselor trainees play: Dealing with trainee resistance. *Counselor Education and Supervision, 11,* 251–256.

Bear, T. M., & Kivlighan, D. M., Jr. (1994). Single-subject examination of the process of supervision of beginning and advanced supervisees. *Professional Psychology: Research and Practice, 25,* 450–457.

Beck, A. T. (1976). *Cognitive therapy and the emotional disorders.* New York: International Universities Press.

Beck, J. S. (1995). *Cognitive therapy.* New York: Guilford.

Benjamin, A. (1990). *The helping interview.* Boston: Houghton Mifflin.

Berg, I., & Jaya, A. (1993). Different and same: Family therapy with Asian-American families. *Journal of Marital and Family Therapy, 19,* 31–38.

Berger, S. S., & Buchholz, E. S. (1993). On becoming a supervisee: Preparation for learning in a supervisory relationship. *Psychotherapy, 30,* 86–92.

Bernard, J. M. (1979). Supervisor training: A discrimination model. *Counselor Education and Supervision, 19,* 60–68.

Bernard, J. M. (1997). The discrimination model. In C. E. Watkins, Jr. (Ed.), *Handbook of psychotherapy supervision* (pp. 310–327). New York: Wiley & Sons.

Bernard, J. M., & Goodyear, R. K. (1998). *Fundamentals of clinical supervision* (2nd ed.). Boston: Allyn and Bacon.

Bohart, A., & Greenberg, L. (1997a). Empathy and psychotherapy: An introductory overview. In A. Bohart & L. Greenberg (Eds.), *Empathy reconsidered* (pp. 3–32). Washington, DC: American Psychological Association.

Bohart, A., & Greenberg, L. (Eds.). (1997b). *Empathy reconsidered.* Washington, DC: American Psychological Association.

Borders, L. D. (1986). Facilitating supervisee growth: Implications of developmental models of counseling supervision. *Michigan Journal of Counseling and Development, 17,* 7–12.

Borders, L. D., Bernard, J. M., Dye, H. A., Fong, M. L., Henderson, P., & Nance, D. W. (1991). Curriculum guide for training counseling supervisors: Rationale, development, and implementation. *Counselor Education and Supervision, 31,* 58–80.

Boyd-Franklin, N. (1989). *Black families in therapy: A multisystems approach.* New York: Guilford.

Bozarth, J. (1997). Empathy from the framework of client-centered theory and the Rogerian hypothesis. In A. Bohart & L. Greenberg (Eds.), *Empathy reconsidered* (pp. 81–102). Washington, DC: American Psychological Association.

Brammer, L. M., Shostrom, E. L., & Abrego, P. J. (1992). *Therapeutic counseling and psychotherapy: Fundamentals of counseling and psychotherapy* (6th ed.). Englewood Cliffs, NJ: Prentice Hall.

Branden, N. (1971). *The disowned self.* Los Angeles: Nash.

Brown, L. (1994). *Subversive dialogues: Theory in feminist therapy.* New York: Basic Books.

Brown, L. S., & Ballou, M. (1992). *Personality and psychopathology: Feminist reappraisals.* New York: Guilford.

Bubenzer, D. L., Mahrle, C., & West, J. D. (1987). *Live counselor supervision: Trainee acculturation and supervision interventions.* Paper presented at the Annual Convention of the American Association for Counseling and Development, New Orleans, LA.

Buie, D. (1981). Empathy: Its nature and limitations. *Journal of the American Psychoanalytic Association, 29,* 281–307.

Casas, J. M. (1988). Cognitive behavior approaches: A minority perspective. *The Counseling Psychologist, 16,* 106–110.

Castillo, R. J. (1997). *Culture and mental illness.* Pacific Grove, CA: Brooks/Cole.

Corey, G. (1996). *Theory and practice of counseling and psychotherapy* (5th ed.). Pacific Grove, CA: Brooks/Cole.

Corey, G., Corey, M. S., & Callanan, P. (1998). *Issues and ethics in the helping professions* (5th ed.). Pacific Grove, CA: Brooks/Cole.

Cormier, S., & Cormier, B. (1998). *Interviewing strategies for helpers: Fundamental skills and cognitive behavioral interventions* (4th ed.). Pacific Grove, CA: Brooks/Cole.

Corsini, R., & Wedding, D. (Eds.). (1995). *Current psychotherapists* (5th ed.). Itasca, IL: Peacock.

Daw, J. (1997). Cultural competency: What does it mean? *Family Therapy News, 28,* 8–9, 27.

Dean, L., & Meadows, M. (1995). College counseling: Union and intersection. *Journal of Counseling and Development, 74,* 139–142.

Dillon, J. T. (1990). *The practice of questioning.* New York: Routledge.

Edwards, C., & Murdock, N. (1994). Characteristics of therapist self-disclosure in the counseling process. *Journal of Counseling and Development, 72,* 384–389.

Egan, G. (1976). *Interpersonal living: A skills/contract approach to human relations training in groups.* Monterey, CA: Brooks/Cole.

Egan, G. (1998). *The skilled helper* (6th ed.). Pacific Grove, CA: Brooks/Cole.

Ekman, P., & Friesen, W. V. (1967). Head and body cues in the judgment of emotion: A reformulation. *Perceptual and Motor Skills, 24,* 711–724.

Ekman, P., & Friesen, W. V. (1969). Non-verbal leakage and clues to deception. *Psychiatry, 32,* 88–105.

Enns, C. B. (1993). Twenty years of feminist counseling and therapy: From naming biases to implementing multifaceted practice. *The Counseling Psychologist, 21,* 3–87.

Farberman, R. K. (1997). What's leading America astray? *American Psychological Association Monitor, 28* (9), 1, 15.

Forrest, D. V. (1983). Employee assistance programs in the 1980's: Expanding career options for counselors. *Personnel and Guidance Journal, 62,* 105–107.

Gazda, G. M., Asbury, F. S., Balzer, F., Childers, W. C., Phelps, R. E., & Walters, R. P. (1995). *Human relations development: A manual for educators* (5th ed.). Boston: Allyn and Bacon.

Gilligan, S. (1997). *The courage to love: Principles and practices of self-relations psychotherapy.* New York: Norton.

Goldberg, D. A. (1985). Process notes, audio, and videotape: Modes of presentation in psychotherapy training. *The Clinical Supervisor, 3,* 3–13.

Goldenberg, H., & Goldenberg, I. (1998). *Counseling today's families* (3rd ed.). Pacific Grove, CA: Brooks/Cole.

Goodyear, R. K., Brinley, R. G., & Kivlighan, D. M., Jr. (August 1997). *Dimensionality of the supervisee role: Supervisees' and supervisors' perceptions.* Paper presented at the annual meeting of the American Psychological Association, Chicago, IL.

Hackney, H., & Cormier, L. S. (1996). *The professional counselor* (4th ed.). Boston: Allyn and Bacon.

Haley, J. (1997). *Leaving home* (2nd ed.). New York: Brunner-Mazel.

Hansen, J., Rossberg, R., & Cramer, S. (1994). *Counseling: Theory and process* (5th ed.). Boston: Allyn and Bacon.

Hardy, K. V., & Laszloffy, T. (1995). The cultural genogram: Key to training culturally competent family therapists. *Journal of Marital and Family Therapy, 21*, 227–237.

Harper, R., Wiens, A., & Matarazzo, J. (1978). *Nonverbal communication: The state of the art.* New York: Wiley.

Hays, P. A. (1995). Multicultural applications of cognitive-behavior therapy. *Professional Psychology: Research and Practice, 26*, 309–315.

Hillman, J. (1996). *The soul's code: In search of character and calling.* New York: Random House.

Horney, K. (1970). *Neurosis and human growth.* New York: Norton.

Hudson, P. O., & O'Hanlon, W. H. (1991). *Rewriting love stories: Brief marital therapy.* New York: Norton.

Hutchins, D., & Cole-Vaught, C. (1997). *Helping relationships and strategies* (3rd ed.). Pacific Grove, CA: Brooks/Cole.

Imber-Black, E., Roberts, J., & Whiting, R. (Eds.). (1988). *Rituals in families and family therapy.* New York: Norton.

Ivey, A. (1994). *Intentional interviewing and counseling* (3rd ed.). Pacific Grove, CA: Brooks/Cole.

Ivey, A., Gluckstern, N., & Ivey, M. B. (1993). *Basic attending skills.* North Amherst, MA: Microtraining Associates.

Ivey, A. E., Ivey, M. B., & Simek-Morgan, L. (1997). *Counseling and psychotherapy: A multicultural perspective* (4th ed.). Boston: Allyn and Bacon.

Jenkins, A. H. (1997). The empathic context in psychotherapy with people of color. In A. Bohart & L. Greenberg (Eds.), *Empathy reconsidered* (pp. 321–342). Washington, DC: American Psychological Association.

Jordan, J. (1997). Relational development through mutual empathy. In A. Bohart & L. Greenberg (Eds.), *Empathy reconsidered* (pp. 343–352). Washington, DC: American Psychological Association.

Jourard, S. M. (1963). *Personal adjustment.* New York: Macmillan.

Kanfer, F. H., & Gaelick-Buys, L. (1991). Self-management methods. In F. H. Kanfer & A. P. Goldstein (Eds.), *Helping people change* (4th ed., pp. 305–360). New York: Pergamon.

Kanfer F. H., & Goldstein, A. P. (Eds.). (1991). *Helping people change* (4th ed.). New York: Pergamon.

Kantrowitz, R., & Ballou, M. (1992). A feminist critique of cognitive-behavioral therapy. In L. S. Brown & M. Ballou (Eds.), *Personality and psychopathology: Feminist reappraisals* (pp. 70–87). New York: Guilford.

Karasu, T. B. (1992). *Wisdom in the practice of psychotherapy.* New York: Basic Books.

Karen, R. (1992). Shame. *Atlantic Monthly, 269*, 40–70.

Kazdin, A. E. (1982). The separate and combined effects of covert and overt rehearsal in developing assertive behavior. *Behavior Therapy and Research, 20*, 17–25.

Kelley, C. (1974). *Education in feeling and purpose.* Vancouver, WA: The Radix Institute, c/o C. Kelley, 13715 Southeast 36th St., Vancouver, WA 98684.

Kelley, C. R. (1979). Freeing blocked anger. *The Radix Journal, 1* (3), 19–33.

Knapp, M. L., & Hall, J. (1992). *Nonverbal communication in human interaction* (3rd ed.). Orlando: Holt, Rinehart and Winston.

Kottler, J. (1991). *The compleat therapist.* San Francisco: Jossey-Bass.

Kramer, P. D. (1993). *Listening to Prozac.* New York: Viking.

Kramer, S. (1990). *Positive endings in psychotherapy.* San Francisco: Jossey-Bass.

Kutzik, A. J. (1977). The medical field. In F. W. Kaslow (Ed.), *Supervision, consultation, and staff training in the helping professions.* San Francisco: Jossey-Bass.

Lanning, W. (1986). Development of the supervisor emphasis rating form. *Counselor Education and Supervision, 25*, 191–196.

Lazarus, A. (1976). *Multimodal behavior therapy.* New York: Springer.

Leong, F. T. L. (1994). Emergence of the cultural dimension: The roles and impact of culture on counseling supervision. *Counselor Education and Supervision, 34*, 114–116.

Lewis, H. B. (1971). *Shame and guilt in neurosis.* Lido Beach, NY: International Universities Press.

Liddle, B. J. (1986). Resistance in supervision: A response to perceived threat. *Counselor Education and Supervision, 26,* 117–127.

Lowen, A. (1965). *Breathing, movement, and feeling.* New York: Institute for Bioenergetic Analysis.

Lum, D. (1996). *Social-work practice and people of color* (3rd ed.). Pacific Grove, CA: Brooks/Cole.

McGoldrick, M., Anderson, C., & Walsh, F. (Eds.). (1989). *Women and families: A framework for family therapy.* New York: Norton.

McMullin, R. E. (1986). *Handbook of cognitive therapy techniques.* New York: Norton.

McNeil, B. W., Stoltenberg, C. D., & Pierce, R. A. (1985). Supervisees' perceptions of their development: A test of the counselor complexity model. *Journal of Counseling Psychology, 32,* 630–633.

Meichenbaum, D. (1993). Stress inoculation training: A 20-year update. In P. M. Lehrer & R. L. Woolfork (Eds.), *Principles and practice of stress management* (2nd ed., pp. 373–406). New York: Guilford.

Mellody, P. (1989). *Facing codependence.* New York: Harper & Row.

Mesquita, B., & Frijda, N. (1992). Cultural variations in emotions: A review. *Psychological Bulletin, 112,* 179–204.

Midori Hanna, S., & Brown, J. (1995). *The practice of family therapy.* Pacific Grove, CA: Brooks/Cole.

Miller, A. (1981). *The drama of the gifted child.* New York: Basic Books.

Miller, G., & Wooten, H. R., Jr. (1995). Sports counseling: A new counseling specialty area. *Journal of Counseling and Development, 74,* 172–173.

Miller, S. (1985). *The shame experience.* Haberford, PA: Analytic Press.

Miller, S., Wackman, D., Nunnally, E., & Miller, P. (1988). *Connecting with self and others.* Littleton, CO: Interpersonal Communication Programs.

Minuchin, S. (1974). *Families and family therapy.* Cambridge, MA: Harvard University.

Morrison, J. (1995). *The first interview: A guide for clinicians.* New York: Guilford.

National Association of Social Workers. (1996). *Code of ethics.* Washington, DC: Author.

O'Donohue, W., & Crouch, J. (1996). Marital therapy and gender-linked factors in communication. *Journal of Marital and Family Therapy, 22,* 87–101.

O'Hanlon, W. H. (1987). *Taproots: Underlying principles of Milton H. Erickson's therapy and hypnosis.* New York: Norton.

O'Hara, M. (1997). Relational empathy: Beyond modernist egocentrism to postmodern holistic contextualism. In A. Bohart & L. Greenberg (Eds.), *Empathy reconsidered* (pp. 295–320). Washington, DC: American Psychological Association.

Ohlsen, M. M. (Ed.). (1983). *Introduction to counseling* (pp. 133–144). Itasca, IL: Peacock.

Olk, M., & Friedlander, M. L. (1992). Role conflict and ambiguity in the supervisory experience of counselor trainees. *Journal of Counseling Psychology, 39,* 389–397.

O'Neill, T. D. (1993). "Feeling worthless": An ethnographic investigation of depression and problem drinking at the Flathead Reservation. *Culture, Medicine, and Psychiatry, 16,* 447–469.

Ozer, E. M., & Bandura, A. (1990). Mechanisms governing empowerment effects: A self-efficacy analysis. *Journal of Personality and Social Psychology, 58,* 472–486.

Paisley, P., & Borders, L. D. (1995). School counseling: An evolving specialty. *Journal of Counseling and Development, 74,* 150–153.

Patterson, L. & Welfel, E. (1994). *The counseling process* (4th ed.). Pacific Grove, CA: Brooks/Cole.

Pedersen, P., & Ivey, A. (1993). *Culture-centered counseling and interviewing skills.* Westport, CT: Praeger.

Perls, F. (1969). *Ego, hunger, and aggression.* New York: Vintage.

Perls, F. (1973). *The gestalt approach and eyewitness to therapy.* Palo Alto, CA: Science and Behavior Books.

Premack, D. (1965). Reinforcement theory. In D. Levin (Ed.), *Nebraska symposium on motivation* (pp. 123–180). Lincoln: University of Nebraska Press.

Rabinowitz, F. E., Heppner, P. O., & Roehlke, H. J. (1986). Descriptive study of process and outcome variables of supervision over time. *Journal of Counseling Psychology, 33,* 292–300.

Robinson, T. (1997). Insurmountable opportunities. *Journal of Counseling and Development, 76,* 6–7.

Rogers, C. (1957). The necessary and sufficient conditions of therapeutic personality change. *Journal of Counseling Psychology, 21,* 95–103.

Rosado, J. W., Jr., & Elias, M. J. (1993). Ecological and psychocultural mediators in the delivery of services for urban, culturally diverse Hispanic clients. *Professional Psychology: Research and Practice, 24,* 450–459.

Rosenthal, T., & Steffek, B. (1991). Modeling methods. In F. H. Kanfer & A. P. Goldstein (Eds.), *Helping people change* (4th ed., pp. 70–121). New York: Pergamon.

Rubinstein, M., & Hammond, D. (1982). The use of videotape in psychotherapy supervision. In M. Blumenfield (Ed.), *Applied supervision in psychotherapy* (pp. 143–164). New York: Grune & Stratton.

Seligman, M. (1990). *Learned optimism.* New York: Pocket Books.

Simpkinson, A., & Simpkinson, C. (Jan./Feb. 1992). Man talk/woman talk. *Common Boundary,* pp. 30–33.

Skovholt, T. M., & Ronnestad, M. H. (1992). *The evolving professional self: Stages and themes in therapist and counselor development.* New York: Wiley & Sons.

Smith, E. (1985). *The body in psychotherapy.* Jefferson, NC: McFarland.

Smith, H., & Robinson, G. (1995). Mental health counseling: Past, present, and future. *Journal of Counseling and Development, 74,* 158–162.

Solomon, B. B. (1976). *Black empowerment: Social work in oppressed communities.* New York: Columbia University Press.

Sommers-Flanagan, J., & Sommers-Flanagan, R. (1994). *Foundations of therapeutic interviewing.* Boston: Allyn and Bacon.

Steinem, G. (1992). *Revolution from within: A book of self-esteem.* Boston: Little, Brown.

Stevenson, H., & Renard, G. (1993). Trusting olé wise owls: Therapeutic rise of cultural strengths in African-American families. *Professional Psychology: Research and Practice, 24,* 433–442.

Stoltenberg, C. D., & Delworth, U. (1987). *Supervising counselors and therapists: A developmental approach.* San Francisco: Jossey-Bass.

Stoltenberg, C. D., Pierce, R. A., & McNeill, B. W. (1987). Effects of experience on counselors needs. *The Clinical Supervisor, 5,* 23–32.

Sue, D. W. (1992). The challenge of multiculturalism: The road less traveled. *American Counselor, 1,* 6–15.

Sue, D. W., & Sue, D. (1990). *Counseling the culturally different.* New York: Wiley.

Sue, S. (1998). In search of cultural competence in psychotherapy and counseling. *American Psychologist, 53,* 440–448.

Sweeney, T. J. (1995). Accreditation, credentialing, professionalization: The role of specialties. *Journal of Counseling and Development, 74,* 117–125.

Tannen, D. (1990). *You just don't understand.* New York: Random House.

Tannen, D. (1993). *Gender and conversational interaction.* New York: Oxford University Press.

Teyber, E. (1997). *Interpersonal processes in psychotherapy* (3rd. ed.). Pacific Grove, CA: Brooks/Cole.

Utz, P. W. (1983). Counseling college students. In M. Ohlsen (Ed.), *Introduction to counseling.* Itasca, IL: Peacock.

Walen, S. R., DiGiuseppe, R., & Wessler, R. L. (1992). *A practitioner's guide to rational-emotive therapy* (2nd ed.). New York: Oxford University Press.

Watson, D., & Tharp, R. (1997). *Self-directed behavior* (7th ed.). Pacific Grove, CA: Brooks/Cole.

Watson, O. M. (1970). *Proxemic behavior: A cross-cultural study.* The Hague: Mouton.

Watzlawick, P., Beavin, J. H., & Jackson, D. D. (1967). *Pragmatics of human communication.* New York: Norton.

Wehrly, B. (1995). *Pathways to multicultural counseling competence.* Pacific Grove, CA: Brooks/Cole.

West, J. D., Bubenzer, D. L., Pinsoneault, T., & Holeman, V. (1993). Three supervision modalities for training marital and family counselors. Special Section: Marriage and family counselor training. *Counselor Education & Supervision, 33,* 127–138.

Wilson, G. T. (1995). Behavior therapy. In R. Corsini & P. Wedding (Eds.), *Current psychotherapies* (5th ed., pp. 197–228). Itasca, IL: Peacock.

Winter, M., & Holloway, E. L. (1991). Relation of trainee experience, conceptual level, and supervisor approach to selection of audiotaped counseling passages. *Clinical Supervisor, 9,* 87–103.

Wolpe, J. (1990). *The practice of behavior therapy* (4th ed.). New York: Pergamon.

Woolams, S., & Brown, M. (1979). *TA: The total handbook of transactional analysis.* Englewood Cliffs, NJ: Prentice Hall.

Worden, M., & Worden, B. (1998). *The gender dance in couples therapy.* Pacific Grove, CA: Brooks/ Cole.

Worthington, E. L., Jr. (1987). Changes in supervision as counselors and supervisors gain experience: A review. *Professional Psychology: Research and Practice, 18,* 189–208.

Worthington, E. L., Jr., & Roehlke, H. J. (1979). Effective supervision as perceived by beginning counselors-in-training. *Journal of Counseling Psychology, 26,* 64–73.

Wynne, M. E., Susman, M., Ries, S., Birringer, J., & Katz, L. (1994). A method for assessing therapists' recall of in-session events. *Journal of Counseling Psychology, 41,* 53–57.

Yager, G. G., Witham, M. V., Williams, G. T., & Scheufler, C. E. (1981). *Tips for the inexperienced counselor: How to maximize your time in supervision.* Paper presented at the North Central Association for Counselor Education and Supervision Annual Meeting, Milwaukee, WI.

INDEX